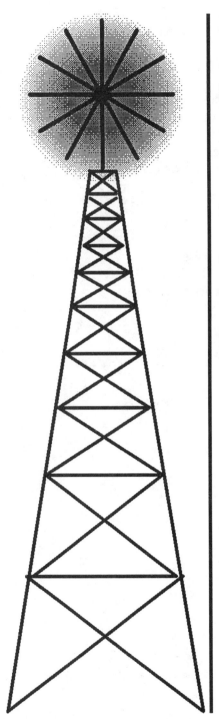

SEIZING THE AIRWAVES

A Free Radio Handbook

edited by

Ron Sakolsky &

Stephen Dunifer

AK
PRESS

© Copyright: 1998 Ron Sakolsky and Stephen Dunifer

ISBN 1-873176-99-6

Library of Congress Cataloging-in-Publication Data
A catalog record for this title is available from the Library of Congress.

British Library Cataloguing-in-Publication Data
A catalogue record for this title is available from the British Library.

Published by:
AK Press
P.O. Box 12766
Edinburgh, Scotland
EH8 9YE

AK Press
P.O. Box 40682
San Francisco, CA
94140-0682

Cover collage, book design and layout work donated by Freddie Baer.

TABLE OF CONTENTS

PART I: MOVING FROM CORPORATE ENCLOSURE TO FREE RADIO

PART III: SETTING THE TECHNOLOGY FREE

ACKNOWLEDGMENTS

Ron wishes to thank his partner-in-crime, Sheila Nopper, for her myriad labors which helped bring this project to fruition. To Ramsey and Bill for a place to hang his raincoat during the course of the research. To Freddie Baer for that first pot of designer tea. To Stephen Perkins, the man with the suitcase. To Sue Gardner, for bringing the noise to Canada. To Michael Townsend, who knows that a working class hero is something to be. To Jason Arnold, transcriber par excellance of the University of Illinois at Springfield, which provided some of the technical support for this project. To Lizzie Borden's flaming birth. And to DJ Elijah, wherever he may be...

Stephen wishes to thank his attorneys of record, Luke Hiken and Allen Hopper, and Peter Franck and Alan Korn of the National Lawyers Guild's Committee on Democratic Communications for their incredible legal support and dedication to the defense of First Amendment rights. Special recognition goes to FCC agent David Doon, former agent, Phillip Kane, FCC attorney, David Silberman, and the rest of the FCC bureaucracy whose unique response to micropower radio has contributed to the overall success of this movement. And thanks to the entire crew of Free Radio Berkeley who have made it possible to be where we are today, especially Radman, Captain Fred, Tom Schreiner, and technical support volunteers, Matt Dott, Doug Forbes and Govinda Dalton.

We would both like to acknowledge Laura Hermann of the Loyola Radio Conference for providing the radio-active setting wherein your co-editors struck up the conversation which eventually became this book. Finally, we gratefully acknowledge the hydra-headed micropowered free radio movement without which this book would not be possible, and most particularly, the man who started it all, Mbanna Kantako.

The following magazine articles appear in reworked, updated and expanded form in these pages:

Ricardo Omar Elizalde. "Pirate Radio: Voices of Discontent," *Frontera #4*, 1996 (PO Box 30529, Los Angeles, CA 90030-0529).

Lorenzo Komboa Ervin. "Attack on Black Liberation Radio," *Slingshot* (Spring, 1997) (3124 Shattuck Ave, Berkeley, CA 94705).

Ron Sakolsky. "Radio-Activity: Community Animation You Can Dance To," *Cultural Democracy* (Spring 1990).

_____ ."Anarchy on the Airwaves: A Brief History of the Micro-Radio Movement," *Social Anarchism* (#17, 1992).

_____ . "Black Liberation Radio," *Index on Censorship* (Vol 22, #2, February, 1993) (Writers and Scholars International Ltd, 32 Queen Victoria St, London, EC4N 4SS UK).

_____ . "Radio Resistor: An Interview With Stephen Dunifer, Oakland, CA, December, 1995," *The Bleeding Edge* (#1, 1996) (PO Box 1233, Springfield, IL 62705).

_____ . "Frequencies of Resistance: The Micropower Radio Movement Goes Global," *Social Anarchism* (#23, 1997) (2743 Maryland Ave, Baltimore, MD 21218).

Peter Spagnuolo. "Steal This Radio," *The Shadow* (#38, May-June, 1996) (PO Box 20298, NY, NY 10009).

Illustration by Carol Genetti

"Unlicensed broadcasting creates chaos on the airwaves. It's anarchy on the airwaves.... Your honor, this opens up such a can of worms."

Statement of David Silberman, Attorney for the General Counsel's Office of the FCC in the case of "U.S.A. vs. Stephen Paul Dunifer" from Transcript of the Proceedings before U.S. District Judge Claudia Wilken (Northern District of California) on January 20, 1995.

PREFACE

FREE SPEECH

A Fable

Stephen Dunifer

In a far distant country lived a people called the Mericans. A proud, stoic lot were they. Unlike many surrounding lands they had overthrown the mantle of obedience to a feudal monarchy and established what was called a republic. Creating a document known as the Declaration of Independence they set forth certain principles such as life, liberty and the pursuit of happiness as their primary goals. Elaborating further on this, they created a Constitution which reluctantly established certain basic rights of every citizen, known as the Bill of Rights. Such things as freedom of speech, equal protection under the law, protection from unreasonable search and seizure and so forth. All of these sought to redress and prohibit the type of mistreatment they had received under the prior monarchy they had done away with. All of this sounded very well and good. As time turned the pages of history it became obvious that certain legal concepts were not stated but very well established and enforced. As the country grew with every advancing wave of industrial development and technology even the less astute among its citizens realized that something was amiss in the Land of Liberty. Unfortunately the means of communication had, for the most part, resided in the hands of those who could own them. In fact, in earlier times printing presses had been licensed by the king. Such restrictions prevented dissenting views from reaching a mass number of the citizens of Merica. What information and contrary views that did leak out were attacked without mercy

Illustration by Sean Vile

by the captains of industry, affectionately known as the Robber Barons. Despite smashing of printing presses by the hirelings of what had become a ruling elite, citizens committed to the basic tenets of the Constitution persisted in their efforts under the banner of Freedom of Speech.

Technology continued its march forward in the land of Merica. Other forms of communication were developed. One of these was known as Radio. Unlike newspapers and books, it carried the spoken word to all who had a radio receiver. A person spoke or sang into an instrument known as a microphone which converted the sound vibrations into electrical impulses which were converted into radio waves by a unit called a transmitter. A radio receiver picked up these radio waves and converted them back into sound vibrations that were made audible by a loudspeaker. Radio receivers began proliferating by the tens of thousands. Communities and various organizations found they could set up their own transmitters and broadcast their views to all who might listen. This was far easier than owning big printing presses.

Being their somewhat slow reacting selves, the ruling elite finally caught on to what a money making proposition radio was. They could use it to sell more commodities and convince people that slavery was freedom. Only one problem stood in their way, many dissenting voices had already taken to the airwaves in the naive belief that freedom of speech was the right of every citizen. Shaking the puppet strings of those they controlled in government, they pulled the usual trick of creating yet another regulatory body over which they would have full control. This regulatory body finally became known as the Federal Communications Commission. Restoring order to what they called "chaos" of the airwaves, the FCC proceeded to silence all of the small voices. They turned over the ownership of what was supposed to be the common property of the people to the Robber Barons.

Every time citizens took a notion to exercise their right of free speech on the airwaves the FCC was there to squash such acts of temerity. It called such initiatives acts of "piracy." An odd notion since the citizens were merely attempting to reclaim what had been stolen from them in the first place.

As the years rolled on an even more effective medium of advertising and social control was developed. It was known as Television. Being very expensive to set up and maintain it remained well beyond the means of all but the very wealthy to own. As radio broadcast equipment evolved technically it became easier and cheaper to set up a community radio station which would reflect the greatest diversity of voices. To forestall this possibility the FCC enacted even more rules which forbade the licensing and operating of an FM radio station with less than 100 watts of power. Once again they acted to prevent all but the wealthy from having a voice. It was akin to saying that everyone had the right to free speech, but you had to own your own solid gold podium from which to speak.

After passing through a rather tumultuous time known as the sixties in the land of Merica, it was becoming rather painfully obvious to many citizens that there was a wide difference between the reality of their situation and what was promised to them by their Bill of Rights. Some maintained that the government existed more to protect the haves from the have nots than actually enforcing the rights of every citizen.

But what was one to do? With every means of communication being concentrated into fewer and fewer hands any true discourse within civil society became impossible. Thanks to a steady drum beat of advertising many citizens were being convinced that freedom just merely meant choosing from fifty brands of breakfast cereal, twenty brands of toothpaste or twelve brands of soap. Convenience yes, but definitely not personal freedom and liberty, however.

A few intrepid individuals decided that enough was enough and set up their own community broadcast stations without FCC approval. Upon discovering one of these operations, self-described as micropower radio by its operator, the FCC huffed and puffed, threatening severe fines and all the wrath of regulatory hell upon it. Unimpressed and secure within a house built with the brick of political conviction and liberty, this community station, Black Liberation Radio was not taken off the air by the FCC.

Some other folks impressed by this effort and alarmed over the massive media propaganda machine decided to take several courses of action. A legal committee was formed to defend the rights of micropower broadcasters. Shortly following that another citizen decided to directly challenge the authority of the FCC both on the airwaves and ultimately in court. Since they have always had their way with the courts the FCC sought an injunction to silence this community station known as Free Radio Berkeley. As surely as pride goeth before a fall, the FCC had the shock of their bureaucratic lives when the judge refused their injunction request on constitutional grounds.

During that time micropower broadcasting became a campaign of electronic civil disobedience. As more citizens realized they could provide an outlet for the many voices in their communities, micropower stations sprouted up like mushrooms after a night's rain. Encouraged by the legal victory and the technical expertise provided by Free Radio Berkeley in the form of inexpensive transmitter kits, hundreds of micropower or free radio stations took to the airwaves all across the land of Merica.

For many it was a way to actively realize what had been promised by the Bill of Rights but never truly allowed by the government — free discourse across any medium of a citizen's choosing. It was also the further realization that any true democracy rests on the free exchange of ideas, news, information, cultural and artistic expression.

And now, good citizen, the next chapter in this fable is up to you. How will you write it? Will you take part in this movement to democratize not only the airwaves but all means of communication? It does not take much in the way of resources to put a community voice on the air. In fact, the cost can be kept to

$1000 or less. Are you satisfied with format and formula radio? Does the media reflect the diversity of your community? Do you believe in the First Amendment and the right to tell the truth? Why not consider putting a micropower FM radio station on the air in your community? Technical advice and equipment are offered by Free Radio Berkeley while legal support and expertise is provided by the National Lawyers Guild's Committee on Democratic Communications. Contact information is as follows:

Free Radio Berkeley
1442 A Walnut St. #406
Berkeley, CA 94709
(510) 464-3041
email: frbspd@crl.com

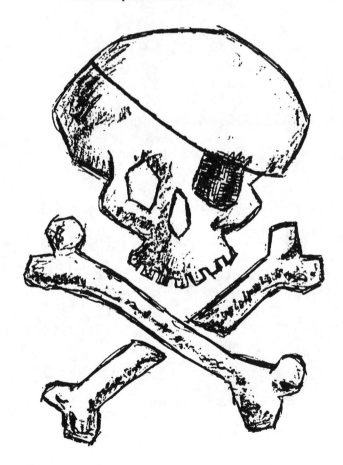

Illustration by Ron Sakolsky

INTRODUCTION

RHIZOMATIC RADIO AND THE GREAT STAMPEDE

Ron Sakolsky

Let us conjure up a vision of a Wild Radio Stampede disrupting the territorialized lines of Authority artificially drawn in the air surrounding Mother Earth. The seismic flows of land, sea, and air waves reconceptualized as rhizomatic possibilities. Let the leaden segmentary lines imposed by capitofeudalism explode into detached shimmering lines of flight. Rampaging sound wave tubers where each stem is itself a rootstock emitting new roots everywhere along its sonic path. Unstoppable drifting planetary waves of radio sound laughing in the sedentary face of the dominant mediacracy's uniformity. Immersion then becomes a metaphor not for entrapment, but for escape as receiver and producer become one in an oceanic roar sounding in its composite signal like a combination of Hiroshi Yokoi's 24 hour FM radio transmissions in Japan programmed according to tidal patterns and Tetsuo Kugawa's micropower radio broadcasts, inspired by the radio experiments in "direct speech" of the Italian Autonomists. The Autonomist trick of *The Serpent of Desire Eating Its Own Tail* as performed by Felix Guattari and the Schizzes, a "molecular revolution" on a mixtape.

Kugawa and Guattari, entwined in the worldwide free radio rhizomes proliferating not underground but in the air; the technician and the theorist both inspired by the heady days of the Italian Autonomia (Autonomy) movement of the late Seventies. Using a hard-won 1975 Italian Constitutional Court's ruling declaring that the state monopoly of the airwaves was illegal, the Autonomia movement remained highly visible in the hundreds of diverse and unregulated miniaturized stations that engaged daily in a guerrilla warfare of the airwaves, such as Radio Alice in Bologna, the station whose programming was chronicled by Guattari himself.

Unlike conventional radio (which in a U.S. context means commercial, public or, increasingly, community), what Guattari called "popular free radio" does not seek to impose programming on targeted segments of a mass audience using marketing criteria. Instead, it aims at changing the professionally-mediated relationship between listener and speaker, and even challenging the listener/speaker dichotomy itself. In one sense, then, it is an expansion upon Bertolt Brecht's 1927 proposal for democratization of radio which called for the apparatus of radio to be changed over from distribution to communication, making it possible to transmit as well as receive. From an Autonomist perspective, Italian radio would be opened up to non-professionals and the hierarchical one way flow of messages would be replaced with egalitarian multiple flows. This new arrangement stood in marked contrast to the authoritarian approach to radio as a vehicle for the shaping of opinion either by the dominant culture or by an oppositional political party. In the latter case, Guattari was going beyond Brecht in concerning himself with the potentialities of radio for creating new spaces for freedom, self-management (*autogestion*) and the immediate fulfillment of desire rather than merely disseminating the party line and/or mobilizing supporters in the traditional leftist manner.

What better way to accomplish this immediacy goal than the phone-in! In fact, what we today refer to as "talk radio" owes an unacknowledged and probably unknown debt to the Autonomists. Typically, the potentially radical phone-in vehicle is drained of its potency within the contemporary authoritarian radio context of pre-screening, censorship, and the use of such control technology as delay devices by swarmy radio windbags like Rush Limbaugh. Yet phone-ins to Autonomist radio collectives in the Italian context took the form of people reading their poetry, singing their songs, playing their instruments, or shouting their manifestoes into the air. They called from their squats to deride their would-be landlords, their housework to skewer their husbands, their workplaces or picket lines to attack their bosses, or from their beds to denounce work itself. Unmediated communiqués, expressed in a popular language that was lively, direct and often ribald. As one caller to Radio Alice put it in defense of charges of obscenity against the station, "Desire is given a voice, and for them, it is obscene" (Lotringer and Marazzi, p. 131).

Speaking truth to power in terms of desire not only targeted capitalists, but, as in Bologna, where the Communist Party held public office and yet promoted policies of law and order and austerity; it was the authoritarian left itself which was challenged. In its own words, "Radio Alice will give a voice to anyone who loves mimosa and believes in paradise; hates violence but strikes the wicked; believes they're Napoleon but knows they could just be aftershave; who laughs like the flowers ... to smokers and drinkers, jugglers and musketeers, the absent and the mad" (Lumley, 1990, p 305). As to the youth revolt component of Autonomia, in some ways, 1977's "Generation of Year Nine" (as they called themselves in mock reference to the year 1968 in the Jacobin calendar) sought to connect with and update the libertarian impulses of the Sixties that had been reterritorialized in later years. This quest then was not a search for roots, but what Guattari has called rhizomatic links that would deterritorialize the airwaves and offer a way out of the oh so manageable bureaucratic box constructed for radio. Beyond Italy, the resulting free radio movement surfaced not only in Japan as previously noted, but was in evidence throughout Europe in the Seventies and Eighties playing itself out on the airwaves in a plethora of pirate radio stations that erupted in the Netherlands (e.g. *Vrije Keizer Radio*), West Germany (e.g. *Radio Dreyeckland*), Spain (e.g. *Radio Luna*), Denmark (e.g. *Radio Sokkeland*), France (e.g. *Radio Libertaire*), Belgium (e.g. *Radio Air Libre*), and the United Kingdom (e.g. *Radio Arthur*). Today, some of these pirate stations continue to exist, while others have been legalized and hence restratified, still others have disappeared. Yet new ones have been born all across the planet in the flames of the Nineties. Circling somewhere in the aether remains the vision of nomadic radio pirates whose transmitters navigate the air waves liberating them on behalf of the voiceless, marginalized and downtrodden and viewing those waves as treasures in themselves which have unjustly been confiscated and debased by the rich and mighty; a touchstone image for current free radio activists throughout the world.

This analogy, of course, brings up the controversy that surrounds the term "pirate" in micropower radio circles. Personally, I have never objected to the term pirate. When they asked Willie Sutton why he robbed banks, his reply was, "That's where the money is." Wobbly folksinger Utah Phillips says his mother used to call bank robbers "class heroes," and Queen Latifah seems to agree. Now since I do not believe that the money that has been privately accumulated by banks is any more the result of an equitable distribution of wealth than that the oligopoly over the airwaves that presently reigns is a fair distribution of a public resource, I would contend that the term radio pirate as it is commonly used is a positive poetic metaphor relating to the redistribution of resources between the haves and have nots. Sure, the naive vision of piracy is often simplistically based on an image of heroic swashbuckling romanticism, but the history of piracy is itself very complex. Those called pirates have ranged from despicable slave traders and imperial guns-for-hire to radical adventurers and utopian visionaries.

In fact, Gabriel Kuhn (Klausmann, 1997) makes a convincing argument that the former were not really pirates at all, but simply sea robbers and fillibusters rather than the embodiment of his Dionysian pirate ideal — the Stirnerite ego operating on a life-affirming active energy and driven by a Nietzschean will to power that excluded the reactive energy of those linked to statist and mercantile systems of domination. As Kuhn points out, many pirates were themselves escaped slaves and some pirate captains — like Mission — would immediately liberate all the slaves on the ships which they commandeered. Others, like Charles Bellamy, considered themselves libertarian socialists, and all lived by the anarchist code of mutual aid even if not acknowledged as such. It is, of course, the latter type of pirate with which most free radio advocates, including myself, identify.

In historical terms, piracy often offered seafarers an alternative to the hierarchical rigidity of naval life or the exploitative working conditions of the commercial ships. In fact, pirate ships were often characterized by a share the wealth ethos and allowed for a degree of gender equality and sexual freedom unheard of on both land and sea. Prominent women pirates took to the high seas in pursuit of liberty (Stanley, 1995, Klausmann, et al, 1997), and homosexuality was often an accepted part of shipboard life. (Burg, 1983). Pirate utopias have existed in the Bahamas (Nassau), the Caribbean (Hispaniola and Ranters Bay), Madagascar (Libertalia), and among the corsairs of North Africa (Republic of Sale).

Peter Lamborn Wilson makes a strong case on behalf of the idea that because of their anarchic forms of organization, the Moorish pirates could be considered our democratic forefathers, both on shipboard and in their commonwealths and intentional communities on land. Often "Articles" or "ships constitutions" unlike those of government man-of-wars or merchant ships called for the election of officers, including captains and quartermasters who received as little as 1 1/2 times the share of the booty as received by crewmen. In spite of the walking the plank Hollywood trope, corporal punishment was often outlawed and disagreements resolved at a drumhead court or by duels on shore. As Wilson puts it, "Pirate ships were true republics, each ship (or fleet) an independent floating democracy ... The Buccaneer way of life had an obvious appeal: interracial harmony, class solidarity, freedom from government, adventure and possible glory" (Wilson, 1995, p 191). Making an earlier case for democracy under the Jolly Roger, radical historian Marcus Rediker has emphatically noted, "Pirates constructed a culture of masterless men. They were as far removed from traditional authority as any men could be in the early eighteenth century" (Rediker, 1987, p 286). For Kuhn (Klausmann, 1997) pirate captains were more akin to Pierre Clastres' "primitive" chief and Deleuze and Guattari's nomadic guerilla than to authoritarian rulers interested in disciplinary power and capital accumulation.

Of course it's certainly true that pirates could be violent. Yet apart from the privateers employed by the nation state, the replacement of the outlawed non-state violence of the pirates with the legally sanctioned military violence of the sovereign nation states which banded together to crush piracy as a threat to *their own* monopoly on violence in international affairs, was hardly an improvement (Thomson, 1994). In the system that has evolved, pirates are seen as stateless, and so, in terms of international law, do not exist except as terrorists, while competing nation-states are seen as legitimate global actors; albeit within the current context of multinational shadow governments.

Are radio pirates plundering and hijacking the airwaves from their rightful state and corporate owners, or are they better conceived of as state-free rebels using culture jamming tactics to challenge the power of the media monopoly and the authority granted by government's normalizing regulations which have created a new interlocking system of enclosure, not merely on land, but in the air itself? Whether called pirate radio, micropower radio, low watt radio, liberation radio or free radio; collectively we constitute a movement that has the capability of bridging the gap between the social and individualist strains of anarchist theory and practice, and offering a libertarian alternative to both corporate and state controlled radio that has an even broader appeal.

Michel Foucault's strategic advice on "living counter to all forms of fascism" prizes "mobile arrangements over systems" (Foucault in Delueze and Guattari, 1983, p XIII), and brings to mind the image of Stephen Dunifer beginning his then clandestine broadcasts with a mobile radio unit in his backpack in the Berkeley hills or that of Mbanna Kantako defiantly vowing to run his Springfield, Illinois radio station off of a bicycle, if necessary, should he be busted by the FCC. These radio activists have in turn inspired countless others in their wake so that presently a virtual free radio stampede is underway as new micropower stations go on the air every day. A stampede can be envisioned as mobility called into being by spontaneous action. "Every animal knows, and humans are no exception, that when there is a stampede you must join in or get out of the way. Try to stop it, and you will be crushed." (Doe, 1996, p 181). Join the Great Radio Stampede!

Fools Paradise
Spring 1997

References Consulted

Anonymous. *Radio Is My Bomb: A DIY Manual for Pirates* (London: Hooligan Press, 1987).

Bey, Hakim. *Immediatism* (San Francisco: AK Press, 1994).

Burg, B.R. *Sodomy and the Pirate Tradition* (New York: New York University Press, 1984).

Critical Art Ensemble. *Electronic Civil Disobediance* (New York: Autonomedia, 1996).

Deleuze, Gilles and Guattari, Felix. *Anti-Oedipus: Capitalism and Schizophrenia* (Minneapolis: University of Minnesota Press, 1983).

A Thousand Plateaus: Capitalism and Schizophrenia (Minneapolis: University of Minnesota Press, 1987).

Doe, Jane. *Anarchist Farm* (Gualala, CA: III Publishing, 1996).

Guattari, Felx. *Soft Subversions* (New York: Semiotext(e), 1996).

Klausmann, Ulrike, Meinzerin, Marion and Kuhn, Gabriel. *Women Pirates and the Politics of the Jolly Roger.* (Montreal: Black Rose Books, 1997).

Lotringer, Sylvere and Marazzi, Christian. *Italy: Autonomia* (New York: Semiotext(e), Vol III, No. 3, 1980).

Lumley, Robert. *States of Emergency: Cultures of Revolt in Italy from 1968 to 1978* (New York: Verso, 1990).

Rediker, Marcus. *Between the Devil and the Deep Blue Sea* (Cambridge, MA: Cambridge University Press, 1987).

Stanley, Jo, ed. *Bold In Her Breeches: Women Pirates Across the Ages* (London: Pandora, 1995).

Strauss, Neil and Mandl, Dave. *Radiotext(e)* (New York: Semiotext(e) #16, 1993).

Thomson, Janice. *Mercenaries, Pirates and Sovereigns: Statebuilding and Extraterritorial Violence* (Princeton, NJ: Princeton University Press, 1994).

Toop, David. *Ocean of Sound: Aether Talk, Ambient Sound and Imaginary Worlds* (London: Serpents's Tail, 1995).

Wilson, Peter Lamborn. *Pirate Utopias* (New York: Autonomedia, 1995).

Inspirations Channeled

Chapman, Robert. *Selling the Sixties: The Pirates and Pop Music Radio* (London: Routledge, 1992).

Dery, Mark. *Culture Jamming* (Westfield, NJ: Open Magazine Pamphlet Series, 1993)

Fiske, John. *Power Plays, Power Works* (New York: Verso, 1993).

Girard, Bruce. *A Passion For Radio: Radio Waves and Community* (Montreal: Black Rose Books, 1992) (Available in English, French and Spanish translations).

Harrison, R.K. *Alternative Radio Handbook* (Orlando: Self-Published, Box 547014, Orlando, FL 32854).

Helms, Harry. *The Underground Frequency Guide* (San Diego, CA: DX/SWL Press, 1990).

Hind, John and Mosco, Stephen. *Rebel Radio: The Full Story of British Pirate Radio* (London: Pluto Press, 1985).

Kahn, Doug and Whitehead, Gregory. *Wireless Imagination: Sound, Radio and the Avant Garde* (Cambridge: MIT Press, 1992).

Keith, Michael. *Signals in the Air: Native Broadcasting in America* (Westport, CT: Praeger Press, 1995)

Kostelanetz, Richard. *Radio Writings* (Union City, NJ: Further State(s) of the Art, 1995).

Levy, William/deRidder, William. *Radio Art: The End of the Graven Image* (Amsterdam: Gallery 'A,' undated).

McHenry, Keith. *Rent Is Theft* (S.F.: Food Not Bombs, 1997)

Milam, Lorenzo. *Sex and Broadcasting: A Handbook on Starting A Radio Station for the Community* (San Diego, CA: Dildo Press, 1975).

The Radio Papers: Essays on the Art and Practice of Radio Transmission (San Diego, CA: MHO and MHO Works, 1986).

Moorish Orthodox Radio Crusade Collective. *Radio Sermonettes* (New York: Libertarian Book Club, 1992).

Teflon, Zeke. *The Complete Manual of Pirate Radio* (Sea Sharp Press, PO Box 1731, Tucson, AZ, 85702, undated pamphlet).

Vigil, Jose Ignaco Lopez. *Rebel Radio: The Story of El Salvador's Radio Venceremos* (Williamantic, CT: Curbstone Press, 1991).

Weiss, Allen. *Phantasmic Radio* (Durham, NC: Duke University Press, 1995)

Wong, Ken. *Pirate Radio Kills The Ruling Class* (Chi: Checagu Department of Psychogeography, 1996).

Yoder, Andrew. *Pirate Radio Stations* (Blue Ridge Summit, PA: TAB Books, 1990)
_____. *Pirate Radio* (Solona Beach, CA: High Text Publications, 1996).

Yoder, Andrew and Gray, Earl. *Pirate Radio Operations* (Port Townsend, WA: Loompanics Unlimited, 1997).

Zeller, George. *The Pirate Radio Directory* (Lake Geneva, WI: Tiare Publications, 1992).

Illustration by Meme Sabon

PART I

MOVING FROM CORPORATE ENCLOSURE TO FREE RADIO

Illustration by Johann Humyn Being

Illustration by Scott Marshall

THE POLITICAL ECONOMY OF RADIO

Robert W. McChesney

By political economy I refer specifically to how radio broadcasting is owned, controlled and subsidized. Another key component of political economic analysis is to look at how radio broadcasting relates to the social and class structure of society. Although I do not do much of that in this article, such a critique is implicit in the following. And while I concentrate upon radio broadcasting, at times it will be impossible to distinguish radio from television and other sorts of electronic communication. In the long run the same basic issues exist for all communication media.

Historically the rise of crucial new communication technologies like broadcasting has generated national public debates over how best to deploy these resources. This was because spectrum scarcity meant only a handful of broadcasters could operate at any given time in a region, and because the spectrum was seen as a publicly owned resource. It was as a result of such debates, for example, that public systems of broadcasting were established to serve publicly determined goals, not to generate profit. These debates often took place among society's elites, but there has been periodic popular intervention. The extent to which there is non-elite participation into communication policymaking may be a barometer for the level of democracy in a society. As a rule of thumb, if certain forces thoroughly dominate a society's political economy they will thoroughly dominate its communication system, and the fundamental questions of how the communication system should be organized and for what purposes are not even subject to debate. So it is and so it has been with the Communist Party in various "people's republics," and, for the most part, with big business interests in the United States.

It is in the United States that the decline of public debate over communication is the most developed. Yet it might surprise most people to know that this is not because a love for commercial media is genetically encoded in persons born in the United States. It is an acquired taste. When radio broadcasting emerged in the 1920s few thought it had any commercial potential. Many of broadcasting's pioneers were nonprofit organizations interested in public service. It was only in the late 1920s that capitalists began to sense that through network operation and commercial advertising, radio broadcasting could generate substantial profits. Through their immense power in Washington, these commercial broadcasters were able to dominate the Federal Radio Commission. As a result, the scarce number of air channels were effectively turned over to them with no public and little congressional deliberation on the matter.

It was in the aftermath of this commercialization of the airwaves that elements of U.S. society coalesced into a broadcast reform movement that attempted to establish a dominant role for the nonprofit and noncommercial sector in U.S. broadcasting. These opponents of commercialism came from education, religion, labor, civic organizations, women's groups, journalism, farmers' groups, civil libertarians, and intellectuals. The reformers attempted to tap into the intense public dislike for radio commercialism in the years before 1934, when Congress annually considered legislation for the permanent regulation of radio broadcasting. These reformers were explicitly radical; they argued that if private interests controlled the medium and their goal was profit, no amount of regulation or self-regulation could overcome the bias built into the system. Commercial broadcasting, the reformers argued, would downplay controversial, pro-working class and provocative public affairs programming and emphasize whatever fare would sell the most products for advertisers.

The reform movement disintegrated after the passage of the Communications Act of 1934, which established the FCC. The 1930s reformers did not lose to the commercial interests, however, on a level playing field. The radio lobby dominated because it was able to keep most Americans ignorant or confused about the communication policy matters then under discussion in Congress through their control of key elements of the news media and their sophisticated public relations aimed at the remainder of the press and the public. In addition, commercial broadcasters became a force that few politicians wished to antagonize; almost all of the congressional leaders of broadcast reform in 1931-1932 were defeated in their re-election attempts, a fate not lost on those who entered the next Congress. With the defeat of the reformers, the industry's claim that commercial broadcasting was inherently democratic and American went unchallenged and became internalized in the political culture.

Thereafter the only legitimate manner to criticize U.S. broadcasting was to assert that it was uncompetitive or "excessively" commercial, and therefore needed moderate regulation to protect the public interest while not damaging the commercial viability of the industry. The basis for this "liberal" claim for regulation was that the scarce number of channels necessitated regulation, not that the capitalist basis of the industry was fundamentally flawed. This was a far cry from the criticism of the broadcast reformers in the 1930s, who argued that the problem was not simply one of lack of competition in the marketplace, as much as it was the rule of the marketplace per se. It also means that with the vast expansion in the number of channels in the current communication revolution, the scarcity argument has lost its power and liberals are at a loss to withstand the deregulatory juggernaut.

This constricted range of policy debate was the context for the development of subsequent communication technologies including facsimile, FM radio, and television in the 1940s. That the communication corporations had first claim to these technologies was not disputed, even by public-service-minded New Dealers. In comparison to the public debate over radio in the 1930s, there was almost no public debate concerning alternative ways to develop these technologies. By the 1940s and thereafter, liberals knew the commercial basis of the system was inviolate, and they merely tried to carve out a nonprofit sector on the margins. (This was problematical, since whenever these nonprofit niches were seen as blocking profitable expansion, their future was on thin ice.)

By the middle 1930s the U.S. system of commercial broadcasting was thoroughly dominated by two enormous national networks — CBS and NBC — and supported by advertising. Both NBC and CBS argued that they could be trusted with such a prominent role in the U.S. broadcasting system because they would voluntarily act as public service institutions, even if it might detract from their profitability. In addition, the FCC technically reviewed license holders every few years to see that they were serving the "public interest, convenience, and necessity," although they almost never, ever withdrew any broadcaster's license. When television came along in the 1940s, the FCC effectively turned it over to the same networks that dominated radio.

That the commercial system has been very efficient at providing certain kinds of entertainment and satisfying certain kinds of audiences is clear. At the same time, it has also been clear that a purely profit-driven and advertising-supported system ignores many areas that may be of public interest. Almost from the beginning commercial broadcasting has generated criticism that it ignored or downplayed controversial political programming, or entertainment and cultural programming that would not attract huge audiences. In addition, advertisers served as powerful censors of broadcast content, and it was not in their interest to sponsor programming that might undermine their sales messages. Much criticism also centered on the fact that the educational potential of broadcasting was scarcely being tapped by commercial radio and television, especially, though not exclusively, for children. Indeed, by the 1960s it was nearly universally acknowledged that, despite its incredible success and popularity, the commercial broadcasting system had severe defects that were inherent to its nature.

The marginalization of public service values in U.S. communication debates — indeed the elimination of political debates over communication — explains the woeful history of U.S. public radio and television. The defeat of the broadcast reform movement in 1934 led to what might be called the Dark Ages of U.S. public broadcasting. If the 1930s reformers sought a system where the dominant sector was nonprofit and noncommercial, all future advocates of public broadcasting had to accept that the system was established primarily to benefit the commercial broadcasters, and any public stations would have to find a niche on the margins, where they would not threaten the existing or potential profitability of the commercial interests. This made public broadcasting in the U.S. fundamentally different from Britain or Canada, or nearly any other nation with a comparable political economy. Whereas the BBC and the CBC regarded their mandate as providing a service to the entire nation, the U.S. public broadcasters realized that they could only survive politically by not taking listeners or viewers away from the commercial broadcasters. The function of the public or educational broadcasters, then, was to provide such programming as was unprofitable for the commercial broadcasters to produce. At the same time, however, politicians and government officials hostile to public broadcasting also insisted that public broadcasting remain within the same ideological confines as the commercial system. This encouraged U.S. public broadcasting after 1935 to emphasize elite cultural programming at the expense of generating a large following. In short, since 1935 public broadcasting in the United States has been in a no-win situation.

The major function of nonprofit broadcasting in the United States from 1920 to 1960 was, in fact, to pioneer new sections of the electromagnetic spectrum when the commercial interests did not yet view them as profitable. Thus it was educational broadcasters who played an enormous role in developing AM broadcasting in the 1920s, and then FM radio and even UHF television in the 1940s and 1950s. In each case, once it became clear that money could be made, the educators were displaced and capitalists seized the reins. Arguably, too, this looks like the fate of the Internet, which has been pioneered as a public service by the nonprofit sector with government subsidies until capital decided to take over and relegate the pioneers to the margins. The 1930s broadcast reformers were well aware of this tendency and refused to let the FCC push them into new technologies where there would be no access to the general public. After 1935, the proponents of public broadcasting had no choice in the matter. (In many cases, such as the Internet, satellites and digital communication, these technologies were developed through research funds provided by the federal government. Once the technologies proved profitable, however, they were turned over to private interests with negligible compensation.)

Even with these limitations, the commercial broadcasters were wary of public broadcasting and fought it tooth and nail well into the 1960s. After many halting starts, Congress passed the Public Broadcasting Act of 1967, which led to the creation of the Corporation for Public Broadcasting, and soon thereafter of PBS and NPR. The commercial broadcasters finally agreed not to oppose public broadcasting, primarily because they believed the new public system could be responsible for doing the unprofitable cultural and public affairs programming that critics were constantly lambasting them for neglecting. There was a catch, however. The initial plan to have the CPB funded by a sales tax on the purchase of new radio sets and television sets, somewhat akin to the BBC method, was dropped, thus preventing public broadcasting a stable source of income necessary for planning as well as editorial autonomy. At the outset it was determined that Americans would have a public system, but it would be severely handicapped. We would have only a system the commercial broadcasters would permit.

Although U.S. public broadcasting has produced some good fare, the system has been supremely compromised by its structural basis, and it is farcical in comparison to the powerful public service systems of Europe. Indeed, in international discussions of public broadcasting, the term "PBS-style system" is invoked to refer to a public system that is marginal and ineffective. It is the fate that the BBC, CBC and others wish to avoid.

Moreover, public radio and television stations in the major markets have become decidedly conservative (in the generic, not political, sense of the term) institutions. The Carnegie Commission — whose 1967 report was instrumental in the formation of U.S. public broadcasting — envisioned local elected community boards actively participating in the management and programming of the public stations. This notion has slid into oblivion and rather cumbersome bureaucracies have settled in. Often, especially in the largest markets, the leading figures on the public television boards are drawn from the very wealthiest and most powerful people in the community. Public broadcasting, despite these drawbacks, has produced and continues to produce outstanding programming. In my hometown of Madison, Wisconsin, it is a precious resource with a much broader audience than found elsewhere. Even those who are critical of public broadcasting acknowledge that it has an important niche in the market. The problem is that it is just that, a niche, and a niche serving only a sliver of the community.

The funding system is the primary culprit. The U.S. government only provides around 15 percent of the revenues; public stations depend on corporate donations, foundation grants, and listener/viewer contributions for the balance. In effect, this has made PBS and NPR stations commercial enterprises, and it has given the large corporations that dominate its subsidy tremendous influence over public broadcasting content, in a manner that violates the fundamental principles of public broadcasting. It has also encouraged the tendency to appeal to an affluent audience, rather than a working-class audience, because upscale viewers/listeners have far more disposable income. Ironically, it is this well-heeled base of support that gives public broadcasting the leverage it has in negotiations for federal monies, as much as any argument for "public" media. If the federal subsidy were fully eliminated, the bias toward corporate interests and an upper-income target audience would be magnified.

This is why the "second" public TV and radio stations as exist in many U.S. communities are so very important. In particular, radio, as a strikingly inexpensive medium is especially well-suited to being a community medium. In addition to "second" public stations, we need to encourage nonprofit community and low-power radio stations. These stations have less resources than the commercial or establishment public stations, but they are much closer to the notion of public broadcasting found globally. These stations tend to have much closer ties to elements of the community not found in the Blue Book, at elite universities, or in affluent suburbs. They tend to be interested in reaching sectors of the community that commercial broadcasters and mainline public broadcasters tend to neglect: poor people, young people, artists, political dissidents, community groups, and minority groups. In short they tend to have a much greater vitality — or the potential for it — than the established public stations. Nobody would suggest we only need one commercial station to accommodate an entire community, so why is it that one public broadcaster is expected to be all inclusive?

With the digital revolution, the technical and legal boundaries between broadcasting and telephony in the 1934 Communications Act have broken down. Indeed, the barriers between all forms of communication are breaking down, and communication laws everywhere are becoming outdated. Congress passed, and President Clinton signed into law, the Telecommunications Act of 1996 to replace the 1934 law. The overarching purpose of the 1996 Telecommunications Act is to deregulate all communication industries and to permit the market, not public policy, to determine the course of the information highway and the communications system. It is widely considered to be one of the three or four most important federal laws of this generation.

Even by the minimal standards of the 1934 Act, the debate surrounding the 1996 Telecommunications Act was a farce. Some of the law was actually written by the lobbyists for the communication firms it affects. The only "debate" was whether broadcasters, long-distance companies, local telephone providers, or cable companies would get the inside track in the deregulatory race. Consistent with the pattern set in the middle 1930s, the primacy of corporate control and the profit motive was a given. The range of legitimate debate extended from those like Newt Gingrich, who argue profits are synonymous with public service, to those like Vice-President Al Gore, who argue there are public interest concerns the marketplace cannot resolve, but can only be addressed once the profitability of the dominant corporate sector has been assured. The historical record with communication regulation indicates that although the Gore position can be gussied up, once the needs of corporations are given primacy, the public interest will invariably be pushed to the margins.

This situation exists for many of the same reasons the broadcast reformers were demolished in the 1930s. Politicians may favor one sector over another in the battle to cash in on the highway, but they cannot oppose the cashing-in process, without risking their political careers. Both the Democratic and Republican parties have strong ties to the large communication firms and industries, and the communication lobbies are among the most feared, respected and well endowed of all that seek favors on Capitol Hill. The only grounds for political independence in this case would be if there were an informed and mobilized citizenry ready to do battle for alternative policies. But where would citizens get informed? Only through the news media, where news coverage is minimal and restricted to the range of legitimate debate, which, in this case, means almost no debate at all. That is why the Telecommunications Act was covered (rather extensively) as a business story, not a public policy story. "I have never seen anything like the Telecommunications Bill," one career lobbyist observed. "The silence of public debate is deafening. A bill with such astonishing impact on all of us is not even being discussed."

The debate over communications policy is restricted to elites and those with serious financial stakes in the outcome. It does not reflect well on the caliber of U.S. participatory democracy, but it is capitalist democracy at its best. The politicians of both parties promised the public that the Telecommunications Act would provide a spurt in high-paying jobs and intense market competition in communications, a "digital free-for-all" as one liberal Democrat put it. An even cursory reading of the business press at the same time would reveal that those who benefited from the law knew these claims to be half-truths or outright lies. These are oligopolistic industries that strongly discourage all but the most judiciously planned competition. It is more likely that deregulation will lead to merger activity, increased concentration, and continued "downsizing." And, as the U.S. 1996 Telecommunications Act "unleashes" the U.S.-based transnational media and communication firms to grow through mergers and acquisitions with minimal fear of regulatory intervention, this effectively gives the green light to further consolidation of the global market these firms dominate. As such, the U.S. Telecommunications Act is to some extent a global law.

The most immediate consequence of the passage of the Telecommunications Act of 1996 has been the immediate and rapid consolidation in corporate concentrated ownership of U.S. radio stations. This is unconscionable and appalling. Corporations dominate nearly every nook and cranny of our media culture. Why not reserve all or most of the radio spectrum for nonprofit and noncommercial utilization?

Illustration by Keith McHenry

BROADCAST CONFIDENTIAL *

Lee Ballinger

Jeff McCluskey sits on his ass in an office in Chicago and tells the radio stations of America what records to play. If you want to get his attention, send a check. McCluskey's consulting company has all the major record labels as clients and maintains what he calls "close relationships" with over sixty of America's biggest radio stations. Using the $6 million a year he takes in from record companies, McCluskey pays each station from $15,000 to $100,000 a year in return for exclusive access to the station program directors. Those program directors know what to do when McCluskey tells them which records to play.

As any regular *Jeopardy* watcher could tell you, the correct question here is: How much airplay does a record get if it's put out by an independent company that can't afford to hire Jeff McCluskey or the other parasites of the record promotion industry?

The passage of the Telecom Act on February 8, 1996 is making things worse. Yet there is at least one good thing about this truly frightening piece of legislation: it puts the opportunities and dangers that face the microbroadcasting movement in sharp focus.

The Act allows for corporations to own many more radio stations than they were previously allowed, including *eight* in the same city. As a result of the mergers and acquisitions generated by the Act, there are already 127 fewer radio station owners now than there were at this time last year. Several billion dollars worth of broadcasting properties have changed hands. For example, in

---

* This article was originally presented as a speech at the International Micropower Broadcasting Conference in Oakland, CA, November 1996.

October SFX Broadcasting bought Secret Communications for $300 million. SFX now owns 75 stations and is a significant player in 20 major radio markets.

In 1995, the top 50 radio chain owners controlled 876 stations, today the top 50 owners control 1,187 stations, an increase of 40 percent in just 12 months. Since bigger broadcasting chains can demand higher consulting fees from record companies, it will make it even more difficult for anyone but the Big Six record companies to get music on the radio. Broadcasting chains that control stations in dozens of markets may soon, according to *Rolling Stone*, demand that they and they alone be allowed to play music by the artists they want to feature.

This process, disgusting as it is, creates opportunities for microbroadcasters to increase their audiences by serving all those left out by the narrow programming of the monopolies. But along with these opportunities comes danger. The huge broadcast chains, having paid hundreds of millions of dollars to expand, will not sit by quietly and allow their investments to be threatened by competition from the likes of YOU.

A case in point is a micro station called Beat Radio in Minneapolis. Alan Freed, who has been a DJ at three Minneapolis radio stations as well as at Power 99 in Philadelphia, went on the air on July 21, 1996 to air a variety of dance sounds that local stations refused to play. With much of the station's airtime handled by local club DJs, Beat Radio soon drew a large and devoted following. It also drew the attention of the FCC, which sent Freed a letter threatening him with prison time. The Minnesota Broadcasters Association filed a complaint about Beat Radio with the FCC, as did several Minneapolis commercial stations. Beat Radio began to suffer high-power interference from another transmitter, which Freed believes could only have been done by licensed stations intent on putting him out of business. Then, at 4:35 PM on November 1, the FCC, accompanied by U.S. Marshals, entered the premises of Beat Radio and seized the station's equipment.

This chain of events can be traced directly back to the National Association of Broadcasters filing a friend of the court brief against Free Radio Berkeley earlier that year, a move that was designed to alert the NAB's corporate membership that unlicensed radio must be crushed. Evidently, radio executives in Minnesota were paying attention.

Behind these actions lie other provisions of the Telecom Act, which makes it a crime punishable by up to five years in prison to distribute, *by any means*, music that is "obscene, lewd, lascivious, or filthy." Using the standards developed over the past ten years by the Clinton-Gingrich administration, this makes felons of everyone, including zine editors and DJs, who help bring artists ranging from Madonna to White Zombie to Wu-Tang Clan to market. The Telecom Act provides the same severe penalty for anyone who, *by any means*, circulates information about abortion.

The harsh truth is that we are up against the people in America who have all the money and all the power. They have already shown that they will not hesitate to use both against us. I say this not to discourage anyone, because we're going to do what we've got to do. But I do want to bring you face to face with the fact that, if we operate as free-spirited lone wolves, we cannot survive the attacks that the future surely holds.

The only way microbroadcasting can get the support it needs to survive is to become the voice of a new America, an America that has just begun to swing into action. Think back over the torrent of activity in 1996 ... The Million Man March in Washington, which followed closely on the heels of a march there by 300,000 women. In October, over 30,000 Latinos went to Washington to push for a $7 an hour minimum wage and health care for all. 250,000 attended the Stand Up for Children rally and delegates representing one million workers founded the Labor Party in June (the Labor Party, by the way, is helping to launch a microstation in Los Angeles). These "big number events" rest on a firm foundation of countless smaller, often hidden events, ranging from gang truce meetings to housing takeovers by the homeless to the strike being waged by the Hotel and Restaurant Workers Local 2850 which is ongoing even while they host this 1996 International Micropower Broadcasting Conference in Oakland.

This process was summed up well by Napoleon Williams of Black Liberation Radio in Decatur, Illinois, when he recently told *Rock & Rap Confidential*: "Before I was sent to prison on trumped-up charges, only a small number of people listened to me when I explained what was really going on in America. While I was in prison, the people here faced bitter strikes, like the one at Caterpillar, and a lot of middle-class white people got beat up by the cops and the corporations. Now I'm out of prison and back on the air and these people are listening to me, calling in, and becoming a part of the station. Maybe we should change our name to 'People's Liberation Radio.'"

In that light, let me end by issuing a few friendly challenges ...

Downsizing in manufacturing and service industries continues to sweep across the country. The result has been extremes in wealth and poverty never before seen in America. Downsizing has created eight million homeless and 80 million people living below the poverty line. These people have no voice in the media. *Micropower radio must be the voice of America's poor, regardless of age or race.*

As a result of NAFTA and its ongoing aftermath, the destinies of poor and working people in Mexico, the U.S., and Canada are joined more closely than ever before. For instance, in order to control the deteriorating political and economic situation in Mexico, the international bankers are pressing the Mexican military to restore order. The police forces of 25 Mexican states are now

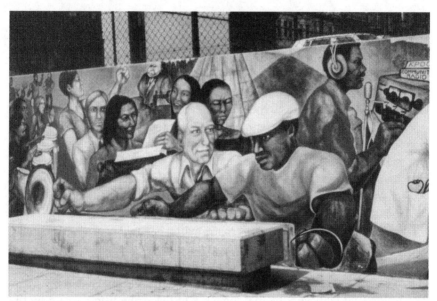

Photo by Tim Drescher of a detail from the mural "Our History is No Mystery" by the Haight-Asbury Muralists (Miranda Bergman, Jane Norling, Arch Williams, Jo Tucker, Myles Stryker and Thomas Kunz), San Francisco, 1977.

commanded by military officers. Southern Mexico is under military occupation. As the Mexican social pot boils over, more and more people will migrate northward to escape hunger and repression. *Micropower radio must facilitate communication throughout the entire zone of NAFTA occupation, from Chiapas to the Yukon to South Carolina. From there, microradio can help us all extend a hand to the rest of the hemisphere.*

Music is the conscience of the world and a prime source of inspiration and information. Commercial radio refuses to play much of the music that is on the charts, let alone the wealth of sounds from the underground. Commercial radio is undemocratic, taking its orders from a handful of professional consultants. Commercial radio is corrupt, gladly taking money from record companies through third parties. *Micropower radio must be the voice of our music and our culture.*

The Democratic party has abandoned us. "Liberal" Democrats were the instigators of the ongoing wave of music censorship. "Liberal" Democrats were eager partners in passing the Telecom Bill. Bill Clinton laughed as he signed this bill. *It passed in the House by a vote of 414-16 and in the Senate by a vote of 91-5. Micropower radio must be the voice of all those striving to break away from the political parties of the corporations.*

Micropower radio has a role that goes beyond being the voice of a vital, cutting-edge underground. Micropower radio must set its sights on becoming the voice of a new American majority.

COMMUNITY RADIO AT THE CROSSROADS

Federal Policy and The Professionalization of a Grassroots Medium

Jon Bekken

Three distinctive models of communications — Commercial, Public (government-sponsored) and Community — have evolved in American broadcasting, each characterized by different modes of financing, control, programming and access. Since 1930, U.S. broadcasting has been predominantly commercial, although coexisting with an embattled public sector (McChesney 1993). Community broadcasting established itself as an alternative model with the establishment of KPFA, Berkeley, in 1949.

This chapter examines institutional constraints on community radio in the United States and the ways in which these are reshaping community broadcasting. These constraints fall into three primary areas: the licensing and regulatory process, financing mechanisms, and access to programming. Each has been affected by changing government policy over the last 15 years as policymakers and community broadcasters have sought to incorporate, to varying degrees, community radio into the public broadcasting system. I then turn to a brief discussion of efforts by community activists to operate outside the parameters of government-licensed operations by establishing low-power, community-based FM stations, and conclude by examining the implications of these developments for community access to, and control over, its own media institutions.

GRASSROOTS COMMUNICATIONS

Throughout the world, the public sector has proved to be neither account-able nor accessible to the public. Grassroots organizations have established their own means of communication where the necessary means could be procured. In broadcasting these efforts — known as community, free or neighborhood radio — have developed throughout Western Europe, in the United States and Canada, in Latin America, and elsewhere (Lewis 1984a; White 1983). Despite substantial differences in origin and structure, each developed as a reaction to existing broadcasting systems (whether commercial or public) by excluded groups seeking to meet their own needs and develop their own programs.

Community radio is characterized by access, public participation in pro-duction and decision-making and, predominantly, by listener-financing. The in-tention is that management of the station is in the hands of those who use and listen to it. Though the workings of such stations are never easy, the structure does offer the possibility of accountability to the audience/user in a way state and commercial stations do not. (Lewis 1984b, 141)

Community radio is thus part of a broader struggle for grassroots access to communication media, a struggle not only for freedom of communications but for freedom to communicate (Berrigan 1977; Barbrook 1987). Rather than leave power in the hands of a few experts, "the community station is the locus for a joining of disparate people with differing needs and interests to share in the construction and dissemination of information and entertainment" (Hochheimer 1988, 164). The idea of a right to communicate has recently gained support as the shortcomings of state and commercial services become increas-ingly evident. Such a right "includes the principles of access, participation and self-management in communications" (Lewis 1984a, 1) and a conception of me-dia as "direct instruments for active groups or movements to produce their cul-tural identity" and create new social relations (Mattelart and Piemme 1980, 336).

> Community radio ... is not some electronic Iskra, calling the masses to battle ... It is not even a facility for a closed circle of professional journalists, however "ideologically sound," to mediate between lis-teners and social events. Rather, what is subversive about community radio is the way it can challenge the division between broadcasters and consumers in our society. (Barbrook 1985, 71-72)

Breaking down this division entails more than simply allowing ordinary citizens access to the airwaves (important though this is); it entails participa-tion in the production and management of communication systems and owner-ship and control of the means of communication.

In Europe, community radio began as an unlicensed (pirate) service, sometimes going on to gain legal recognition — though often at the cost of government regulation, or of opening the door to commercial broadcasters as well. While pirate broadcasters are often closely integrated with social movements and explicitly activist in tone, this illegal status leaves them vulnerable to suppression and creates barriers to wider community involvement. In North America community radio developed as a licensed service, although growing numbers of community broadcasters are turning to unlicensed operations in order to circumvent the Federal Communications Commission's inhospitable regulatory framework and the shortage of available frequencies (Hallikainen 1991; Radio Free Detroit 1992; Radio Free Venice 1991; Rodriguez 1991; Drew 1993).

LICENSING

The licensing and regulatory procedures adopted by the Federal Communications Commission serve as an insurmountable obstacle to many community broadcasting efforts, and tend to discourage true self-management and community control. KKFI, a community radio station in Kansas City, found that it took more than ten years from conception to going on-air (KKFI 1987). Lorenzo Milam (1986), who helped establish five community radio stations, provides harrowing detail on the difficulties of navigating the bureaucratic processes to obtain a broadcasting license. Dennis Gross, an organizer of Dallas station KCHU, found that it took four years to complete the necessary paperwork:

> there's the application for construction permit form from the Federal Communications Commission, and the application for STL and SCA form from the same body; there's the Federal Aviation Authority (sic) form to construct a tower. The Internal Revenue Service has an army of them for tax-exempt status. ... If you took all the forms, and stacked them all together, and took Dennis Gross, and stacked him next to them, they'd both stand at about 4'9". (Milam 1986, 110)

Few community-based institutions have the bureaucratic savvy or staying power to see this process through years of delays, or to handle the barrage of paperwork. Milam was involved in founding several stations precisely because he had developed expertise in shepherding applications through the bureaucratic maze, and because he could get his hands on the necessary funds. Other stations developed their own experts or, after the founding of the National Federation of Community Broadcasters, relied on NFCB experts.

Once a station is on the air, the constraints imposed by the licensing and regulatory process continue. Community radio stations (like all broadcasters) are required to maintain programming and engineering logs; to comply with FCC regulations governing indecency, equal time, technical standards, etc.; and to periodically apply for license renewal. In addition, FCC regulations require that stations be operated only by licensed personnel. While obtaining a Restricted Radiotelephone Operator Permit is relatively simple, the majority of the population is thereby precluded from direct access to the airwaves and can broadcast only with the assistance and mediation of a licensed operator. The FCC did exempt broadcast personnel at noncommercial stations from a $35 application fee after months of protest from community broadcasters (FCC waives $35 fee 1991). Similarly, state and federal authorities require the filing of periodic financial reports and tax forms, and require that certain hierarchical forms (Boards of Directors, Chief Engineer, etc.) be observed.

And the FCC now requires that FM radio stations operate at least 100 watts, although it does allow unlicensed transmitters with a maximum coverage radius of 200 feet (Hindman 1990, 2-3; Federal Communications Commission 1991). By increasing its minimum power requirements from 10 watts in 1980, the FCC barred many localized and low-budget operations from broadcasting, even while permitting hundreds of licensed and unlicensed all-commercial operations difficult to reconcile with traditional public service doctrines (Harris 1990; Bagdikian 1992).

The need to meet FCC regulations for record-keeping, technical standards and uninterrupted service ensures that "there will be a nucleus of professional workers" and a division of labor between administration, engineers and programmers (Barbrook 1985, 73). Some stations have operated without any paid staff; a few even offering 24–hour service on an all-volunteer basis. But in practice even these stations depend upon a core of dedicated volunteers who have acquired the technical and bureaucratic skills to maintain compliance with state regulations and keep the station on the air, and who thus wield greater power and influence than can other participants. While most community broadcasters attempt to minimize the effects of this division of labor, FCC and other government policies inexorably pull in the opposite direction.

GOVERNMENT FINANCING

Until the 1960s federal funds were not available for public radio and most noncommercial stations were operated by educational institutions for in-house purposes (Carnegie Commission 1979). In 1967, public radio stations became eligible for Educational Broadcasting Facilities Program grants (now the Public

Telecommunications Facilities Program [PTFP]) to purchase transmitting and studio equipment. Although no formal regulations barred community broadcasters from receiving these grants, they were not made available in practice until the late 1970s, following lobbying by the National Federation of Community Broadcasters (NFCB) which then assisted local stations in obtaining these funds.

PTFP funds now play a major role in financing new community radio stations, and in enabling existing broadcasters to upgrade facilities or replace worn-out equipment. For example, KKFI, Kansas City, MO, received $204,200 in PTFP matching funds to build its 100,000 watt station (KKFI 1987). Before the advent of PTFP funding, no community radio station could have hoped to raise these sorts of funds, or to broadcast at such high power levels. PTFP funds are not the only governmental monies available for community radio. Several community broadcasters have obtained grants for arts programming through state and federal arts agencies. These grants are often not tied to specific programming, but made available to meet general operating expenses. CETA funds enabled many stations to hire paid staff, some for the first time, before that program was abolished in 1981. And community broadcasters have actively pursued, with varying levels of success, Corporation for Public Broadcasting funds.

In addition to financing National Public Radio, television's Public Broadcasting System and individual program producers, the Corporation for Public Broadcasting offers Community Service Grants. To qualify, radio stations must have an annual budget of at least $195,000 in non-federal funds, at least five full-time employees, programming that does not duplicate that of other local public stations, and a broadcast schedule of at least eighteen hours daily (CPB raises fundraising hurdle 1991). In 1998, the CPB will add requirements that broadcasters either demonstrate average quarter-hour listenership of 15 percent (12 percent in large markets) or financial support from 18 to 20 percent of coverage area residents (Corporation for Public Broadcasting Board 1996).

These requirements are particularly difficult to meet for stations targeting minority and low-income communities or in small and medium-sized communities with a smaller potential base of support (Barlow 1989). Community broadcasters have been unsuccessful in efforts to count the value of volunteer staff time towards their non-federal support, and only a handful — notably the Pacifica stations — have met the requirements (Robertiello 1991; Hindman 1990, 6; NFCB 1987). In pursuing Community Service Grants, however, many stations have embarked upon ambitious expansion programs. WEFT (Champaign, IL), for example, expanded its paid staff and broadcast power in an unsuccessful effort to qualify for CPB funding which left insufficient funds for station operations and undermined the role and authority of volunteers (Stein 1988).

Since few community broadcasters can meet the program's staffing and budget requirements (let alone the new Arbitron standards), the Corporation introduced two programs to facilitate integration of community broadcasters into the public broadcasting orbit (Chadwick 1990). A Station Development Grant program permits broadcasters to qualify for CPB funds incrementally over a five-year period. Participating stations must have at least three full-time employees and spend more than $75,000 in non-federal funds annually. Qualifying stations are also integrated into the public radio satellite program service as CPB pays connection fees. Stations which cannot meet these initial requirements may seek one-time Program Acquisition Grants which cover access fees and provide funds for purchasing and promoting satellite-distributed programming.

Both programs offer very real incentives to community broadcasters to pursue the public radio model. WEFT, for example, applied for and received a Program Acquisition Grant in hopes of securing increased listenership and, hence, support. The decision was controversial; station volunteers protested the Board of Directors' decision to go further into debt to acquire the satellite dish necessary to participate in the program (Bekken 1990; Robertiello 1990).

These and other government programs encourage professionalization. Columbia's KOPN increased its paid staff from one full-time to 25 full and part-time positions between 1976 and 1980, after operating for its first two years without any paid staff at all. Only one-and-a-half staff positions were paid out of listener funds — the others were funded through grants which provided more than half of KOPN's income. In 1981, KOPN received $30,000 in CPB funds but was in the process of losing its other remaining federal funds, and thus the staff positions required to retain CPB funding (Palmquist 1981a, 1981b). KOPN retained CPB funding only by soliciting underwriting and operating weekly bingo games (Poses 1983). In 1993 a collapse in bingo revenues led to renewed financial crisis. The station responded by developing a "more homogenous, predictable" sound based upon the Adult Album Alternative format and heavy use of the American Public Radio satellite feed. The National Federation of Community Broadcasters used KOPN as a pilot for its CPB-financed Healthy Station Project, aimed at increasing the station's budget by developing a more commercial sound (Teutenberg 1993; KOPN 1993; LaPage 1994; Board of Directors 1994). While the NFCB considers the Healthy Station Project a success, many participating stations objected to recommendations for homogenized programming that would appeal to a more upscale audience (Jacobson 1994).

As government support of community radio becomes increasingly important, concerns are being raised over the impact these funds will have on community broadcasters' independence and integrity. Pacifica Foundation vice president Peter Franck (1979, 181) noted that

Pacifica has .... presented voices and views, some unpopular, which otherwise would have been absent from the airwaves. ... Such programming has led on occasion to criticism by public officials, subpoenas from investigating bodies and court challenges. Listener sponsorship, the support of many subscribers, made Pacifica's independence and innovative programming possible.

"The vitality of the democratic processes in this country needs a strong listener-supported community radio movement," Franck argued (1979, 191), opposing proposals supported by the National Federation of Community Broadcasters (1979) to allow advertising. Nor did Franck favor government operating subsidies:

> Funds should be made available in a way that does not increase dependence on a continued flow of funds ... Clearly the grant of funds for the construction of new facilities or for the improvement of existing facilities is a one-time kind of thing and does not generate dependence.
>
> General, un-earmarked funds, as in the Corporation for Public Broadcasting's present Community Service Grant (CSG) program, encourages dependence on a continuing flow of such funds ... We fear that a station which was getting a large part of its operating budget from the United States government would have hesitated to attack J. Edgar Hoover in 1963, or would have hesitated to have a reporter in Hanoi in the early 60s. (Franck 1979, 192-93)

I quote Franck not because his views are representative of community broadcasters — the National Federation of Community Broadcasters' pleas for easier access to public funding (NFCB 1979 and 1987; Thomas 1979, 1981a and 1981b; Robertiello 1991) seem more typical — but because he raises issues that few community broadcasters have seriously grappled with. Most have eagerly pursued federal funding with little consideration to related institutional constraints (whether in the form of increased dependence, staff time needed to pursue and administer grants, or the structural changes needed to qualify for funding and the impact these might have on the station's character and mission). Even where such concerns are raised, they are generally given short shrift. At WEFT, for example, station volunteers voted against seeking further PTFP equipment grants because they consumed staff time needed for other purposes, entangled the station with the government contrary to the philosophy of the station's membership, and was not clearly a benefit to the station since it required matching grant funds with donated funds.

WEFT's board expressed "its appreciation of the Associates' concern," but voted unanimously (with one abstention) to seek the funds anyway (WEFT Board of Directors' Minutes 1988, 2).

When NFCB's president testified against proposed federal budget cuts, he noted

> I myself started in public radio some 10 years ago at a station that received not a dollar of tax funds. ... Looking back, I know we did some great things, but we worked for poverty-level wages, and our ability to attract and keep competent, professional staff was severely limited.... Community radio has come a long way from those days ... [and] Federal assistance has played a crucial role. (Thomas 1981b, 200)

Thomas described stations built without Federal assistance as "crippled projects" without the technical or economic foundations essential for effective broadcasting.

Yet most community radio stations were built under such conditions, and were thereby forced to rely on the communities they served for expertise, funds and labor. Where community radio once depended entirely on volunteers not only for programming but also for administration and support services, state and federal sources of funding enable and require stations to develop a core paid staff for station operations — ranging from administrative and technical functions to professional programmers. These professionals now argue for severing their station's remaining reliance on volunteers.

Mark Fuerst, station manager at Philadelphia's WXPN, views volunteer programming and the power volunteers exercise over programming decisions as anachronisms that must be overcome. A core of paid on-air personnel would in this view enable station management to require more "professional" programming from remaining volunteers and result in improved listenership and financial support. Fuerst admits that such a policy would meet with fierce resistance from existing volunteers and listeners, but argues that it is a logical extension of the earlier shift from volunteer to professional administrative staffs. Extending hierarchy and professionalization into the programming sphere is, in this view, the next logical step in the institutionalization of community radio (Fuerst 1988; see also Buchter 1990).

The process of professionalization, however, has led to intense conflicts between volunteers and listeners on the one hand, and station management on the other (Miami judge orders volunteer deejays reinstated 1991; Behrens 1991; Kurtenbach 1988). Volunteers and listeners have organized strikes, financial boycotts and alternative slates for elected board seats, and have demanded formal mechanisms for ensuring community control (Noton 1994; Kneedler 1993). These struggles have arisen even at Pacifica flagship KPFA, where subscribers contend that the station is increasingly undemocratic, driven by corporate and foundation funding, and indistinguishable from mainstream media outlets (Save KPFA 1993; Noton 1994). Pacifica managers responded to the controversy by prohibiting on-air discussion, illegally closing board meetings to the public, and hiring a union-busting consultant to aid in its efforts to eliminate unpaid staff's union protection (Blankfort 1996).

SATELLITE PROGRAMMING

Professional broadcasting ideology and financial incentives thus combine to create a vision of "community radio" quite unrecognizable to those who have sought to break out of traditional, hierarchical models of media practice. These trends are further reinforced by reliance on satellite technology for program dissemination and, particularly, on the institutional forms and practices that have emerged to govern the satellite system. Until a few years ago, community broadcasters could obtain external program material only through expensive telephone feeds or on tape. While both Pacifica and the NFCB operated program exchanges, these were primarily a medium whereby volunteer programmers could disseminate locally-produced programs with wider appeal. The overwhelming majority of community radio programming was produced in-house.

With satellite program distribution, strong incentives towards reliance on non-local programming come into being. This programming — often produced with (relatively) lavish financial backing from corporations, foundations or the government — is generally of higher technical quality than can be expected from volunteer programmers and frees program directors from reliance on what volunteers are willing or able to produce. Instead they can schedule programs off the satellite to meet perceived audience desires and/or needs or to replace recalcitrant volunteers.

The satellite link makes possible greater — and more contemporary — coverage of national issues and news. But the economic and institutional arrangements governing satellite access and usage foster greater reliance on institutionally-sponsored, professionally-produced programming. Not only must a community radio station spend several thousand dollars for equipment to receive programs off the satellite, it must also pay annual access charges (Greene 1987; Satellite Distribution/Interconnection 1988). This entitles stations to free or nominally-priced usage of many programs on the satellite, although National Public Radio and American Public Radio charge substantial fees for their programs (few community broadcasters carry NPR programming, APR's programs are sold individually and are carried by some stations — KOPN, for example, carries Monitor Radio, as does Seattle's KUCM). Yet producers must pay to place their material on the satellite and meet their program costs. Pacifica's live coverage of the Iran-Contra hearings included periodic fund appeals (with an 800 telephone number) in an effort to recover costs (Stum 1987). More commonly, however, producers resort to corporate or other underwriting.

The availability of satellite-distributed programming gives paid staff a stronger hand in setting programming, as they are no longer dependent upon volunteers or the community to meet their objectives. Albuquerque's KUNM replaced volunteer programmers with satellite-distributed classical and jazz music programs despite bitter opposition by volunteer programmers and listeners (Glick 1987a, 1987b). And many community stations now carry the Corporation for Public Broadcasting-financed "World Cafe," a daily world music feed described as "a texture, a profile of programming that gives your station a sound and a style in listeners' minds so they tune in over and over again" (Singer 1990, 10). However, this audio wallpaper has drawn heated criticism and been financially disastrous for some stations (*Radio Resistor's Bulletin* 1993a; Kneedle 1993).

Satellite distribution is initially attractive both to producers and to broadcasters who gain access to a wide variety of programs that can be used to fill gaps in available programs and serve unmet community needs. Unlike tape exchanges, satellite transmission makes possible rapid transmission of programming, particularly for the handful of stations with the facilities to put programs onto the satellite. With tape-based distribution each program is individually purchased or exchanged, encouraging reliance on local production. Flat-rate satellite access charges and federal funding transform the economic and organizational constraints on national programming. Once a station has committed resources to meeting the annual access fee it costs little more to carry additional externally-produced programs.

The economics of satellite distribution also work to bar most community productions from the air. To distribute programs on tape requires only modest investment, well within the resources of most volunteers. Access to the satellite, while subsidized, is comparatively expensive. Fairness & Accuracy in Reporting, for example, paid $6,000 a year to distribute its half-hour weekly program over the satellite in 1994. Funding agencies — whether corporate, governmental or philanthropic — are unlikely to support volunteer productions, or to finance programs inconsistent with their objectives and values. Thus satellite distribution increases dependence upon external funding, strengthens the hands of paid staff in setting programming policy (particularly as they seek to develop more consistent, professional "sounds"), and erodes community members' power over (and access to) their media institutions.

UNLICENSED BROADCASTERS

Even as government policies work to incorporate community broadcasters into the public broadcasting model, however, a new wave of unlicensed broadcasters is challenging both this model and the very right of the government to determine who will be permitted to broadcast (Sakolsky 1992; Markoff 1993). Mbanna Kantako has operated Black Liberation Radio (now Human Rights Radio) in Springfield, Illinois since 1986. His unlicensed station broadcasts black music and literature, political and social commentary, and confrontations with the police — often turning his microphone over to local residents (Shereikis 1990; Rodriguez 1991; Bishop 1991; Larsen 1991). Similar stations are broadcasting across North America, and their operators actively encourage others, offering technical information and a video showing how to set up a low-power transmitter (Sakolsky 1990; Kneitel 1991; How To Build Your Own Radio Transmitter 1992; Edmondson 1988). Kantako says FCC policies put radio broadcasting

> out of the reach of the people that we're trying to reach — people who live in public housing ... who have no hope at all ... of ever achieving any economic success in this country. ...
>
> That regulation [requiring a minimum 100-watt transmitter] systematically excludes the disadvantaged. ... When you're facing the conditions that our community in particular is facing, you have a duty as a human being to do whatever you can to try to turn those conditions around. And we feel that communications is one of the things that we have to take control over. (Kantako 1990)

Similarly, Radio Free Detroit (1992) has argued that FCC policies are designed "to enforce and maintain corporate control of the media," and that freedom of speech necessarily entails the right to communicate free of both government and corporate control. Unlicensed broadcasters have argued that since the FCC as a matter of policy does not license stations operating at less than 100 watts, low-power broadcasting is unregulated unless it causes interference with existing broadcasters. In California, Radio Free Venice (1991) notified the Federal Communications Commission that it would commence unlicensed broadcasting, citing the Federal Communications Act and the First Amendment to argue that the act applies only to interstate communications. A

Hawaii broadcaster seeking to serve a remote, sparsely populated district which received no FM signals went on the air after being denied permission to operate a 10-watt station (Hallikainen 1991). (See Phipps [1991] for an earlier, and unsuccessful, argument that government licensing of intrastate broadcasting was an unconstitutional infringement of free speech rights.) And the National Lawyers Guild's Committee on Democratic Communications is assisting unlicensed broadcasters in appeals before the FCC and the Ninth Circuit Court of Appeals (*Democratic Communiquè* 1993, *Radio Resistor's Bulletin* 1993b). While the FCC remains intransigent, its arguments have thus far fallen flat in court (Dunifer 1995, 1996).

Although unlicensed broadcasters have historically operated clandestinely, many low-power broadcasters now operate openly, encouraging community participation. Their stations are not merely alternative, they are oppositional, "giving community people a chance to have a vehicle for the direct expression of their ideas and needs ... breaking the silence that is a product of the media monopoly" (Sakolsky 1990, 4). As such, they represent a continuation of the community broadcasting model.

CONCLUSIONS

Community broadcasting in the United States has generally operated within the constraints imposed by the licensing and regulatory processes. Although these constraints impose very real barriers to full democratic control and grass-roots communications, particularly by fostering reliance on experts and bureaucracy, broadcasters' dependence upon their communities for financial support and volunteer labor served as an important countervailing force. Station management or the legally-empowered corporate boards could not act without regard for the wishes of their community of listeners and volunteers.

Recently, however, the institutional environment in which community radio operates has been transformed. Federal funds have made possible state-of-the-art broadcasting equipment and enabled many stations to hire relatively well-paid, professional staffs. Federal policies have encouraged community broadcasters to increase signal strength to a point where it is no longer possible for many listeners to hope to participate in running their "community" radio station. The development of (relatively) large paid staffs and budgets made possible by the increased availability of funds has left many stations dependent on continued infusions of outside funds, and has undermined the possibility of self-management and genuine community control. Similarly, corporate and governmental support for programming — both in sponsorship of particular programs and, more generally, through the satellite network — serves to devalue the efforts of volunteers while encouraging professionalization and centralization of programming.

Community broadcasters generally welcomed the infusion of federal funds. These funds have made possible more sophisticated and reliable broadcast facilities, paid staffs, professionally-produced programming, operating funds and access to satellite distribution services. To many community radio stations, accustomed to operating on bare-bones budgets, this has seemed a golden opportunity. Yet a heavy price has been paid for these funds. Writing twenty-five years ago, Theodore Roszak (1968) argued for the central importance of two factors in grassroots communication:

> The first is independence. Pacifica is ultimately responsible to no one but its own listeners — to no sponsor, to no institution, to no creature of the state. ... Secondly, Pacifica has always been characterized by an inveterate amateurishness, which, at last, is the station's finest quality. ... There would quite simply be no Pacifica if programme participants were not willing to contribute their words and works ... if members of the community were not willing to help out continually at everything from remodelling the studios to editing the news each day. (Roszak 1968, 327-28)

Whatever their purpose and short-term benefit, government policies have created strong institutional pressures towards professionalization and bureaucratization, undermining efforts at grassroots communications. While the emergence of unlicensed, low-power broadcasters offers an important alternative, they face government reprisals (including fines and seizure of equipment) as a result of their at-best questionable legal status.

Writing in the British context, Richard Barbrook (1987, 109, 125-26) argues:

> The Left should be interested not just in advancing the democratic rights of certain communities to broadcast, but also in overcoming the separation of the working class as a whole from the means of electronic communications. ... These stations represent a space where more democratic and accountable methods of collective working in the mass media can be tried, albeit limited by the continued existence of market pressures in and around them.

> Such spaces have, in many places, been opened. But countervailing pressures threaten to undermine these efforts at community control over its own media institutions, and to incorporate them into the public sector. The example of community radio points to the necessity of examining regulatory and funding mechanisms with an

eye to their implications for grassroots communications — for the right "to seek, receive *and impart* information and ideas through any media and regardless of frontiers" set forth in Article 19 of the Universal Declaration of Human Rights.

REFERENCES:

Bagdikian, Ben H. (1992): "Pap Radio." *The Nation,* April 13, pp. 473, 488.

Barbrook, Richard (1987): "A New Way of Talking: Community Radio in 1980s Britain." *Science as Culture* (Pilot Issue), pages 81-129.

Barbrook, Richard (1985): "Community Radio in Britain." *Radical Science Journal* 16, pages 53-77.

Barlow, Bill (1989): "Harlem Community Radio." *Democratic Communique* VIII(3), Winter, pages 17-18.

Behrens, Steve (1991): "Great Divide: Two Views of Public Radio Clash in Colorado." *Current,* May 27, pages 1, 10.

Bekken, Jon (1990): "WEFT and the Bird." Unpublished Discussion Paper.

Berrigan, F.J. (ed.) (1977): *Access: Some Western Models of Community Media.* Paris, UNESCO.

Bishop, Don (1991): "Kantako Continues Unlicensed FM Broadcasts." *The Ace,* July 1991, pp. 16-17.

Board of Directors, New Wave Corp. (1994): "What's New is Good News at 89.5." *KOPN Program Guide,* Winter, p. 2.

Buchter, Eric (1990): "Is Your Station a Radio Club?" *Community Radio News,* February, pages 10-12.

Carnegie Commission on the Future of Public Broadcasting (1979): *A Public Trust.* New York, Bantam Books.

Chadwick, Lynn (1990): "CPB Established Radio Expansion Programs." *Community Radio News,* February.

"Corporation for Public Broadcasting Board Adopts New Performance Standards for Public Radio Grantees" (1996). Press Release, January 22.

"CPB Raises Fundraising Hurdle for Public Radio Grants" (1991). *Current,* May 27.

Democratic Communiquè (1993): "Micro Radio." vol. XI(3), Fall, p. 6.

Downing, John (1984): *Radical Media.* Boston, South End Press.

Drew, Jesse (1993): "Micro Radio: Filling Gaps in the Commercial Broadcast Spectrum." *Extra!,* November/December, p. 27.

Dunifer, Stephen (1996): "Free Radio Berkeley Update." *Free Radio Press* 15, Fall 1996.

Dunifer, Stephen (1995): "Bay Area Micros Lead Movement." *Radio Resistor's Bulletin* 10, March 1996, p. 6.

Edmondson, Brad (1988): "Radio Free Obscurity." *UTNE Reader,* January/February.

"FCC Waives $35 Fee for Noncommercial Radio Operators" (1991). *Current,* October 21, page 4.

Federal Communications Commission (1991): "Permitted Forms of Low Power Broadcast Operation." Public Notice dated July 24, reprinted in *The ACE,* November, pp. 22-23.

Franck, Peter (1979): Statement, Hearings before the House Subcommittee on Communications, June 26, pages 180-206. *The Communications Act of 1979,* Volume IV. Washington, Government Printing Office.

Fuerst, Mark (1988): "Authority and Decision Making." *NFCB Updates,* August.

Glick, Andrea (1987a): "Radio Programmer Convicted in Format Change Dispute." *Current,* December 8, page 28.

Glick, Andrea (1987b): "Public Radio Keeps Reaching for the Numbers." *Current,* July 21, pages 1, 16-18.

Greene, John (1987): "Report to the listener." *KRCL Program Guide,* September/October, page 4. (KRCL, Salt Lake City)

Hallikainen, Harold (1991): "Crossing Swords with Pirates." *The Ace,* October, pp. 11-12.

Harris, Joyce (1990): "Radio Transmitter is New Sales Aid." *Arkansas Gazette,* November 8, page 3C.

Hind, John and Stephen Mosco (1985): *Rebel Radio.* Pluto Press. London,

Hindman, Douglas (1990): "Community Radio in the United States and Canada: A Comparison of Regulatory and Financial Influences on Programming and Development." Paper presented at Association for Education in Journalism and Mass Communications, Minneapolis.

Hochheimer, John (1988): "Community Radio in the United States: Whom Does it Serve?" *RTV Theory and Practice* 3, pp. 160-84.

"How to Build Your Own Radio Transmitter" (1992). *The Democratic Communiqué* X(2), Summer, pp. 4-5.

Jacobson, Don (1994): "'Experience Talks' About the HSP." *Radio Resistor's Bulletin* 9, December 1994, pp. 7-8.

Kantako, Mbanna (1990). Interview with author, originally broadcast July 26 on WEFT-FM, Champaign.

KKFI (1987): *A History of KKFI FM 90.1.* Kansas City, self-published.

Kneedler, Tim (1993): "CURSEstory." *CURSEword* 7, November, pp. 3-5.

Kneitel, Tom (1991): "That Was Then, This Is Now." *Popular Communications,* March, pp. 4, 72-75.

KOPN (1993): "Wake Up To New Morning." *KOPN Program Guide,* Summer, p. 1.

Kurtenbach, Ron (1988): "Centralization Robs Power." *KZUM Horizons,* Spring, page 6. (KZUM, Lincoln)

Larsen, Elizabeth (1991): "Radio Free America." *UTNE Reader,* Jan./Feb., pp. 22-24.

LePage, David (1994): "The NFCB Talks About Healthy Station Project." *Radio Resistor's Bulletin* 9, December 1994, page 6.

Lewis, Peter M. (ed.) (1984a): *Media for People in Cities: A Study of Community Media in the Urban Context.* Paris, UNESCO.

Lewis, Peter M. (1984b): "Community Radio: The Montreal Conference and After." *Media, Culture and Society* 6, pp. 137-150.

Lewis, Peter M. (1977): *Different Keepers: Models of Structure and Finance in Community Radio.* London, International Institute of Communications.

Lewis, Peter M. and Jerry Booth (1990): *The Invisible Medium: Public, Commercial and Community Radio.* Washington, Howard University Press.

Markoff, John (1993): "Pirate Battles to Keep the Airwaves Open." *New York Times,* October 24, pp. 1, 18.

Mattelart, Armand and Jean-Marie Piemme (1980): "New Means of Communication: New Questions for the Left." *Media, Culture and Society* 2, pp. 321-338.

"Miami Judge Orders Volunteer Deejays Reinstated on Air" (1991). *Current,* October 21, page 3.

"Micro Power Broadcasting the Free Speech Movement of the '90s." *Reclaiming the Airwaves,* May/June 1994.

Milam, Lorenzo W. (1986): *The Radio Papers: From KRAB to KCHU.* San Diego, MHO & MHO Works.

National Federation of Community Broadcasters (NFCB) (1987): "Tiered Levels for Community Service Grants." *Representation,* October, pages 3-4.

National Federation of Community Broadcasters (1979): Comments before the Federal Communications Commission. *Commission Policy Concerning the Noncommercial Nature of Educational Broadcast Stations,* Docket #21136. Appended to Thomas (1981b).

Noton, Peggy (1994): "Independent Radio's Problems and Prospects: An Interview with Peter Franck, Former President of Pacifica Radio." *Z Magazine,* March, pp. 51-57.

Palmquist, Jean (1981a): "Future of KOPN." *New Wave,* May, page 3. (KOPN, Columbia)

Palmquist, Jean (1981b): "8 Years Done — Cuts Loom Ahead." *New Wave,* April, page 1. (KOPN, Columbia)

Phipps, Steven (1991): "Unlicensed Broadcasting and the Federal Radio Commission: The 1930 George W. Fellowes Challenge." *Journalism Quarterly* 68(4), Winter, pp. 823-28.

Poses, Jonathan (ed.) (1983): *KOPN-FM: History of a Community Radio Station, 1973-1983*. Columbia, KOPN.

"Radio Free Detroit: The Sound of Rebel Radio" (1992). *Fifth Estate* 26(3), Winter 1992, page 7.

Radio Resistor's Bulletin (1993a): "From CURSEword." May-June, p. 5.

Radio Resistor's Bulletin (1993b): "Urgent Breaking Information." December, un-numbered insert.

"Radio Free Venice Claims Constitutional Rights" (1991). *The Ace,* August and September.

Robertiello, Jack (1991): "Public Radio's 'Bottom Half' Seeks Reforms." *Current,* July 22, pages 1, 13.

Robertiello, Jack (1990): "Radio Expansion On Track." *Current,* Nov. 19, p. 3.

Rodriguez, Luis (1991): "Rappin' in the Hood." *The Nation,* August 12/19, pp. 192-95.

Roszak, Theodore (1968): "The Case for Listener-supported Radio." *Anarchy* 8(1) (#93), November, pages 321-329.

Sakolsky, Ron (1992): "Zoom Black Magic Liberation Radio: The Birth of the Micro-radio Movement in the USA." In: Bruce Girard (ed.): *A Passion for Radio.* Montreal, Black Rose Books.

Sakolsky, Ron (1990): "Radio-Activity: Community Animation You Can Dance To." *Cultural Democracy* 39, Spring, pp. 3-5.

"Satellite Distribution/Interconnection" (1988). *NFCB News,* August, p. 3.

Save KPFA (1993): "Censorship at KPFA!" (leaflet).

Shereikis, Rich (1990): "Making Radio Waves." *Columbia Journalism Review,* July/August.

Singer, Stephen (1990): "National Show Makes Bid for Music Audience." *Current,* Oct. 22, pp. 1, 10.

Spark, Clare (1987): "Pacifica Radio and the Politics of Culture." In: Donald Lazere (ed.): *American Media and Mass Culture: Left Perspectives.* Berkeley, University of California Press.

Stein, Jeff (1988): "WEFT: End of the Beginning or Beginning of the End?" Unpublished discussion paper.

Stum, Marlin (1987): "KRCL Joins the Space Age." *KRCL Program Guide,* September/October, pp. 6-7. (KRCL, Salt Lake City)

Teutenberg, Jay (1993): "Community Radio on the Rocks." *Radio Resistor's Bulletin* 5, December, pp. 5-6.

Thomas, Thomas J. (1981a): Statement, Hearings before the House Subcommittee on Telecommunications, Consumer Protection, and Finance, April 29, pages 164-77. *Public Broadcasting Amendments Act of 1981.* Washington, Government Printing Office.

Thomas, Thomas J. (1981b): Statement, Hearings before the House Subcommittee on Telecommunications, Consumer Protection, and Finance, March 25, pages 200-02. *Public Broadcasting Oversight of 1981.* Washington, Government Printing Office.

Thomas, Thomas J. (1979): Statement, Hearings before the House Subcommittee on Communications, June 26, pages 160-79. *The Communications Act of 1979,* Volume IV. Washington, Government Printing Office.

WEFT Board of Directors Minutes, January 14 1988. (WEFT, Champaign)

White, Robert (1983): "Community Radio as an Alternative to Traditional Broadcasting." *Media Development* 30, March, pp. 4-9.

Wynne, Randy (1982): "WCUW: Access R`adio." *The Lobe,* September/October, page 7. (WCUW, Worcester)

THE CANADIAN ALTERNATIVE:

A Brief History of Unlicensed and Low Power Radio

Charles Fairchild

Felix Guattari has noted the central institutional paradox of the contemporary media firmament in North America. He contrasts the trend "towards hyper-concentrated systems controlled by the apparatus of state, of monopolies, of big political machines" with moves "toward miniaturized systems that create the real possibility of a collective appropriation of the media." The latter provide control over the means of mass communication to those to whom it has been specifically denied by the former. (Guattari, 1993:85) The diversity of forms miniaturized communicative appropriation has assumed in recent decades is remarkable, but only one has even come close to challenging the legal basis of corporate dominance over public systems of mass culture in the U.S., micropower radio. While the travails of Black Liberation Radio and Free Radio Berkeley are becoming increasingly well-known it is useful to look at the experiences with low-power radio in other countries to compare the FCCs arguments, actions, and attitudes to those of its regulatory counterparts.

One case of particular relevance to the U.S. situation is that of Canada. In what follows I will describe the historical role unlicensed and low-power radio has played in Canada and how the current community radio sector there is in part the result of a series of low-power experiments in various parts of the country. I will argue that the central differences between the experiences of the U.S. and Canada have been the kinds of political pressure applied by grassroots and institutional radio interest groups in both countries to relevant government

Illustration by Michael Schwartz

institutions and the role of each country's regulatory agency in alternately attacking or helping to shape a community radio sector. In the U.S. pressure from institutional interest groups has resulted in a convenient tactical alliance which has helped to enact a ban on all radio broadcasting under 100 watts, with a few convenient exceptions. In Canada grassroots political activities have resulted in a steadily expanding community radio sector. The Canadian Radio-television and Telecommunications Commission (CRTC) in particular has responded to public pressure and lobbying by drafting a series of carefully-crafted policy accommodations for certain specific interests. The overall policy regime evolved slowly as various issues were inserted into the policymaking mechanism by these interests. Ultimately I will show that, as with most regimes of broadcast regulation, these accommodations have had numerous and often contradictory consequences, and that several key lessons can be drawn from the Canadian experience, both inspirational and cautionary.

A History of Unattended Development

There is little ambiguity about the fact that community radio in Canada began in small isolated aboriginal communities in the far north of the country and that the first efforts were mostly homemade, unlicensed operations using whatever equipment was at hand. These efforts usually relied on "trail radio" equipment scavenged from government operatives in the RCMP or the Department of Indian Affairs. Residents needed a way to communicate with those out on hunts or on the traplines in order to mitigate the seriousness of possible emergencies and found that the equipment brought in by bureaucratic, entrepreneurial, and law enforcement personnel was ideally suited to these and other needs. (Salter, 1981; Valentine, 1995:35) The earliest known experiment was started in Pond Inlet, Northwest Territories in 1964 where DIA equipment was set up as a small two-way radio system used for sending messages between communities, broadcasting news, important public information, and music. According to one report, "when people realized they could use radio equipment to talk with friends and relatives in neighboring settlements, they scrounged record players, rebuilt the ham radio equipment to operate with 10 watts power on the amateur band and started their own station" (Salter, 1981:19-20). The station operated for several years before its signal was discovered accidentally by two pilots flying into Montreal, prompting the CRTC to request they normalize their activities under existing broadcast regulations. (Roth, 1993:317) The station has since become a prototypical example of northern radio in small isolated communities who use their limited available means to accomplish their desired ends.

Another early low-power experiment was called Radio Kenomadiwin, created in 1969 by a group of university students acting under the auspices of the "Company for Young Canadians" who tried to initiate a mobile radio station in conjunction with a group of Ojibway who lived in the Longlac region of Ontario. The goal was to teach the basics of radio production to the aboriginal participants "with the express purpose of documenting a series of scandals in government administration of native affairs" (Salter, 1980:89-90). Contained in a van which travelled between six communities and hooking up to available antennas, Kenomadiwin was intended "to include programming that was local in origin and available in the native language" (ibid.:90). In addition, "it would broadcast local events including meetings, interviews, debates, and talent shows" (ibid.:91). While the effort ultimately took a form somewhat contrary to its original motivations, Radio Kenomadiwin marked an important precedent for others to follow; one of the staff involved in the project was later involved in the creation of Co-op Radio in Vancouver in 1973, one of the first urban community radio stations in Canada. The most important result of these developments was the necessary practical and policy precedents which allowed the development of future community-based radio experiments in southern cities and towns.

The foundations of the current policy regime were laid with the inception of the Canadian Broadcasting Corporation's "Accelerated Coverage Plan" (ACP) which aimed to provide direct CBC services via satellite to any community with more than 500 residents. The CBCs pursuit of its coverage policies began with the creation of a Northern Service in 1958 and continued as it implemented the ACP in 1973; both efforts were designed to enhance official government policies aimed at assimilating the aboriginal population into mainstream Canadian society. The Northern Service broadcast the same programming received in the south and was often made accessible to people who had either no interest in or active hostility towards it. As the CBC presence in the north increased so did local use of transmitters and donations of other equipment, and as part of the ACP, the CBC allowed local communities not only to operate and maintain these Low-Power Radio Transmitters (LPRTs), but also "to decide which CBC radio programs [would] be aired. By simply throwing a switch, local broadcasters [could] communicate directly with an entire community" (Rupert, 1983:56). This was a level of access and participation denied to the rest of the country.

As a result of these efforts organizations representing aboriginal communities and their LPRT sites to the government began to form. These organizations were in part a reaction to the explicitly assimilationist intentions of the government, but were also in part funded by the government. So, for example, when the ACP was approved and implemented without any consultation with northern aboriginals and without any possibility of programming by or for their communities, the government also created the "Native Communication Program" aimed at funding the nascent societies forming in various parts of the country, organizations whose sponsorship was in part a reaction against the direct interests of the government, a contradiction that continues. (Valaskakis, 1992:70-2) Today aboriginal radio and communication societies are numerous and diverse, some representing one community, some representing thirty, some printing newspapers as well as producing radio and television programs in varying amounts of Inuktituk, Ojibway, Cree, Micmac, English, French, and some local languages and dialects. Currently there are over three hundred aboriginal communities using

LPRTs and other community access radio stations in Northern Canada and these are represented by over a dozen regional communication societies which, while suffering from dramatic budget cuts made early in the 1990s, still manage to produce programming, provide much-needed communication services, and distribute information in a variety of media (Stiles, 1985). Most stations survive through volunteer labor and small staffs operating with small budgets and many depend on revenues from radio bingo and paid messages or song dedications for survival, while receiving small amounts of government funding through the regional communication societies (Smith and Bingham, 1992:187).

More recently a number of stations have been established on reserves in southern Ontario and Quebec many of which also began as unlicensed low-power experiments. The activity has been greatest on reserves which in sum form a large part of the Haudenosaunee (Iroquois) Confederacy including the reserve communities of Akwesasne, Kanesatake, Kahnawake, Tynedinaga, and Six Nations. The first station to be established on a southern reserve was CKON, and the current 250 watt station grew in part from an earlier 20 watt operation called "Akwesasne Freedom Radio" which was designed to demystify media technology and to draw in those community members interested in longer-term radio projects. CKON began broadcasting on the Akwesasne reserve near Cornwall, Ontario, in 1982 and the station's supporters have since refused to seek licensing by the CRTC or the FCC, but are instead governed by a proclamation by the Akwesasne Mohawk Nation. This arrangement is acknowledged, but not influenced by the CRTC, while the FCC has refused to recognize the station altogether (Wilkinson, 1988:38; Keith, 1995:88). The stations at CKHQ at Kanesatake and CKRK at Kahnawake also began as low-power stations, between about five watts and 50 watts respectively, although CKRK now operates at 250 watts (Roth, 1993:319). CKRZ at Six Nations also began as an unlicensed low-power operation and continued to operate without sanction from the authorities for several years before exterior circumstances forced it to apply to the CRTC for official status (Fairchild, 1997). About eight other stations are either broadcasting or in development at other Iroquois or Ojibway reserves throughout southern Ontario (ibid.).

The independence of these stations stems from the resolve of their members not to sacrifice the sovereignty and self-determination granted in numerous but mostly ignored treaties between the British Crown and their ancestors. To the CRTC's credit they have not tried to force these stations out of existence nor have they tried to enforce any regulations which are clearly inappropriate to these communities, although they often insist on some involvement in what many reserve residents feel are sovereign airwaves. The current aboriginal radio infrastructure stands as testament to what Roth has called "the history of appropriating airwaves" for uses which are unimaginable to centralized administrative and funding organizations. (Roth, 1993:317)

ACTUALLY-EXISTING LOW-POWER RADIO

The central argument made by the FCC against low-power radio is that such operations would inevitably cause interference with existing broadcasters and while the evidence supporting this argument is limited at best, as Alexander Cockburn notes, "in it's role as the rich folks' cop the F.C.C. has been soliciting complaints from licensed broadcasters to buttress its specious claims about interference" (Cockburn, 1995:263). Perhaps the most compelling evidence to contradict the protestations of the FCC is the fact that "low-power" radio stations exist all across the U.S. and Canada and not just in small isolated communities. In addition to the hundreds of LPRTs in northern Canada, broadcasting operations that would be considered illegal in the U.S. due to insufficient wattage operate even on the most crowded radio dials on the continent, including those in southern Quebec, Ontario, and even Metropolitan Toronto.

For example, CHRY 105.5 FM operating from the campus of York University, is a fifty-watt station set in the far northwest corner of Metropolitan Toronto. The campus and the station are set in the much-maligned "Jane-Finch" corridor, a low to middle-income neighborhood named for the intersection of Jane Street and Finch Avenue which is one of the most ethnically diverse areas in Canada. The station's signal only reaches about eight miles or so and as a result its programming is largely reflective of the community it which it is situated, including programs by and for the West Indian and Asian communities in the area. Another low-power station in Toronto is CKRG 800 AM on the campus of York University's francophone Glendon College which specializes in French-language programming. The most important point to keep in mind here is that the Canadian broadcasting regime does not apply blanket prohibitions on types of radio broadcasting based on arbitrary considerations like their radiating power, but takes into account the social context and function of a particular radio station, a story to be picked up shortly.

As part of his court case Free Radio Berkeley founder Stephen Dunifer argued that low-power broadcasting in Canada could act as a model for licensing related efforts in the U.S. The Commission countered by arguing that since there are far fewer Canadian radio stations using more or less the same number of frequencies, interference is not a consideration, an argument that is not entirely accurate or in some cases even relevant. The obvious fact ignored by the FCC is that Canadian regulators have long had to account for the huge number of U.S. radio stations whose signals have extensive reach into Canada and which have constrained domestic development for decades. This is not a reciprocal concern for U.S. stations because of long-standing international agreements which guarantee the U.S. control of the vast majority of continental and regional "clear-channel" frequencies. In fact, in cities like Windsor, which is just across the river from Detroit, as well as Montreal and Toronto, the radio and television bands are actually more crowded than those of comparably-sized U.S. cities precisely because of allowances made for U.S. broadcasters. Yet despite this imposed reality, in Windsor, Toronto, and Montreal the CRTC has found room for several radio stations of fifty watts and under including CKHQ, CKRK, CFRU at the University of Guelph (near Toronto), and CJAM at the University of Windsor (Wilkinson, 1988:18).

Perhaps most surprisingly, a large number of low-power AM broadcasters exist all across the U.S. as well, but these are the correct kind of low power broadcasters, the kind which "offer travelers news and information on attractions and parking and weather at airports, along highways, and in parks all across the country" (Scully, 1993:35). Further than this, the number of applications by local governments for these kinds of services have increased dramatically in recent years and the AM band has even been increased in size recently to accommodate these local information services and new commercial stations as well. (ibid.) No consideration has yet been given to competing possibilities as the imagined realm of the "public interest" isn't nearly as flexible as the FCC's logic. What should be clear is that claims by the FCC that low-power radio operations would cause unacceptable interference with existing broadcasters remain at best unsubstantiated, selectively applied, and in some cases entirely irrelevant.

THE POLITICS OF POLICY

Community radio policy in Canada was designed to simultaneously accommodate and control community radio and the series of policy decisions regarding the form which began in the early 1970s has left a mixed legacy. In comparison with the complete policy vacuum in the U.S., however, the situation is drastically more beneficial for the form in general. There are two issues which are particularly important for the purposes of comparison: the character and extent of political pressure applied by advocates of "community radio" in both countries and the reaction to this public pressure by each country's respective regulatory agency.

In the U.S. organized political pressure on the FCC regarding community radio did not come from grassroots activists, but from an institutional alliance between National Public Radio (NPR) and the National Federation of Community Broadcasters (NFCB). Laboring under the impression that the available slots on the FM band were rapidly disappearing, the NPR/NFCB alliance began to push for what they called the "professionalization" of public and community radio. As Barlow notes, in the 1980s both organizations convinced "the FCC to limit the number of 10-watt low-power noncommercial FM broadcast operations in favor of their high-powered and better-financed counterparts" (Barlow, 1988:99). Further than this, however, NPR and the NFCB presented the following recommendations to the FCC: 1) stations of less than 100 watts will be required to move to the commercial spectrum, if any room is available. If not they will be allowed to stay in the noncommercial band only if they can prove that they will not interfere with any other stations. 2) Low-power stations will no longer be protected from interference, in effect losing all practical spectrum-use rights. 3) Low-power stations must operate at least 36 hours a week and at least five hours a day. 4) Stations broadcasting less than twelve hours a day will be required to share their frequencies in agreements created and enforced by the FCC (Fornatale and Mills, 1983:181). As has been noted elsewhere, the FCC has gone well beyond even these strident provisions. The most unexpected consequence of the attempted consolidation of noncommercial radio in the U.S. has been the micropower radio movement itself, in part a result of the NFCB/CPB alliance. A movement was created comprised of precisely those operations whose existence the alliance aimed to prohibit, founded by those whose interests this same alliance repeatedly claimed to serve.

Most interesting is the adoption by the FCC in the Dunifer case of the core concept which propped up the arguments used by the public radio alliance: spectrum scarcity. In 1980 representatives of NPR and the NFCB argued that since FM frequencies were scarce, the limited space in the noncommercial portion of the FM band should not be taken up by "unprofessional" operations with the kind of limited range and (implicitly) limited appeal of low-power radio. But spectrum scarcity, where it can be said to exist at all, is not a natural condition, but an imposed one, created by the spectrum management and use policies of the FCC, not by the activities of 10 watt broadcasters. More specifically, it has been the deregulatory policies the FCC has followed since 1980 which have put the most pressure on remaining frequencies. Deregulation has resulted in the drastic over-licensing of the FM band and a subsequent and predictable wave of bankruptcies, convenient facts for those who are now building continental networks by scooping-up a large number of stations at bargain-basement prices from overextended entrepreneurs trying to get out of a business in which monstrous "economies of scale" predominate (Bagdikian, 1992; Andrews, 1992). The most important fact to understand in relation to the arguments of spectrum scarcity adopted by the NPR/NFCB alliance is that as deregulation began in earnest in 1980 the reaction of those claiming to represent community radio did not fight the policy or offer any practical alternatives, but instead made numerous accommodations with the FCC and in the end became major beneficiaries of a disastrous policy. It is clear that the legal inadmissibility of low-power radio is not due to any potential interference problems that might arise nor is it due to a crowded spectrum, but to the self-interest of those who are most able to divide the spectrum up between themselves and influence policymakers to transform this self-interest into law.

In Canada political pressure on the CRTC was most effectively applied by grassroots aboriginal groups, francophones both inside and outside of Quebec, and student radio groups. The CRTC responded by drafting a carefully-designed regulatory policy over the period of two decades which has both enhanced and protected community radio while simultaneously institutionalizing the form and incorporating it into the national broadcasting infrastructure. As a result the form has been largely immune from the encroachment or usurpation by hostile entities because the regulations clearly set out an unambiguous and enforceable definition of the structure and mandate of community radio while allowing these policy definitions to remain uniquely flexible and adaptable to the social function and context of particular stations, thus remaining relevant to the three founding streams of the form (CRTC, 1985; 1992). Most importantly, despite the CRTCs general reluctance to vigorously monitor and enhance community participation in some areas, the broadcast regulator has made a good faith attempt to deal with those representing public access radio in a constructive manner and has not enacted a series of arbitrary and unduly restrictive rules designed to constrain the development of community radio in the numerous diverse contexts in which it was created.

More precariously, community radio stations now have numerous mundane regulatory responsibilities to fulfill and difficult programming can still shake a station to its foundations. For example, the conditions of license for all stations, commercial, community, or public, require adherence to a detailed programming agreement with the CRTC called the "Promise of Performance" which applies for the duration of the license. Any significant change of programming also requires a change in the conditions of the license. While this affords marginal stations some protection from their own enforced obsolescence at the hands of wealthier and more ambitious commercial stations bent on incorporating marginal cultural forms, it also prevents bold new programming statements from being made between license renewals. While the CRTC remains a mostly reactive organization, in that they respond to specific criticisms rather than seeking them out, there always remains the implicit and arbitrary threat to the viability of a license. It is the classic trade-off of broadcast regulation: in order to exist you must eventually acknowledge total regulatory authority. But since community stations are usually unaided and mostly marginalized by the same central authorities who also hold their licenses, despite having to fulfill programming obligations similar to those of pampered commercial stations, regulatory authority can often be as much of a burden as a protection.

The Canadian experience with unlicensed and low-power radio shows demonstrates both the promise and the peril of the form. On the one hand true public access community radio has been legitimized by the state and despite the chronic financial difficulties of many stations, the form is legal, clearly defined, and firmly established in every region and city in the country. The main lesson for U.S. activists to take away from these developments is that nothing is as important as a clear and practical working definition to set the terms through which community radio can find its voice and govern its everyday operations. This definition doesn't necessarily have to be sanctioned by the state nor must it be enshrined in law, but it must exist and it must sooner or later come to define the agreed-upon limits of the form. The kind of collective definition found in Canada has allowed for change based on consensus, not force and this in turn has built solidarity between stations. All stations who have accepted the general definition of community radio are now implicitly allied with one another. If one station is attacked all stations are attacked and what happens to one can happen to all; thus the possible range of responses is wider and stronger. With this in mind it becomes less difficult to imagine a series of low-power storefront radio operations across the U.S. whose only responsibilities are to register for the use of regional frequencies set aside for community access and to reflect and record the needs and desires of their participants, listeners, or detractors.

REFERENCES

Andrews, Edmund L. "A New Tune For Radio: Hard Times." *New York Times* : March 16, 1992, Sec. 4, p. 6.

Bagdikian, Ben. "Pap Radio." *The Nation* :254 (14): 473, 1992.

Barlow, William. "Community Radio in the U.S.: The Struggle for a Democratic Medium." *Media, Culture and Society*: 10 (1): 81-105, 1988.

Cockburn, Alexander. "Beat the Devil: Low-Watt Sedition." *The Nation*: 261 (8): pp. 262-3, 1995.

CRTC. *The Review of Community Radio*. Canadian Radio-television and Telecommunications Commission, April 23, 1985. CRTC Public Notice, 1985-194.

CRTC. *Policies For Community and Campus Radio*. May 29, 1992. CRTC Public Notice, 1992-38.

Fairchild, Charles. *Community Radio and Public Culture, being an examination of media access and equity in the nations of North America*. Ph.D. dissertation, State University of New York at Buffalo, 1997.

Fornatale, P., and Mills, J. *Radio in the Television Age*. Woodstock, NY: Overlook Press, 1980.

Guattari, Felix. "Popular Free Radio." In *Radiotext(e)*: N. Strauss ed., New York: Autonomedia, 1993.

Keith, Michael. *Signals in the Air: Native Broadcasting in America*. Westport, CT: Praeger, 1995.

Roth, Lorna. "Mohawk Airwaves and Cultural Challenges: Some Reflections on the Politics of Recognition and Cultural Appropriation After the Summer of 1990." *Canadian Journal of Communication* :18 (3): 315-331, 1993.

Rupert, Robert. "Native Broadcasting in Canada." *Anthropologica* : 25 (1): 53-61, 1983.

Salter, Liora. "Two Directions on a One-Way Street: Old and New Approaches in Media Analysis in Two Decades." *Studies in Communication* : 1 85-117, 1980.

Salter, Liora. *Community Radio in Canada*. Canadian Broadcasting Corporation, Office of Community Radio, 1981.

Scully, Sean. "Broadcasters wary of plan to move low-power AM's." *Broadcasting and Cable*:: May 10, 1993, 35-6, 1993.

Smith, B., and Brigham, J. "Native Radio Broadcasting in North America: An Overview of Systems in the United States and Canada." *Journal of Broadcasting and Electronic Media* : 36 (2): 183-194, 1992.

Stiles, Mark. *Broadcasting and Canada's Aboriginal People's: A Report to the Task Force on Broadcasting Policy*. Department of Communications, Ottawa: Government of Canada, 1985.

Valaskakis, Gail. "Communication, Culture, and Technology: Satellites and Northern Native Broadcasting in Canada." In *Ethnic Minority Media: An International Perspective*: S. Riggins ed., Newbury Park, CA: SAGE Publications, 1992.

Valentine, Lisa Philips. *Making It Their Own: Severn Ojibwe Communicative Practices*. Toronto: University of Toronto Press, 1995.

Wilkinson, Kealy. *Community Radio in Ontario — a dynamic resource, an uncertain future*. Ministry of Culture and Communications, Government of Ontario, 1988.

"THE AMERICAN PEOPLE ARE WITHOUT A VOICE"

An Interview With Louis Hiken

Ron Sakolsky

Ron Sakolsky (RS): What do you find particularly important about the Stephen Dunifer case? What interests you about it?

Louis Hiken (LH): To me what this case has brought to light is the degree to which the American people are without a voice. The media is so monopolized today. The case deals with the whole question of the facade of free speech that we have in this country which, in fact, means that you're allowed to say whatever you want in your own living room, but any attempts to try and communicate with anybody else in your community, unless you do it by yelling in a park or on a street, go unheard or have to be filtered through the commercial interests that decide what's to be broadcast and what's not. For somebody like Stephen Dunifer, it was the Gulf War that brought that reality home, when the media was so clearly a pawn of the Pentagon mouthing the instructions given to them by their rulers. It just shocked many people to a point of saying, 'For God's sake, if we're going to speak in this country at all we have to somehow control the means of communication.' We have to have access to a means of communicating that doesn't require us to go through Disney or Westinghouse or GE or the billionaire corporations that now dominate the airwaves.

RS: What are the issues in the Dunifer case now before Judge Claudia Wilken?*

---

*Since this interview was done in 1996, Judge Wilken has again ruled against the FCC, and in favor of Stephen Dunifer, on constitutional grounds. We have added an addendum on the legal implications of her November 12, 1997 decision at the end of this article.

Illustration by Guy Colwell

LH: Judge Wilken is faced with a body of law that has been built up over a series of decades, that has been defined and dominated by the FCC and commercial broadcasters. She's not taking it upon herself to say 'I don't like what's going on.' She has to judge the context of the law as it's presented to her. Now the history of this case is that the FCC issued what they call a Notice of Apparent Liability to Stephen, which is a notice saying, 'It's been brought to our attention that you are broadcasting without a license in violation of the law and you therefore owe us $20,000. If you disagree with us, let us know.' We, at that point, responded. We being myself, his attorney, and the National Lawyers Guild's Committee for Democratic Communications, which was a group that had been trying to deal with this problem of the monopolized media on an international level as well as a national one. We said to the FCC, 'Look, you provide no vehicle whatsoever whereby the poor can communicate over the airwaves. You've given the airwaves 100 percent to the commercial broadcasters and that *violates* the statutory authorization you have to responsibly define who uses the airwaves and to license accordingly. They responded by saying, 'No, we disagree. What we're doing is fine. Pay us $20,000.' That's where it sat. We at that point had a right to file a petition for review or a petition to appeal that decision, which we filed. They sat on that for years.

Stephen did not stop broadcasting. He continued to broadcast because he continued to feel that the position that we set forth in our arguments was correct and that he had a lawful right to broadcast because the FCC was violating its own authorization, its own authority. The FCC then went into Federal District Court, and asked Judge Claudia Wilken to enjoin Dunifer from broadcasting. We raised before her the same constitutional issues that we had raised before the Commission. We pointed out that they had not yet even ruled on what we had presented to them, and that there were constitutional infirmities that at least deserved a trial in which there was a likelihood we would prevail, and that they should not issue an injunction unless we had no legal standing to challenge it.

She evaluated the case at that point based upon those factors, and found, number one, that it made no sense for them to have sat on our appeals for two years and then come to her for an injunction when they should have at least ruled on our request first so that she had the benefit of their own analysis of it. The second part of her opinion said to the FCC that she was not going to issue an injunction, because they hadn't shown any likelihood of irreparable harm and injury. The FCC then went back and issued their own ruling. They then returned to her court, and said that she didn't have jurisdiction to hear the argument. They said that they had the legal right to come into court and ask for an injunction, but we didn't have a right to challenge the regulatory scheme and the FCC's statutory conduct as our defense. We pointed out that, 'Wait a minute, number one, *you're* the ones who came into this court seeking the court's jurisdiction; we didn't. Number two, *you* took the position in another case called "FCC versus Dougan" that it was the District Court that should have jurisdiction to hear a challenge to a Notice of Apparent Liability. Now that you have a District Court that you don't like, you're saying it's the Court of Appeals that should have the jurisdiction.'

She has not yet issued a decision because there are complicated constitutional issues involved. The FCC is trying to rephrase it as an attack upon a regulatory scheme, but they are not authorized to regulate the airwaves however they choose. We're not saying that the FCC is not an agency authorized to license or regulate communications in the interest of the American people. We're just saying the airwaves are not their gift from Congress to give only to the rich, or only to white people or only to their relatives. That's a constitutional delegation question, and not merely a question of some minor procedure that is properly dealt with as a regulatory question.

RS: So it sounds like part of the issue here is the allocation of who gets access to the airwaves. How would you see an appropriate reallocation vis a vis micropower radio?

LH: We have no problem with a certain portion of the radio spectrum going to commercial broadcasters. We feel though that, constitutionally, the American people themselves have a right to another portion of the spectrum space, and that microbroadcasters represent an interest that is *absolutely precluded* from any access to the airwaves at this time. If you want to broadcast a city council meeting in a small town, who's going to do it under the current regulatory scheme that the FCC has devised? Nobody is going to broadcast the Emeryville City Council meeting unless there's a station in Emeryville, and there isn't one because the FCC now sells their stations at the rate of about $50-80 million apiece. So, you're talking about church groups and community groups and political groups and social groups, *none* of whom have access to what is a *public* freeway, the airwaves, because the FCC has defined access solely on the basis of financial power. They are whoring for commercial broadcasters instead of carrying out their legal responsibility to administer the airwaves in the interests of the American people.

With micropower radio you're talking about a person in any city or village in this country being able for about three or four hundred dollars to go on the air and speak to the people in their community about their concerns and their feelings and their beliefs! They don't have to have somebody's approval because what they're saying is or is not politically correct. They don't have to be complying with some commercial broadcasters' sense of what's going to sell products or not. Right now, there's a greater discrepancy between the rich and the poor in this country, more than any nation in the western hemisphere. We are facing crises economically and socially that are really unparalleled. The idea that the American people have no access to any means of communication to talk to themselves about how to solve these problems but instead have to sit and listen to the political solutions being offered by the rich is nonsense.

The FCC is *absolutely* tied in to those financial interests with no interest whatso*ever* in giving the American people a voice. There is no access whatsoever to hear what people are saying, what their concerns are, what their solutions to problems are, and when you start looking at that with a magnifying glass you realize that nobody, *nobody*, has access that's not controlled and dominated by the rich. I think we're living during a period where marketplace economics are the God of Justice and Truth, and it merely is replicated in the radio spectrum. Communications is a very different concept than selling products, and if you're going to define access to communications systems by what is commercially viable, you, for all intents and purposes, *silence* the democratic communications that a nation has got to have. So the question is where do the people then conduct those discussions, and where does that dialogue take place?

RS: Some people who are in favor of the big commercial broadcasters have argued that because they're so big they reach many more people and therefore they're much more acceptable to give the airwaves to than a small station that has a very narrow focus. Would you care to comment on that?

LH: It is clearly true that a 100,000 watt station reaches more people than 500 microradio stations. And it's surely easier to police one station than it is 500 stations. But if you're talking about communications as a concept, when you have the ability to have 500 stations on the same frequency as one station; that's a choice. That's a political choice! In San Francisco for instance you could have seven stations on the very same frequency at the same time, none of them interrupting each other because of the way FM signals are broadcast. That gives access to a significant number of people who can talk about the issues that are affecting their communities in their areas. Now who can say that it's better to have only easy listening music on that same frequency, selling automobiles and beer, and that *that* is in the American interest; but that the seven stations that could also be on that same frequency talking about what's going on with crime and what's going on with investment and what's going on with politics and religion, are not an interest that should be recognized? All that we say to the FCC is that they've got to recognize that the concept of democratic communications is as important and equal a concept as commercial sales and that *both* have to have a place in anything that they're going to regulate whether it's over the television or whether it's over the radio.

RS: We don't really know, even if its decided that micropower radio stations should be licensed, what form that licensing would take as far as the government is concerned. Do you have a particular preference that you would like to see? It seems to me the range is anywhere from self-regulation where you simply have agreements between stations, to informal registration, to actually having an FCC approved license.

LH: Our hope and expectation is that if the FCC were to allocate a certain portion of the spectrum for microradio that it would vary from place to place. How many people and how many interests would want to be on and for how long could be worked out relatively informally, either through the kind of post card that you send in with a CB radio saying here's what I'm using and here's the frequency, to any kind of first come first serve allocation for the remainder of the spectrum space. There's a lot of variables on how that could be done, and we're prepared to present to the court a series of different alternatives as to what we feel the best way to do it would be.

RS: It sounds to me from what you were saying that this mail-in registration would, in your opinion, satisfy the requirement of FCC licensing. Is that correct?

LH: Well it might vary from area to area. You're talking about a different thing if you're in the middle of Wyoming where you're lucky to get one or two stations versus, say, Manhattan. It might be that in one area you require more specificity and more of an identification as to the ability of the people to broadcast in a way that won't interrupt. Most importantly, any licensing procedures should be based on a notification process rather than a financial qualification. That's the major distinction. We don't oppose notification to the FCC so they can regulate. What people oppose is this financial qualifying that they have created that basically excludes 99.9 percent of the American people from access.

RS: Right. Now do you think this kind of notification system is likely to be the form that licensing takes as the court rules, or do you think that there might be some other possibilities that would be based on more of a regulatory process that involves not simply notification but justification, commercial fees, and all the rest. What do you expect in terms of this court decision? Do you expect a favorable decision, and what would that entail in terms of regulation?

LH: I don't know what's going to happen. I do know that the FCC is not about to allow Claudia Wilken to issue a decision that challenges their authority and procedures without a fight. They will appeal to the 9th Circuit and to the Supreme Court rather than comply.

RS: So you think it might ultimately go to the Supreme Court?

LH: I think it's very likely. We're sure not going to accept a lower court decision that says only the rich can broadcast. The FCC is surely not going to accept a decision that says anybody can broadcast. So, (chuckles) if you're saying what do I think it's ultimately going to look like, I think eventually the American people are going to insist upon the ability to speak to each other without having to go through Disney. I think that's ultimately what's going to happen. Now if you're saying to me, is that going to be by means of a court decision or is it going to be the same way the CB radio licensing was changed, I tend to think the latter is what's going to happen. There'll just be people saying this is crazy that we can't talk to each other, and so I'm going to just *do* it!

RS: Is that what you're saying was the way that CB licensing was changed?

LH: Yeah. When CB radio was first started, the FCC wanted to license them, but so many people just went on the air without a license that the FCC changed it and said, all right, it's a notification system.

RS: That's a very interesting analogy. CB radios, however, didn't interfere with commercial broadcasting privilege in the same way that micropower radio might do.

LH: Not commercially. It did much more with safety vehicles, much more so than microradio does, but interestingly enough that didn't (chuckling) concern the FCC so much. (laughter ...)

RS: So this is a tougher nut to crack in a way?

LH: Absolutely, I mean look at what's going on. Look at who's running the show. I think the way it's going to change is the way Mbanna Kantako changed it. He said, 'Look, there's no way in the world that African Americans in this community are going have a voice on the radio unless we create our own station. I don't care what the FCC says and I don't care what the court says; it's more important for me to talk to my community.'

RS: What Mbanna says very clearly is that if the FCC has the power to grant a license then they also will have the power to revoke it. So he's not interested in licensing at all. Sometimes there seems to be a divide between the people in the micropower movement who are trying to challenge the licensing procedures to allow for more access to licensing vis a vis micropower radio, and those people, like Mbanna, who are saying we don't want anything to do with licensing, which is why he decided not to be part of the court case in the first place. So, it sounds like you see those two wings of the micropower radio movement working together in a way that might eventually overthrow the control of the airwaves by commercial interests.

LH: Absolutely. To me they're not contradictions at all. There are people in this society who tend to think that compromise is a possibility or that people can sit down and reason together, and there are others who come to the conclusion that unless they take what is theirs they're never going to get it.

RS: I posed the same question to Stephen of course and he said — and I'd be interested in your response as well — that challenging the FCC in court has meant that more people have gone on the air, and the more people that go on the air the better because that will increase the momentum for change. So he sees it as a strategic decision. He doesn't necessarily disagree with Mbanna. Each individual station has to make its own choice about what is best to build the movement. Even though he is challenging the FCC through the courts, he recognizes at the same time that change will not come exclusively through the courts.

LH: I think that the law is a forum that is as legitimate a forum for change as any other in this society, education is another forum for changing the public's mind, and civil disobedience is a third. Mbanna's decision not to go that route is probably based upon his own consciousness and recognition that what he represents is *never* given a meaningful voice by the courts of this country, so why waste the time? We've had long discussions with him, and I have a great respect for his integrity and his principled position.

— September 13, 1996

Addendum to "The American People Are Without A Voice:" Court Rejects FCC's Constitutional Catch 22

United States District Court Judge Claudia Wilken has rejected another attempt by the Federal Communications Commission to silence Berkeley Microradio Broadcaster Stephen Dunifer, founder of Free Radio Berkeley. In a 13-page opinion released on November 12, 1997, Judge Wilken once again rejected the government's motion for an injunction to silence microradio broadcasts by local radio pioneer Stephen Dunifer.

In 1995, Judge Wilken rejected the government's first motion for a preliminary injunction against Dunifer's broadcasts. At that time the Court found merit in Dunifer's argument that the FCC's ban on low power, affordable FM broadcasting was a violation of the First Amendment's guarantee of free speech to all in the United States. In a blatant attempt to avoid facing its First Amendment obligations the FCC then urged Wilken to permanently enjoin Dunifer from Broadcasting and at the same time argued that she could not even consider the issue of whether its rules, which prevent him from getting a license, are unconstitutional arguments. The government claimed that only the higher federal courts could consider the constitutional question.

In her November 12, 1997 decision rejecting the Government's position, Judge Wilken pointed to the fact that the FCC had taken exactly the opposite position in the 1994 case of Dougan vs. FCC. In that case, an Arizona microradio broadcaster had appealed an FCC fine (for broadcasting without a license) to the 9th Circuit Federal Court of Appeal, and the FCC had argued that the Court of Appeal had no jurisdiction over the case, and that it had to be heard by the District Court. The Court of Appeals agreed with the FCC and sent the case back to the District Court.

Judge Wilken noted that the Arizona broadcaster had raised the same constitutional arguments in the Court of Appeals that Dunifer is raising. The Court ruled that in sending all of the issues in the Arizona case to the District Court, the Appeals Court recognized that the District Court had jurisdiction over all aspects of the case.

In denying the Government's motion for an injunction "without prejudice," Judge Wilken ordered the Government to file a further brief on the question of whether the unconstitutionality of the FCC's ban on microradio is a valid legal defense to an injunction against broadcasting at low power without a license. Dunifer's attorneys, Louis Hiken and Allen Hopper of San Francisco, will have an opportunity to rebut the government's arguments on this point.

In response to pressure from the commercial broadcaster's lobby, the National Association of Broadcasters (N.A.B.), the FCC has in recent months been stepping up its campaign of harassment against the thousands of micro-radio stations now on the air in this country. Hiken commented "The broadcast industry is clearly afraid of these little community stations which are speaking truth to its power. In trying to do the N.A.B.'s bidding, the FCC demonstrates that it is nothing but an enforcement arm of the commercial broadcast industry and the multinational corporations which own it."

The National Lawyers Guild's Committee on Democratic Communications has represented the Lawyers Guild, San Francisco's Media Alliance, and the Women's International News Gathering Services as a "Friend of the Court" (Amicus) in this case. In its Friend of the Court brief the Lawyers Guild pointed out that FCC regulations make it impossible for all but the very wealthy to even apply for a broadcast license. This, they told the Court is the equivalent of saying anyone could speak from a soap box in the park, but the box had to be made of gold. Guild attorney Peter Franck commented "In an era when Disney owns ABC, the world's largest defense contractor owns NBC and CNN merges with Time which merges with Warner, and when 'public' broadcasting is told to get its money from corporations, microradio may be our last best hope for democracy on the airwaves." He continued "Judge Wilken's decision is a courageous rejection of the Government's attempt to use a legal Catch-22 to avoid facing the fact that its ban on microradio flies in the face of the Constitution."

The legal team representing Dunifer and the Amicae are very pleased with Judge Wilken's reasoned and thorough decision denying the FCC's motion to have the case resolved without a trial on the merits. For almost 70 years, the FCC has catered solely to the interests of commercial corporate giants, through their mouthpiece, the National Association of Broadcasters. These are the pirates, who have stolen the airwaves from the American people, and who represent corporate interests valued at more than 60 billion dollars. Only the Pentagon, the Silicon Valley and the transportation industries possess the financial wallop represented by the NAB and its constituents.

Judge Wilken's decision represents a vision of what it would be like for the American people to be given back their own voice. The decision suggests the likely unconstitutionality of the entire regulatory structure underlying the FCC's ban on low power radio. It forewarns of the total failure of that agency to carry out its statutory obligation to regulate the airwaves in the public interest — that is, in the interest of the American people, rather than the media monopolies that control our airwaves.

The legal team welcomes the opportunity to have a court identify the real pirates of the airwaves — the thousands of microradio broadcasters who seek to communicate with the people of their communities, or the billionaire commercial interests that control the airwaves as if they own them. Is it General Electric, Westinghouse and the Disney Corporation that have the right to control local community radio, or is that a right that belongs to all of the American people, regardless of economic status?

Courtesy: National Lawyers Guild's Committee
on Democratic Communications,
November 13, 1997

FREQUENCIES OF RESISTANCE

The Rise of the Free Radio Movement

Ron Sakolsky

What do the U.S. cities of Watsonville, Salinas and Berkeley in California and Springfield, Illinois have in league with Chiapas, Mexico and the island of Haiti? I'm not referring to some insipid Sister Cities Project masterminded by economic development honchos, Yahoo civic boosters or public relations flaks, but to a grassroots mutual aid project presently taking shape in the cracks of the New World Order.

It is a story that began ten years ago at the John Hay Homes public housing project in Springfield. Sometimes it seems there is a federal law that each state in the U.S. will have a Springfield. It is that generic All-American city where "The Simpsons" takes place, and before that "Father Knows Best;" so while situation comedy fathers change their stripe, from lovable patriarchs to darker Homeresque bumblers, Springfield the town remains at the center of the action. Springfield, Illinois prides itself on being the final resting place of former resident Abraham Lincoln — the mythical Great Emancipator who contrary to his exalted folklore status in fact considered the "white race" superior and freed the slaves in a calculated military move to disrupt the Southern war effort in the Civil War.

In spite of these facts, readily ascertainable by anyone willing to look for them in a public library, Lincoln has been historically deified as some kind of civil rights champion. In actuality, Lincoln's Springfield today is a barely Northern plantation town where subtlely racist Republican pols ceremoniously make the pilgrimage to the bust at his gravesite to ritually rub his by now very shiny

Photo of Mbanna Kantako by Frank Martin

nose for good luck before going into battle each election year, and where the Lincoln Cab Company recently was cited for routinely and unashamedly posting a notice in the dayroom instructing its cabdrivers not to pick up black male passengers. While the latter revelation was cause for public chagrin to the town's tourist industry, it certainly must have come as no surprise to the smug Babbitts, arrogant political insiders, and crass developers who run city politricks, their pretensions to grandeur notwithstanding. As to the cab company, the initial defensiveness of their "so what" reaction was later toned down, but only under pressure from the powers that be to maintain the sanctified Lincoln image unblemished in theory if not in practice. As to the block which is the site of Lincoln's home, it is now primarily known for being the center of the downtown prostitution trade.

Yet out of this sleepy nexus of everyday Midwestern racist hypocrisy and proud xenophobic ignorance, where if you're a liberal you're considered radical and if you're radical you're considered crazy and not suitable for prime time; also come Mbanna and Dia Kantako. Since 1986, they have operated a micropower radio transmitter out of their apartment in open defiance of the FCC. The housing project in which they were originally situated is now demolished. In the guise of "neighborhood revitalization," this now newly available prime real estate will be divided up in what Mbanna calls a "land grab" among such institutional power wielders as: St. John's Hospital, the Illinois Department of Corrections, City Water Light and Power, the University of Illinois at Springfield and, of course, *Lincoln*land Community College. While this scam is politely labeled economic development by Springfield's *State Journal Register* newspaper, the image of pigs at a trough comes more readily to mind. Nevertheless, even before the scheduled demolition the Kantakos vowed to continue their culture jamming efforts at whatever new address they found themselves in the future. After several months spent as the last tenants left in the projects — in order to document the dispersal of their community on the radio — they finally moved their eight watt transmitter to a new location in March of 1997. The station was off the air for only 90 minutes before they set it up again upstairs at a new apartment on Springfield's near Northside only a few blocks from its original location in the projects. As the Kantakos see it, the speed of that move clearly demonstrates the simplicity and adaptability of micropower technology.

Over the years, the programming has consisted of direct phone interviews with everyone from local police brutality victims to Noam Chomsky; a nightly grassroots deconstruction of the Six O'clock News; and, in special situations, doing everything from being the only local media voice that opposed the Gulf War to using their police scanner to give out the locations of local cops during the Mayday uprising at the Hay Homes which occurred around the time of the Rodney King verdict — all these spoken words churning in a dynamic mix of conscious hip hop and reggae. It is here in Springfield that the micropower radio movement that has shaken the foundations of the multinational corporate media empire originated, beaming its then "one watt of truth" from the Hay Homes deep within the belly of the beast out to a network of radio rebels who have been inspired by the Kantakos' model of radical community radio.

The station was originally called WTRA (after the Tenants Rights Association which spawned it), then Zoom Black Magic Liberation Radio, then later Black Liberation Radio, African Liberation Radio, and now Human Rights Radio; names which increasingly reflect its combined global consciousness and neighborhood-based reality. As Mbanna Kantako sees it, the FCC doesn't speak to the human rights of Springfield's African American community. He says, "We weren't around when they made those laws about licensing ... We were sitting in the back of the bus somewhere. So why should we be responsible to obey laws that oppress us." The emphasis is now on human rather than civil rights. As Kantako puts it, "It's about getting this government to cease waging war against our people so that we can exercise the rights to live and be free given to us at birth by the Creator. You get your human rights by accepting your human responsibilities. Human rights is the basis for understanding why you exist. This country says we exist to serve the corporate state. That's a goddamn lie!"

In the United States, in response to the government carrot of licensing status and the stick of antipiracy crackdowns, many once adventurous community radio stations have toned down their oppositional elements and have consciously or reflexively become engaged in a process of self-censorship. One signpost pointing to a road leading in a different direction is the micropower movement, originating not on a college campus or in a university-based community like many of the National Federation of Community Broadcaster (NFCB) stations, but in the heart of the black ghetto.

During the mid-eighties, the John Hay Tenants Rights Association (TRA) was formed to do issue-based, neighborhood organizing. Focusing first on expressway opposition and related school traffic safety issues, it then moved to the issue of the inadequate representation of the Eastside community under the archaic commission form of government. The TRA called instead for community control, opposed school busing, and even challenged the legitimacy of the local black bourgeoise who claimed to represent them in an historic voting rights lawsuit then pending and which eventually replaced Springfield's commission form of government with an aldermanic one. They then opposed an ordinance sponsored by their newly elected black alderman which involved the purchase of scab coal from a Shell-owned mine which violated an anti-apartheid boycott on Shell in response to its South African holdings, and politically skewered the alderman's plan for a weak-kneed civilian review board for the police, proposing instead a much stronger one modeled, as if in premonition of future solidarity, on that of Berkeley, California.

Angered and dismayed by media coverage of these actions and organizing campaigns, the TRA, in 1986, hit upon the idea of a community-based radio station to represent its point of view directly to its constituency and to communicate more effectively with a community which has an oral tradition and a high rate of functional illiteracy. This idea was not unusual in itself. Nationally, ACORN (the Association of Community Organizations for Reform Now) had started to think about community radio as an organizing tool around the same time. However, the ACORN vision was more centralized in focus, more closely tied to coordinating national ACORN organizing goals among the local chapters, promoted relatively high wattage for maximum outreach, featured a professionalized model of radio programming, and was strictly legal.

In contrast, WTRA (as the station came to be called) was based on a decentralized model, had a symbiotic relationship to its community with no official membership base and no national ties, was low watt, disdained professional trappings, and was not only illegal in the eyes of the Federal Communications

Commission (FCC), but defiantly so. Yet, because of Springfield's apartheid housing patterns, it was clear that even a station of less than a watt with a radius of between one and two miles could cover 70 percent of the African-American community, the prime audience which the station desired to reach. Since it was not to be a clandestine station, it would, by its very openness, challenge the power of the federal government.

Given the TRA's noncompliance with FCC rules and regs, though it continued to be involved in more mainstream community organizing activities, its primary funding agent, the Campaign for Human Development canceled its grant. Fortunately, before that cancellation, $600 in grant money had already been spent to purchase the equipment necessary to set up the radio station. All that remained was to find an empty spot on the dial and start broadcasting.

The FCC model for radio broadcasters is based on scarcity. Asserting that the electromagnetic spectrum is finite, in the public interest, the FCC agrees to act as the impartial gatekeeper for access to the airwaves, even though, as is typically the case with community radio, the signal is kept within state boundaries and involves no interstate communication and digital technology is rapidly expanding the points of access available. However, another explanation of federal radio communications policy might start with a question recently posed by Kantako, as founder of the TRA and "deprogramming" director of the radio station since it has been on the air, "Why is it that in this country you cannot buy a radio transmitter fully assembled, but you can buy an AK-47?" It is from the Kantakos' apartment that the station emanates, and their living room is a gathering place for political activists, neighbors and friends to discuss the issues of the day. It is a focal point for community animation in which grievances are aired and aspirations articulated around the radio transmitter.

Just before the original FCC cease and desist order was issued, Kantako had broadcast a series of shows which involved community people calling in and giving personal testimony about police brutality, or as Kantako calls it "official government-sponsored terrorism." Springfield's Police Chief at that time, Mike Walton, quickly complained about the illegality of the station to the FCC, and in April of 1989, the feds knocked on Kantako's door demanding that he stop broadcasting or face a fine of $750 (that's $150 more than the start-up cost of the station's equipment) pursuant to Section 301 of the Communications Act of 1934 for being an unlicensed station. Upon shutting down the station for a little less than two weeks to reflect on the situation, Kantako recalled from history that during slavery there had been laws against the slaves communicating with one another. As he once pointed out, at a conference in Chicago on "Censorship On The Radio," which was put together by Lee Ballinger, associate editor of *Rock and Rap Confidential*, FCC regulations are selectively enforced. He calls the FCC the "thought patrol." "If you are saying, 'Don't give a damn about nobody. Get you a house. Get you a dog. Get you a swimming pool, and the hell with everybody else,' then they will not only leave you on the air, they'll give you a bigger transmitter! But if you start talking about people coming together to fight against the system that's oppressing all of humanity, all across the planet, then they will find you. There is nowhere you can hide."

So, he decided to go back on the air as an open act of civil disobedience, risking having his equipment taken, with fines that could go as high as $10,000 and criminal penalties of as much as $100,000 and one year in prison. By this act, WTRA was not simply resuming operations, but consciously challenging the exclusion of low income people, particularly African-Americans, from the airwaves and offering an affordable alternative. Since 1978, for the FCC to license a station, it requires a minimum of 100 watts (replacing the old minimum standard of 10 watts). Start up costs for such a station are between $50,000-$100,000 (including equipment costs, engineering surveys, legal fees and proving to the FCC that you're solvent.) These requirements effectively silence many potential radio voices due to excessive costs.

As Kantako has put it, "It's kind of like those black tie dinners at $25,000 a plate. You can come, if you've got $25,000. For anything you need to survive, they put a price tag on it, and if you don't have it, you don't survive. They call our broadcasting controversial. We call it survival material." In relation to the police, such survival material began to include broadcasting local police communications live from a police scanner set up in his apartment to monitor the police, and, in a more humorous vein, doing a recording at a Central Illinois barnyard of oinking and squealing pigs to be aired later for a full 90 minutes as a "secretly-recorded meeting at the Springfield police station."

While he likes a good joke at the expense of the police, when he flipped the switch to go back on the air, Kantako was very serious about his historical mission in picking up the torch laid down by Huey Newton and Bobby Seale by patrolling the police guerrilla-radio-style as a sort of "electronic Black Panther" strategy. In his words to the press that day, "Somebody tell the children how WTRA served as an advocate for the people when the police wouldn't police themselves ... Somebody tell the people how we fought police brutality by broadcasting the personal testimonies of African American victims." While he was not arrested, the FCC made clear to him that he was in violation of the code. In spite of the fact that the station was well under 10, much less 100, watts, the only exemption to the FCC's licensing requirement seems to be for extremely low power operations — 250 microvolts per meter — that can be heard no more than 25 yards away. So, unless it upped its wattage 100 fold, which would be financially impossible, Kantako's station would not qualify for an FCC license.

Kantako is calling the FCC's bluff by demanding that the government pay more than just lip service to the First Amendment's guarantee of free speech and the 14th Amendment, which provides equal protection under the law. In terms of the latter, while blacks compose 12 percent of the nation's population, they only own two percent its radio stations for an exclusion rate of 600 percent, which is even more dramatically high if class and gender are brought into the picture. Providing equal protection by waiving license requirements or by setting up a separate amateur or personal category for low power community broadcasting licenses are political choices which the FCC seems unwilling to offer to the citizenry at the present time. Yet the 1934 Federal Communications Act calls for "fair, efficient and equitable" distribution of radio services.

The types of voices heard on WTRA when it started and those heard on the station today have changed somewhat over the years. This change represents a situation in which equitable access to radio for young people has decreased as a direct result of the government clampdown on the station. While so far the FCC has not invaded Kantako's apartment and stolen his equipment, the local constabulary had upped the ante with a constant barrage of police harassment directed at anyone who had something to do with the station when it was located in the projects. This particularly affected the youth who were once the mainstay of the station and who, like the station, were unlicensed, being essentially teenagers learning radio skills and doing live hip hop mixes on the air, laying down a revolutionary sound track for the Nineties.

At the start there were as many as 16 young people regularly on air. All 16 were expelled from school by the school authorities and their police patrols for, as Kantako puts it "anything from reading books on Malcolm X to not wanting to eat the red meat." Today, the youthful voices in the station are primarily the Kantakos' own home-schooled kids. Moreover, in addition to radio, many youth have been involved in the TRA's Marcus Garvey Freedom Summer School and/or the Malcolm X Children's Library, consigned to the wrecker's ball with the demolition of the projects.

It is because of police retaliation that many stations choose to be clandestine, but the fact that the FCC and the Springfield police have not more directly attempted to shut the station down is probably related to its very visibility, both nationally and internationally. So, as some people have speculated, the destruction of the projects had the added appeal, for the powers that be, of smoking out the radio station without the need to mount a police invasion. They just never expected that it would start up so quickly again elsewhere.

While the FCC and the Housing Authority has sought to discredit the station is by calling it a pirate operation, Kantako has never liked the pirate label. Firstly, for him, the term "pirate" conjures up piracy on the high seas and the connection between that piracy and the slave trade made it an unacceptable name. Secondly, the name has been associated with radio hobbyists, vanity broadcasting and radio hijinx, and Kantako is a serious programmer with a political message. Thirdly, the name "pirate" emphasizes illegality (what it isn't, rather than w hat it is), leaving out the chance to define itself positively. Finally, pirates are typically clandestine. So in spite of the pirate's romantic outlaw image and the history of clandestine political broadcasting, the micropower term seemed more appropriate to Kantako.

All of the above usages of the term pirate are, of course, a far cry from the original radio pirates of the Twenties that came on the air and usurped the frequencies and call letters of licensed stations in order to pass themselves off as those stations whose credentials they hijacked. In fact, in recent times, this kind of trickery is more frequently done by the government than by privately operated pirate stations. For example, during the Gulf War, *Clandestine Confidential* (Feb. '91) reported a CIA pirate that probably used the studio of Radio Cairo to wage psychological warfare against the Iraqi troops and to provide disinformation to the Iraqi population by masquerading as Radio Baghdad, complete with the same introductory theme, bridge music and a hired actor impersonating Saddam Hussein. In a similar vein the Voice of Free Iraq was almost certainly a British operation.

As to its politics, a distinguishing feature of the Kantakos' station has always been its oppositional stance. During the recent war in the Middle East, it was the only station in Springfield that was vigorously critical of the U.S. government, with both the commercial stations and the university-based one (then called WSSU) busily involved in collaborating with the process of manufacturing consent. As Kantako has said, "If anything, what people should have got out of the Persian Gulf Massacre is how tightly the media is controlled by the military industrial complex ... Your station will get community support if you start telling the people the truth because all over the planet folks are dying to hear the truth and one way this multinational conglomerate has stayed in charge is by purposely making the people ignorant."

In addition to counter-hegemonic news and commentary, the station has had a music policy that offers a "yard-to-yard" mix of hip hop, reggae and African-based music with a political flavor that consciously eschews racist, sexist or materialistic (my Mercedes is bigger than yours) music. As Kantako says, "Our music format is designed to resurrect the mind, not keep the mind asleep." In the past he has played "talking books" on black history, culture and liberation struggles that he received from the audio service for the blind but these days he's more likely to have his family members read directly from those books in a voice that's more familiar to their hoodies while at the same time providing role models for engaged literacy to the community.

Aside from content, another way that the micropower radio movement intrinsically challenges cultural hegemony is on the networking level. It is based on a model of organization concerned more with spreading information than with hierarchical control. In the early days of the movement, Kantako even produced a 20 minute video on how to set up your own micropower radio station which he distributed widely around the country to those wanting to get started. This homemade video, in combination with Japan-based Tetsuo Kugowa's series of U.S. micropower radio workshops (one of which was videotaped in part by Paper Tiger TV and combined with Black Liberation Radio footage for widespread distribution under the title "Low Power Empowerment"), and a passel of alternative press articles, sparked the micropower radio movement in its early days. I once asked Kantako what his vision was for the micropower movement, since it is a term he coined himself. He replied, "I would like to see lots of little stations come on the air all over the country so you could drive out of one signal right into another. If you had a gap, you could run a tape until the next one came into range. I'm not interested in big megawatt stations. When you get too big, you get what you got now in America which is basically a homogenized mix of nothing, a bunch of mindless garbage which keeps the people operating in a mindless state. We think that the more community-based these things become, the more the community can put demands on the operators of these stations to serve the needs of that community."

So, in my anarchist visionary mode, I see myself in a car cruising the USA of the future with a map of micropower radio stations lighting my way from coast to coast, reflecting the wide array of cultural diversity that exists beneath the surface gloss — a vision that is the antithesis of the lockstep national unity of the New World Order. I smile broadly as I recall a 1991 radio interview with Kantako by Tobi Vail, the drummer for Bikini Kill, in which he was asked what he would do if the FCC came and took his equipment. "We're prepared," he said, "to be a mobile station until we get some equipment again. We can run our station off of a 10 speed bike if necessary." Then, when asked, "How can our listeners support you in your struggle? Should we write the FCC?" Mbanna's immediate reply was, "Go on the air! Just go on the air!"

At one time Kantako was thinking of hooking up with the "lefty" National Lawyer's Guild whose Committee on Democratic Communications wanted to challenge those FCC regulations on his behalf in a First Amendment case. In the end, he chose to concentrate his activity on the local station and not get involved in what he calls the "sanitized lynching" of the court system. As he once told me, "Anything the government gives you, they can take away ... Don't no government give you freedom of speech. Don't no government own the air ... How the hell we gonna argue with them about their laws? That is insanity.

We've already tried that for 500 years. I don't give a shit about their laws. Now this is what I call real revolution. You're exposing the system so the people can't have faith in it no more."

Moving into the vacuum created by Mbanna's exit from the case has come Berkeley's free radio activist, Stephen Dunifer who began broadcasting in April of 1993 from the Berkeley hills with a homemade 15 watt transmitter which he carried in a backpack. Ultraliberal Berkeley is, of course, on the exact opposite end of the political spectrum from Springfield, and Stephen Dunifer's radio activism is not the kind of explosive issue it would undoubtedly be in the more conservative climes of Illinois' capital city. In fact, Free Radio Berkeley has been joined in the Bay Area by San Francisco Liberation Radio, Radio Libre, and is the base for the Food Not Bombs Radio Network.

As an anarchist, Dunifer is certainly no proponent of government solutions to problems of democratizing communication, but he has been willing to take up the legal struggle as a way of carving out a kind of autonomous island in a sea of media monopoly. The station he created in April of 1993, Free Radio Berkeley, which now has a range of eight-to-ten miles, was once clandestine but is at this point a 30 watt, 24 hours/day, seven days/week volunteer operation of about 50 people. Organized as a collective, Free Radio Berkeley counters the conventional radio model of hierarchical managerial control, playlists and demographics, with workers' self-management. Its efforts have spawned a host of other liberation radio stations around the country and a burgeoning world-wide movement. While he is quick to cite Mbanna Kantako as his inspiration, both for starting his own station and for standing up to the FCC thought police, it was *his* January 20, 1995 and November 12, 1997 court victories, in the "United States of America versus Stephen Dunifer," that have sparked the current growth of the micropower radio movement. In these decisions Federal Judge Claudia Wilken refused to grant the FCC an injunction against Free Radio Berkeley — the first time they have ever been denied an injunction to shut down an unlicensed station — and the later decision once again raised Dunifer's claims that the FCC had violated his constitutional right to free speech.

When asked in Berkeley about his legal strategy in December of 1995, he told me: "Basically we want to build a movement of solidarity around grassroots democracy, around decentralized communication, around free radio, around micropower broadcasting. We have a window of opportunity here and it's going to remain open for a while. We need to explore it to the fullest while we're still under the protection of the court. Of course, no matter what the system ultimately decides, we intend on going ahead with it in one way or another, with or without legal approval. It's one of the most critical movements to happen in this decade."

In regard to the global dimensions of this movement, Dunifer has twice visited Haiti, where he acted as a technical consultant to the network of Haitian micropower radio stations (such as Radio Timon) presently beginning to flex their muscles with the support of the *Lavalas* (Cleansing Flood) party, whose logo is of people sitting equally around a table. While treated as an unsavory criminal by the U.S. government, Dunifer has found a supporter for his ideas in former President Aristide (who himself has been the subject of an ugly U.S. government disinformation campaign), and with his help Dunifer seeks to place a transmitter at the center of that *Lavalas* table.

On the day he left Haiti after his first visit, Dunifer met with Aristide himself to discuss the possibilities for setting up micropower radio stations throughout the island, reserving 50 percent or more of the spectrum for either public or grassroots community radio. Previously, Dunifer had supplied transmitters clandestinely after the rightist military coup against Aristide, and now he was back to openly bring Do It Yourself radio to Haiti. By the use of off-the-shelf technology and common electronic components, Free Radio Berkeley has been able to provide communities with a low power FM station (20-50 watts) at a cost of between $1,000 and $2,500, depending on the audio equipment utilized. Micropower radio makes perfect sense in a country where the predominant language is Creole, but where most of the media, particularly print, is in French, the colonial language of the elite. Given the language barrier and the fact that most Haitians are illiterate, the appeal of a myriad national network of urban and rural micropower radio stations broadcasting in Creole is apparent. It is Dunifer's hope to supply the "people's technology" and the training to realize this vision regardless of the more conservative thrust of U.S. foreign policy. Contrary to the media's version of consensus reality carefully orchestrated by the U.S. government; in Haiti, the democracy movement is not supported by U.S. intervention, but rather is opposed by U.S. financed paramilitary units like FRAPH, the threat of renewed U.S. military intervention, and World Bank/IMF economic pressures toward the "privatization" of state enterprises rather than the *Lavalas* party's emphasis on their "democratization."

This kind of internationalist radio activism is not new for Dunifer. Since 1994 his transmitters have, via the Free Communications Coalition in Berkeley, been placed in the hands of political activists in the barrios of Mexico City. In one case the downtown station known as Radio TeleVerdad (located on a central traffic island) was raided by Mexican police, but has since gone back on the air. Other transmitters have also found their way to the Zapatista rebels and other insurgent Indian groups in Chiapas, who have used a combination of armed rebellion and nonviolent direct action to push for their own autonomous regions within Mexico.

For his part, Dunifer envisions an exchange program in which some people from peasant communities in Chiapas would visit Haiti and vice versa to promote unity by using community radio as a tool in confronting NAFTA and GATT. He has called GATT, Greed Allowed To Triumph (a new acronym no doubt awaits GATT's successor, the World Trade Organization or WTO; might I suggest Willing To Oppress). As to NAFTA, he'd like to turn it upside down so that it stands for North American Free Transmission of Anarchy. Imbedded in the pointed humor of the above acronyms is Dunifer's recognition of both the global nature of communications media and the need to keep them out of the exclusive control of the multinational corporations.

His new project, International Radio Action in Education (IRATE) will attempt do just that. Its agenda is essentially to pose the cultural policy question of what communications media would be like if they weren't dominated by the global corporate state? For one thing direct lateral connections between embattled ethnic enclaves in the US and those nations from which they originally sprang could be facilitated without the mediation of the megawatt radio dinosaurs, Disney or CNN. For example, take the Chicano farmworker communities of Watsonville and Salinas in California, both of which now have micropower radio stations and are newly finding their voices on the airwaves broadcasting in Spanish and making connections with Chiapas via the free radio movement. The aim is to not only provide transmitters and related equipment, but the technical know-how to manufacture, repair, set up and maintain those transmitters and stations. Recently, technical consulting and support was also provided to ARPAS, a community radio association in El Salvador when in late 1995 the government raided 11 community radio stations and seized their equipment. Equipment and training have also gone to Guatemala, Nicaragua and the Philippines.

And what about using micropower radio as a local community organizing tool with spontaneous impact? Dunifer recounted a story to me about a June 26, 1995 protest march in San Francisco that had been called in support of Mumia Abu Jamal (currently an imprisoned and censored would-be radio radical himself). The torchlight demonstration ended in an unconstitutional mass arrest. Quite a number of the people arrested had shows on Free Radio Berkeley. As they were being hauled off to the big "time out chair" downtown, they shouted out the studio phone line number for the station and phone calls to the studio from sympathizers were put on the air. A lot of folks from the East Bay community, which is covered by the Free Radio Berkeley signal, heard *directly* within minutes that their friends were being arrested in a random police sweep, as a result both of these calls and arrestee phone calls to the studio made from the jail itself (where the station's phone number had been scrawled onto the wall above the phone). The station in turn orchestrated a phone campaign to deluge the D.A. and the mayor's office with phone calls demanding that people be freed. Moreover, it soon became international in scope, as word went out on the Internet about the bust, and San Francisco quickly became the site of intervention on behalf of free speech by advocates from around the world.

If there is a *deja vu* feeling to the above scenario, perhaps it best recalls the famous Wobbly free speech fights from the early part of this century. When Wobs were jailed for soapboxing on behalf of the One Big Union, the word would go out through the IWW grapevine and the hobo jungles to head to the latest site of confrontation so as to get arrested and fill the jails with boisterous singing Wobs until the free speech fight there was won because keeping them jailed was more of a nuisance than it was to let them organize. Dunifer, himself a Wobbly, sees the continuity here in terms of an emphasis on direct action tactics; using, in the San Francisco case, the latest technology to successfully combine micropower radio, telecommunications and the Internet in a mass protest situation. His IWW cohorts at the station agree; as do those at Flea Radio Berkeley, an IWW offshoot which broadcasts live every week from the Ashby Flea Market in Berkeley where, weather-permitting, they have a table containing literature on the free radio movement and the Wobs, and, offer face-to-face participatory programming to any shoppers who have songs, poems and commentary to voice. Moreover, they have also begun to broadcast on the spot coverage of public events and demonstrations where mobile micropowered radio is currently used to offer an alternative to corporate media bias in reporting political activism; airing shows which range from first-hand accounts of the anti-union busting picket lines of workers at the Lafayette Park Hotel to the revelry of the People's Park Hemp Day Festival. All in all, as a result of such activity, the accessibility, safety, and practical potential of micropower radio is increasingly being witnessed on a first hand basis.

For years, people have gotten the "I" in IWW mistaken for "International" rather than "Industrial" (Workers of the World); an honest mistake given the union's internationalist perspective. Perhaps Dunifer's efforts on behalf of the micropower radio movement both in Berkeley and abroad, can utilize human scale technology to unite those engaged in struggles for political, economic and cultural autonomy; from Springfield to Berkeley, from Watsonville to Chiapas and onward to Haiti. In so doing, this approach could simultaneously break down the artificial dichotomy between local and international struggles without sacrificing the particular needs of one to the other. And so, as the century turns, we could give new "state of the art" meaning to the old Wob slogan, "direct action gets the goods."

PART II

ON THE AIR:
VOICES FROM
THE FREE RADIO
MOVEMENT

Illustration by Freddie Baer

Illustration by Keith McHenry

RADIO ACTIVISTS SPEAK OUT!

Micropower Radio
Broadcasters Conference

Dedication by Bill Mandel: This conference is dedicated to the memory of Mario Savio. There are probably some here who have never heard of Mario Savio since this conference includes people from different generations. Thirty odd years ago, Bob Moses, an African-American, organized about a thousand people, white and black, to go down to Mississippi to encourage people to exercise their right to register and vote. Among those thousand people was a young Italian American, from New York originally, named Mario Savio, who was later a student at the University of California.

He was quite unusual in being of working-class origin. In the 1960s, it was rarer to find the son or daughter of a working person at the University of California, than it was even to find a black person at the University of California, and there were damn few of either. Mario and others, including one of my sons, was down South and people were killed, more black than white. When Mario came back to school, he and the other students who had been there simply wanted to set up card tables here at the University of California where they could organize support for the people of Mississippi. Simple as all that! The University in those days had this crazy old rule that they called *in loco parentis* ; that's Latin for acting in lieu of parents, since students were not considered grown up. Students had to be treated like children, and the UCB Administration said you can't do a table. Imagine, my son had spent his honeymoon with a pistol and a chamber pot under the bed in some little town down South, and he was being treated like a child. When you've been through that, you are not going to take any bullshit from University administrators saying you can't speak. The consequence of this was a struggle that not only changed the face of university education in this country, but quite literally began the Sixties. The Sixties began in two places. It began with black students in the South sitting in at lunch counters saying that we want to be able to buy a cup of coffee and with the white kids up here demanding freedom of speech.

Mario was a very modest person. He spoke with a stutter, but when the chips were down, he was a Martin Luther King. He was a great orator. He was a tactician. Here was a kid of maybe 19 at that time who was able to sit one on one with the President of the University of California and bargain things out. I was involved with the Free Speech Movement along with Mario a little over 30 years ago. Because he led the Free Speech Movement, Mario represents the spirit of what we are trying to do here, and, to me, the dedication of this conference in his memory is a totally appropriate way of saying that we are going to carry on the fight that he, among others, initiated.

Napoleon Williams (Black Liberation Radio, Decatur): While I commend Steve and the National Lawyers Guild for fighting the FCC on free speech grounds, I beg you to understand that I don't recognize the government as having any power over Black Liberation Radio. Let me tell you about how the government operates. I'm the father of two kids that I missed a visit with simply because I chose to come here. I'm a weekend father. My kids have been placed in foster care and get to come home from five o'clock Friday evening to five o'clock Sunday. Now I beg you to understand that nothing has ever happened to my kids, nobody has ever accused anybody of doing anything to my kids. My kids were simply taken in a game where it was break up the family and you break up the radio station. In other words my kids may very well be the youngest political prisoners in this country. I refuse to recognize a government that will not help me get my kids back, but will do everything that they can to silence me from telling the story about the taking of my kids. So my radio work at Black Liberation Radio Station is an act of civil disobedience. They can't silence Black Liberation Radio. What can they do, take it? When they take it, I'll get another one, and another one, and another one (applause).

I believe that determination is a message that we must leave here and let these people know that, regardless of the outcome of Stephen Dunifer's case, they are not going to silence, nor stop, nor hinder the microradio movement. It's important that we take it upon ourselves to do everything that we can to make people understand that this is not about if this is going to be won in court. This is going to be decided by the people. It's going to be decided by whether or not we have the courage to fight a system that is so out of whack, so out of control, that we don't have a voice in the mainstream media. I think it's stupid to sit back and recognize people who are oppressing you or follow their rules for coming out from under their oppression. I think it's important that each and every one of us get the word out immediately that we are watching Stephen Dunifer's case and, if anything, the courts will make it worse by deciding that we shouldn't broadcast.

I intend to put as many radio stations on the air as I can. As a matter of fact, I was visited by the FCC last week and they asked me under whose authority was I operating. I told them, I guess, God. I ain't having no problem keeping it up or keeping it going. I can't really tell you whose authority. They wanted to come in and inspect the station. I told them, 'Inspect it for what?' 'To see if you're operating legally,' they said. I don't want to operate legally! See, I don't want to be approved by a system that is messing me over. I speak on the radio like people hanging out on the corners. As a matter of fact I go out of my way to come up with curse words. I have made 'bourgeois handkerchief-headed-nigger' and 'low-life-racist-cracker' household words (applause) in the city of Decatur, Illinois. It would take a low-life-racist-cracker to separate and persecute two black kids from a black mother, with her standing in the hallway wanting her kids back, for no other reason than his hatred of Napoleon Williams and a radio station. It would take bourgeois-handkerchief-headed-niggers to let something like that go on right under their nose.

We are a popular station because we are a voice telling people that if we don't stand up we gonna suffer sooner or later from the things that are going on around us. We don't have the option of standing by and doing nothing. If you just stand by and do nothing you'll get caught up in the whirlwind. We must get active. We must leave here and do everything that we can for this movement. If you can, put a station on the air. Just last month I was referred to as the Rosa Parks of Decatur, Illinois because I have refused to be messed over. I have refused to shut up. I use the radio station to get a message out to the people that each and every one of us should refuse to be fucked over and we should refuse to shut up.

Black Rose (Zoom Black Magic Radio): Just being here looking out at this group this evening is very rewarding for me. At one time I had given up to some degree because I felt that what I was fighting for, or what I was attempting to do at that particular time, was to no avail. Then, when I got a letter from Lee Ballinger talking about this gentleman up in San Francisco named Stephen Dunifer, and that he had a bunch of attorneys working with him, I thought, ah, just maybe this whole thing can come to a head. Just maybe there's a chance for us. For the last couple of years I have been building my transmitters and my antennas. I stand on the sidelines scheming about how to get my van together, but I'm watching very closely what takes place between Stephen, the attorneys, and the courts because what they are doing has been a beacon for so many of us. It's given a lot of us the initiative to keep going. Brother Napoleon here is over in Decatur, fighting a whole system by himself, way across country, isolated. I felt like I was a Lone Ranger down in Fresno, California, and then we had new stations pop up Johnny Appleseed style.

People would ask me from time to time 'What do you think about what's going on?' I said, it's long overdue because corporate America is determined to make sure that you and I do not enter into the competitive arena with them. That and censorship is what the whole game is about. They want to make sure that you don't get a chance to get some of the goodies. Brother Napoleon alluded to it a little earlier. I take the position that he does about licensing. I refuse to accept their license. I will not apply because to me a license is giving up a right for a privilege. Once I do that then I destroy everything that I've said that I believe in and I say that what I believe in is a lie. Then too, I refuse to be censored by someone who means me or my community no good. Their intention is really no good (applause). I listen to the speakers here and I think it's not about the black community, the brown community, the white community; it's about the community of *people*. It's about humanity. In this country what we see in this room is very dangerous. It's not supposed to take place. The powers that be don't want us to get together. Broadcast radio is an agent for the powers that be. So you're not going to get any sympathy from them. The National Association of Broadcasters is not going to sympathize. Individuals amongst the ranks might sympathize, but, as a collectivity, they're not going to come out in support because they want to keep their licenses. They're willing to play the game.

If they rule against Stephen, heaven help them because we're not going back. We're not turning around, and you attorneys back there [Alan Korn and Peter Franck] will have more troops. I mean if they shut down one, ten will spring up. So, it's not going away. They don't think that they can afford to let us win, but they can't stop us. If they rule against him, it's out of their hands, and if they don't, it's out of their hands. As far as I'm concerned it is a win/win situation for us and a lose/lose situation for them. Now, we're going to experience hard knocks. They're going to get very brutal. Some of us sitting here have already experienced it. They're going to intimidate, threaten us, and the corporate broadcasting entities can get violent with the blessings of the FCC on the quiet side. The FCC will turn a blind eye to it, but they will commit acts of violence because we're talking big bucks even though I've never tried to make anything in broadcasting myself. Things are going to get rough, but I think we can pull it off if we keep coming together, bringing brothers and sisters together like this and recruiting more people. All I can say is pray for the best. I know we're gonna win!

Stephen Dunifer (Free Radio Berkeley): As an anarchist and a Wobbly, I don't have any faith in the system, but we take our battles where we find them. It was the FCC who took us to court, not us taking them to court. Thanks to members of the National Lawyers Guild's Committee on Democratic Communications, we were able to bring off a victory of sorts in that arena that's held so far. Actually, an historical precedent was set on that fateful date of January 20th, 1995 when we appeared in court with the FCC. The FCC thought it was a slam-dunk operation. They had this attorney out from D.C. who was real full of himself. He was possessed of the opinion that he was coming out to clean up Dodge City, and it was going to be a cakewalk. Well, within five minutes of that court proceeding beginning, it became rather apparent that he was not going to get what he wanted. He spouted off about it, saying that if I was allowed to continue broadcasting there would be chaos and anarchy on the air waves. [Applause]

I said to myself, 'Well, we already got chaos, what we need is a lot more anarchy.' I'm distinguishing those two things because people tend to try to equate anarchy with chaos, violence and general dysfunctionality. What we really have is chaos in the society. Chaos comes from the Greek for gaping mouth. Our society has a broadcast media propaganda machine, made up of corporate and government thought control operations, which creates an insatiable hunger in people for whatever is the newest goody or commodity. It's an insatiable hunger that can never be fulfilled by the means which they offer to you, and that's the whole intent and purpose of it. It's like a McDonald's meal. It fits the propaganda of what your taste-buds have been accustomed to, but it in no way provides for the nutritional requirements of your body. Your body is always left hungry because it's not getting the balanced amount of nutrients it really requires to function in a healthy manner. So therefore you have these perpetual cravings for more, and that's what this whole system is about. That to me is a chaotic system because it is a gaping mouth system; a gaping mouth that is always demanding to be fed more and more shit.

We've come a long way thanks to many people in this movement: pioneers like Black Rose, like Mbanna Kantako, like Napoleon Williams and many other people have made this whole thing possible. Things like this are built incrementally and built on the experience and the energy and the dedication of those who fight for their rights and fight for the rights of everyone. I am particularly glad that we are dedicating this conference to the spirit of Mario Savio because what we are doing represents not just one point in isolation but is part of a continuum in the history of struggle by people for self-determination, free speech, and the right to live their own lives as they damn well please. This means free of coercion, free of repression, and free to be themselves. It means to live their lives as fully as they possibly can do so, and hopefully spend many hours sitting under a tree somewhere eating blackberries. Instead, the system wants to grind us down, wants to keep us running all the time. We can't hang ten and relax somewhere. The free speech movement at Berkeley was spurred on by people with a vision and a heart like Mario and many other people before him in this continuum of struggle who would not put up with the status quo, with the repression in their lives, with the working conditions to which they were exposed, or to whatever odious offenses against their humanity that were thrust upon them by the state and the corporations who own it.

What we are doing now with free radio is the free speech movement of the Nineties. In the early nineteen hundreds, there was a militant labor union known as the Wobblies, the Industrial Workers of the World, still functioning today. They pioneered what were called the free speech fights. Free speech as a public right in a park was not recognized by the U.S. Supreme Court until the Thirties even though we have a Constitution which claims free speech as a right for all people in this country. That document is two hundred years old. Yet only sixty years ago did the Supreme Court say it was OK to speak your mind in a public park without threat of reprisal. The Wobblies would come into a town to organize against oppressive working conditions, working conditions that would maim and kill, that would put children to work under those conditions. They would speak out against this situation by getting up on a soapbox on a corner somewhere. Then the local powers that be, the plutocrats, who owned the sheriff and owned the town would direct their minions to go arrest these people for having the temerity to speak truth to power on a street corner.

But the Wobblies were well organized, and what would happen is when two or three would be arrested for speaking out on a street corner word would go out and within a week the town would experience an invasion of Wobblies. Hundreds would show up, maybe more. In fact, sometimes there got to be so many riding the rails that you had to produce your Little Red Card to prove your membership in the IWW in order to get on a boxcar to get somewhere in time for a free speech fight. They would all show up in that town and pick a street corner. They'd line up by the hundreds and start speaking. The sheriff would be there and his deputies. They'd start arresting people. These free speech fights occurred in Fresno, San Diego, Portland, Seattle, all up and down the West Coast. The sheriff would have these people arrested one by one. All you'd have to do was say, 'Fellow Worker', and it was off to the hoosecow.

So the jail or the school or wherever they had to house hundreds of these Wobblies would be filled to the breaking point. If it's one thing the Wobblies are known for it's for singing and chanting and generally raising hell. So, they'd stay up all night long and chant and sing. In many cases the judges and municipal authorities lived near the jail facilities, and the towns were small enough so they could be heard. They'd keep them up all night long, and this was how they were able to break the back of the prohibition of free speech. Those towns learned that if they cracked down on two or three people speaking on a street corner there was a very good possibility that within a week their town would be overflowing with militant labor activists speaking out and filling their town's holding facilities, and they had to be fed too. That's how the struggle for free speech was really won. By people willing to take the abuse that came about in cold winter conditions when the cells holding people would be flooded with fire hoses. People would be in there with water up to their ankles, up to their knees. People were beaten, killed, but they kept on doing it.

This is the same sort of spirit that underlies any struggle for self-determination or free speech. We can compare that situation with the situation of those civil rights activists at the lunch counters who were dragged off and beaten, as Mario Savio probably experienced first hand. We see the same thing now with what we are doing with micropower radio. We intend to do the same things as the Wobblies did, the same thing as people at the lunch counters did. That is, to force the system to the breaking point. We must engage in this struggle in such numbers and with such energy and intensity that there is no way that the system can accommodate us. That's the only way we can win. I have no illusions about the court process. It has been a great PR vehicle. Our court case has brought this issue out to people, but our legal strategy must be coupled with a campaign of civil disobedience and direct action just like what happened in the South. The court action gives you a certain degree of credibility that the other doesn't, but one doesn't preclude the other. And, in my opinion, it's direct action and militant action that gets the goods. If you are not willing to fight, there's no point to begging your oppressor for a small crumb off the table. No more of that. We don't want another slice of the pie. We want the whole damn pie shop. That's really what's happening here.

We are seeing a struggle going on in this country for self-determination that is similar to the one in Chiapas, in El Salvador or in Haiti. We live at a time when the corporate yoke of what I call neo-feudalism, the powers that be call it neo-liberalism, is descending upon the neck of everyone on this planet. They think they have it made, but I got news for them. People are fighting back!

Antonio Coello (Truth Radio): In Chiapas you can receive information only through a few radio stations that are owned by the government or are commercial. The information that those radio stations broadcast is manipulated so people don't know what is happening out there. One of the motivations of independent radio in Chiapas is to broadcast true information. We are called Truth Radio in the Mayan languages. We want to create a radio where everybody can come up and participate and say what they think about the situation over there. So, we try to get people involved in the process of building this radio station. We invite musicians. We discuss the news with people so they can express what they think about it as to what's good and what's wrong. We have special discussions about certain topics which are important for the people over there like the right of self determination. We transmit from autonomous territory. The autonomists of Chiapas are demanding the right to decide how to use the natural resources and the airwaves too. We're exercising the right of free expression through the airwaves in the autonomous regions. Our transmissions are multilingual because in Chiapas, along with Spanish, there are more than seven Mayan languages. We invite people from the different ethnicities to participate.

The situation right now is critical because of the conflict in the area. We have two radio stations there and both of them are in the conflict area. The Mexican Federal Army interferes with our signal so we have to change our frequency very often. They then change the interfering frequency too. We have to move all over the FM dial trying to avoid the interference they are sending. They don't want us to broadcast our truth words.

We want to link the process of building an independent radio, a free radio, with other sustainable development. For example, using the radio to make agricultural proposals on what to plant at certain times of the year. We try to contribute to the development of the community and the people in general through the radio. Our priority in broadcasting is, first of all, information. We don't yet have access to the Internet, but we would like to have it because then we could get *La Hornada,* an alternative newspaper from Mexico City, and we could spread the news. We also have special programs for human rights so people can know their rights and they can demand respect for their rights. We're also interested in health. A lot of children are dying of diarrhea, and some sicknesses which don't exist anymore here in the First World. We teach how to dig latrines and to boil the water so as not to get sick. We try to contribute to the preservation and the development of the culture by broadcasting in the oral tradition about the history of the Mayan people.

Autonomous radio in Chiapas has a lot of possibilities, but economically our situation is kind of fucked up. We have to travel by donkey sometimes through the mountains because there is no road. It's hard to carry all the radio equipment even though it's pretty small equipment and its not that heavy. You get tired very fast if you are walking with all these things on your back. So, we travel usually by donkey when we can or if necessary we carry all the stuff ourselves. We still have a lot of equipment needs. We just have one mixer and two tape decks. We don't have any CD players. We would like to get a computer for being on the Internet. Because our radio station is not commercial, there's no way to generate money. There's no way to make the radio autosustainable. It has to depend on contributions from the people of the communities which we reach. They can contribute food, corn and beans, but not money to buy tapes.

There is also a project in Mexico which is for creating a network of alternative communication to which we belong. We have two radio stations in Chiapas, but we want to create a national network of autonomous communication throughout Mexico.

Annie Voice (aka Jo Swanson) (San Francisco Liberation Radio): I'm with San Francisco Liberation Radio which operates on the western side of San Francisco. We've been on the air for over three years now and basically San Francisco Liberation Radio is run out of our home so we think of it as our family. Like Antonio, we started off as a mobile operation three years ago, going out in Richard Edmondson's truck once a week and broadcasting from high altitude locations with a little car battery for power. Then, after about a year, Richard was out by himself and an FCC man came up behind him and tracked him down and knocked on the door of the truck. He asked him for his ID and if he could look in the truck. Richard said no, leave me alone and drove away. And so the FCC agent contacted the San Francisco police and told them that there was someone on the loose who was wanted by a federal agent. He didn't tell them why. So Richard was stopped by six squad cars down by the City Center. It was a huge arrest in the middle of the street and traffic was stopped. Then the police found out what it was for and they were almost disgusted with the FCC agent for wasting their time. It ended up with a big article in the *Guardian* which gave us a lot of publicity, and made the FCC and the police look kind of stupid. After that, we realized we had nothing to lose so we decided to broadcast out of our own apartment and that made things a lot easier.

We really have to thank the lawyers who have been helping us because they gave us some good legal advice and we knew we'd have some back-up if we needed it. So, from once a week, we went to seven nights a week and have been doing that ever since. We reach about a ten mile radius. We have our call-in talk shows on Tuesday. Keith McHenry of Food Not Bombs does a call-in talk show, as does Kiilu Nyasha who used to be with KPFA but got bumped off the air during the recent purge. We also have a new animal rights talk show and a Native American rights talk show in the works. Our other programming includes music. We broadcast a lot of hip hop and censored music that you won't hear on mainstream radio plus whatever we can get for free or cheap that's not hatred-oriented. That's probably the one rule we have. We won't broadcast anything that promotes hatred which makes us very different from a lot of stations out there. We also do a lot of Internet news, speeches and announcements. Richard produces a program called The Food Not Bombs Radio Network and sends that out to about 20-25 stations throughout the country. We've got a lot of mail from people who have heard the program and then gone on to start Food Not Bomb chapters where they live and that's been a great inspiration to us. We've even got a pen pal in Italy who heard our show. Richard sends it out on shortwave to about 62 countries. So, we now have a regular contributor who sends us Italian hip-hop music.

In the future I'd like to see even more community participation than there is at this point in microradio. One vision I have is seeing three or four stations in one area sharing the same frequency. If they're all one or two people like our station is, you could have people broadcasting in the morning and other people in the afternoon and other people at night. That way if somebody's antenna gets blown down or something, there's other radio stations that you can still tune into at that frequency. Also, I'd like to see more storytelling on the air. I work with preschool children and I see what a horrendous effect the corporate media has on them! They're all dressed in Walt Disney clothing; it's terrifying! You walk into work and there's 32 little Hunchbacks of Notre Dame smiling at you or Power Rangers. Children are very susceptible to what they see on TV and I think if there were more children's storytelling available we'd be sowing the seeds for a future that's a little more hopeful than what we've got now.

Also in the future I do worry about the corporate crackdown. I see the government giving away the airwaves to large corporations and media outlets. I wonder sometimes if they're doing that just so the corporations will take care of cracking down on us so that they won't have to do it themselves and look bad and spend a lot of money. Maybe Disney will come knocking at our door. I can see Mickey Mouse there with the handcuffs, 'C'mon!' Sometimes I have a little paranoid fantasy that we'll be in their "prisons-for-profit." It'll be like this revolving cycle where they can arrest people for intruding on their airwaves and they can toss them into their prisons where we can all make bluejeans for virtual wages. So, in the future, I've been thinking maybe we could have more radio stations right outside of prisons. We should get more mobile equipment so we can set up outside a prison and run away if necessary. A friend of mine in the American Indian Movement suggested we seek a permit from them. He said, 'We have sovereignty. We'll give you a permit!' That's a good idea.

We've been on the air for three years and it's a big job. You get home from your day job and then you've got to get the news and wind up tapes and everything. It weeds out a lot of people. Anybody who's an idiot generally will go away after a while because there's no money, there's no fame, and there's a lot of work involved. You have to *love* what you're doing and the people who love it are mostly nice people. I talk to a lot of people about microradio whenever I'm traveling around, and I have rarely heard anyone complaining. Everybody from left to right wing believes that freedom of speech and microradio is a good idea.

The only people who really worry about it are the people who are corporate-types. They are afraid they're going to lose money somehow if we're on the air without a license, but the beauty of it is there is no money in microradio so they have nothing to fear.

Liszet Squatter (Radio Vrije Keizer): I'm from Amsterdam, the Netherlands, and I'm from Radio Vrije Keizer or, in English, Radio the Free Emperor. We started in 1979, in a squat, as a radio station for the squatters' community in Amsterdam. We wanted to inform all of the people in Amsterdam and all other fellow squatters about what we were doing there and ask for needed help, like blankets. Today we are mainly a news station. The news we broadcast is about squatting in Amsterdam, nationwide, and internationally, because there are also land squatters in Brazil and don't forget 13th Street in New York. Beyond squatting, we cover issues about anti-fascist matters, feminist issues, queer liberation, and international liberation issues, like the Kurds in Kurdistan and the Zapatistas in Chiapas. We also do a lot of music from independent labels which is very important because, on mainstream radio, bands with their own productions or on small labels don't have any air time at all. It is the same with the news because we have mainly radical news topics not covered by mainstream media. We are one of three free radio stations in Amsterdam. The station is our community's radio station.

We broadcast one day in the week from 11 in the morning until eight in the evening, but we are an action radio station. That means we go on the air whenever needed. It is not only one day a week. We work as a communication device, so when, for instance, the riot cops want to evict squatters, we are going to be on the air to let everybody know where the police are at and what they're doing with the squats. Most of the time the squatters have telephones, and that gets you some very nice coverage when you have a person actually sitting in a squat phoning in to the radio station and telling what the cops are doing outside, how they are trying to get in ... Most of the time the houses are well barricaded so you hear them going like ... I can not do it but it's a horrible sound that you hear over the phone — and then the cops are in there.

I'm lucky to be here because it's pretty expensive to come all this way and the main thing I want to do here is networking. We like to receive cassettes so we can send them to our colleagues all over the Netherlands. We have about five other pirate radio stations across Holland. It's a very small country. We also have information from the Internet. We translate it and read it for our listeners, but the best thing is to have your voice on cassette on our airwaves. Support your local radio!

— November 8, 1996, Oakland, California

"WE'RE PART OF THE RESTORATION PROCESS OF OUR PEOPLE"

An Interview With Mbanna Kantako (Human Rights Radio)

Jerry Landay

Jerry Landay (JL): Why are you on the air?

Mbanna Kantako (MK): Our most important concern is human rights. So we're on the air to stress the idea that people are born with rights, and they come before any government, any judge, anybody on earth. Nobody has a right to write a rule that comes before the rights that you're born with.

JL: What's the point of using radio to do this?

MK: In our community there is serious literacy problem. Plus African people are an oral people. We communicate orally. There needs to be a back and forth conversation.

JL: So you're reading books to people? What books are you reading?

MK: Right now, my wife Dia is reading Jeremy Rifkin's book called *The End of Work*.

JL: Why are you reading that one?

MK: People tend to think that we're on the air because I'm black and I come out of the projects, and that this is a white/black thing. It's a human being thing. It's about the survival of everybody and Rifkin's book talks about the plans of the so-called ruling elite, and how they are going to impact upon everybody. We want to try to share that kind of information with people. It's like a Black Panther political education class on the radio. That's all we're doing. That's where the whole concept came from, but we recognize how the government used those classes as

Photo of Mbanna Kantako courtesy of Dia Kantako

opportunities to attack the Panthers and attack the people that were coming to the meetings. So this is the perfect meeting room right here where people can just hear it on their own. We call our station 'The Peoples' Choice.' When you listen, you choose to listen. We're not dragging you, making you listen. You listen when you're ready to listen. It's just a perfect way of sharing information.

JL: What else has your family read to them besides Rifkin?

MK: My daughter is reading Jonathan Kozal's book *Savage Inequality*. My son is reading a book that is full of folk-tales and fables. We've read Ward Churchill's book *Agents of Repression: the Cointelpro Papers; Seize the Time* by Bobby Seale. We've read Nat Turner. Right now my youngest daughter, is reading a book called, *My Trip to Africa.* We try to read a variety of books. I try to submit books that are age appropriate for our children and at the same time books that are going to help speak to some of the conditions that people see going on around them.

Last night my wife Dia was going over some newspaper articles getting ready for the radio. She said, 'Man if you don't read you won't know nothing will you?' That's it. What we're trying to do is use these books and articles to show people how the information is laying right there. People talk about conspiracy. It ain't no damn conspiracy what this government is up to. It's right there in print. A conspiracy is something done in secret. It's no conspiracy at all. All people have to do is pick it up and be able to analyze.

JL: What's the government up to?

MK: There is a problem. There is a surplus population as they call it. It's threatening the ability of those who have everything to keep everything. Those in power feel the solution is some kind of extermination program, and it's going to manifest itself in different ways. A lot of times when we say this stuff people say, 'Well, that's impossible.' Yet there were people on this land when this government came to these shores, and we saw what they did to them. We weren't here when this government came, but we saw what they did to us. So, we know this government is fully capable of anything. You see now that they've moved from the Industrial Age to the Information Age, they don't need all those workers no more. The only reason that this government says you have a right to exist is that you have a use for them. Well, they don't need you at the job no more, but they know that you're not going to sit around and let them kill you off. So, there's been several things enacted to try and put the population in a real vulnerable position. One is what your witnessing in this neighborhood here, this massive relocation program in which the apartment that this radio station is presently located in will be demolished by the Housing and Urban Development agency.

JL: It's not a relocation program. It's a taking apart program, a dismemberment program.

MK: There you go! We can't just sit around and blame other people for this massive dispersal program. We were trying to come up with a solution. We thought the problem was that people were not communicating, so the solution was what we are doing here — the radio.

JL: Why did they kick Napoleon Williams off the air and confiscate his equipment and haven't done that to you?

MK: It's hard to say. I know this, we've not made it easy for them to leave us alone. They've shown remarkable restraint. [Laughter]

JL: What do you mean, what have you done? You're saying to me that you provoke them?

MK: Well, being alive and being in opposition to what they're saying is provocation enough on our part as far as they're concerned.

JL: What if the Dunifer case gets to the Supreme Court and the Justices who caused most of the problems we're now trying to solve suddenly say, 'OK, you're going to have to reserve a portion of the band for community radio.' And that includes you, and they give you a license, and they say, 'Fine, but you have to stay on this frequency, and you have to operate at five watts or whatever it's going to be, and you're going to have to go and apply for a license every three years.' Would you do that?

MK: No.

JL: Why wouldn't you do that?

MK: 'Cause we're on the air right now and we ain't got none of that stuff. The question is, are there some things that you just have a right to do? We think the right to communicate is a human right. So, I'm not interested in the government authorizing us or giving us permission to do what we have a natural right to do. OK?

JL: OK. Now let's suppose that I go on the air and ten other people do it, and fifty other people do it, a hundred other people do it, including people on the right wing that simply want to come in and interfere with you, and there's no order at all. What do you do then if there's no FCC?

MK: I'm not going to worry about that. I don't think everybody is going to do it. Hey, I've been here ten years. I doubt it. You'll have a few air jocks that come on just for a little ego trip or whatever, but in terms of being there ongoing for a long time, you're never going have that many people. Not that many people are committed enough to do it.

JL: When did you first go on the air here?

MK: November 25th, 1987.

JL: And before that you did some deejaying?

MK: Well, I did some freelance street deejaying.

JL: OK, so how have you changed during that period of time? You're still here. You've been on the air since '87. How have you grown?

MK: Well, I know there is a Creator now ... Back then, I wasn't certain. That's basically how I changed, and that's to me the big change.

JL: Sitting here on the air you had your epiphany?

MK: Well, you know when you get through the things that we've gotten through and you endure for the time we've endured, you just know that being able to maintain this long behind enemy lines is concrete proof that we're not alone.

JL: You ever get disappointed that in all that time the essential problem, the human rights problem, that you're addressing, hasn't been solved?

MK: Well, I haven't been here for over five hundred years, so I can't really complain personally. You do want to be on the scene when it happens because you know it's going to be a beautiful time. But, at the same time, once you grow in the knowledge of who and what you are, you recognize that the goal is when *we* get there, not *me* get there.

JL: I find that doing what I do educates me. Every time I write, I write to find out what it is I'm thinking. Do you find that this activity has educated you?

MK: Yeah, it's rehumanized us. My people have been ground into the dirt. I mean just as low as you can get them. Well, there had to be a recovery time. And, the radio has served as a good therapy for me and my family. We have also developed a sense of community. Just the other night, for example, we was playing the eviction tape at 4:45 in the morning.

JL: Playing the eviction tape?

MK: Well, last week we recorded when they threw me out of the apartment I was using for our youth programs, and we made a program out of it. We're here to educate the people. So we just take encounters, and we educate the people by letting them hear the encounter and see what solutions we brung.

JL: Called eye witness news. . . [Laughter]

MK: But the power of that night has to do with a little brother, he's about thirty years old. At 4:45 in the morning this program was playing, and he come all the way up here in these housing projects which are about to be demolished to ask us if everything was OK. So that's the power of it. I mean here's a midget coming into these projects that are now empty except for me and my family. He thought the eviction was happening right then. If he was listening to the program he would have to think there are hundreds of police and everything over here, but he came at 4:45 in the morning. Reminded me of that song 'Stand' by Sly and the Family Stone where there is midget standing tall and a giant beside him about to fall. That's the satisfaction I get from this station. When I talk with people they tell me that they feel us inside of them. It's not just that they listen to us on the radio. They feel us inside. That's the satisfaction. Knowing that we're a part of the restoration process of our people. And, that's what we're about, the business of restoration. We've been blessed to accumulate a wealth of information and knowledge, but not so we just sit around and pump ourselves up. It's so that we can share it with the people.

JL: What do you call the station now?

MK: Human Rights Radio. Over the years we have gone through a lot of changes and all the name changes reflected our developing consciousness. At the time we started we thought the solution to the problem was tenants' rights. So, the first name of the station was W-Tenants-Rights-Association.

JL: WTRA.

MK: That's right. By '89 though we got really disenchanted with the system. We came more to our senses you could say. We didn't want anything to do with any of the things that would indicate that we were in compliance with the system. So, we dropped the call letters and we took up something called Zoom Black Magic. We were basically just looking for something different. Then we became Zoom Black Magic Liberation Radio. In 1990, we said, 'Well, we need to be more specific about the nature of the problem.' So we called it Black Liberation Radio. At the time we thought all the black people in the world came from Africa and all the whites came from Europe, and that all the white people were bad and all the black people were good. It took us about three or four years to realize that it wasn't necessarily that way. Then we moved to African Liberation Radio, but you can just take the differences between the Sahara and the Serengeti and you know that there is going to be some differences in African people. So, we thought, 'We still need to be more specific.' And we ultimately ended up saying Human Rights Radio because we thought that before we can get people to start talking about what kind of person they are, they have to appear to themselves as worthy of *being* a person. So in the name of human rights we hope to challenge this whole concept of getting permission as opposed to being born with rights. Human rights simply represent the right to be a human being. Civil rights are just basically permission.

JL How does your family contribute to the station?

MK: They are absolutely essential. Because by me being blind, there are a lot of things I don't have access to. At the same time Dia helps me get to material and uses our research to educate our children. You know we teach our own children at home, and just the whole process of running a radio station and keeping up on information, keeps our children aware.

JL: So, are you ever scared?

MK: I go a day at a time. As far as being afraid, what's there to be afraid of when the Creator that made everything in the universe has got your back?

— February 28, 1997*

---

* This interview was conducted at the radio station/apartment of Mbanna and Dia Kantako at Springfield's John Hay Homes Housing Project on the eve of its demolition by HUD.

Photo by Dia Kantako of a
work in progress entitled,
"Human Rights 97/
Criminal Enterprises" by
the Art With A Heart
muralists in Springfield,
Illinois, 1996. This mural
was defaced and then stolen
from the University of
Illinois at Springfield
campus where it was being
painted under the supervi-
sion of Professor Marcelo
Lima. The theft occurred
just before it was to be
unveiled and sent to an
international children's art
show entitled, "Promise to
Children in the World
Today" at the Museum de
LaVillet in Paris France.
Art With A Heart muralists
pictured are Shameka
Thomas, Latoya Sanders,
Konnadi Kantako,
Karimah Dixon, Ebony
Kantako, Mbanna Kantako
Jr., and Tieba Readus.

"GHETTO RADIO" RAP SONG

Konnadi Kantako
Mbanna Kantako Jr.
Ebony Kantako

Verse

Don't touch the dial
Don't touch that radio.
There's a story that we think
You all should know.

About a people who were taken
Far from where they belong.
About a people who keep fighting
Trying to make their way home.

That's us Africans
Still being held by this nation.
The oldest prisoners of war
Still fighting for our liberation.

So kick back relax
While we run this rap.
About another group of us
Who did strike back.

Break

In the concentration camp
They call John Hay.
There arose from the people
T.R.A.

Tenants Rights Association
What these letters stood for.
A group of sistas, and bros.
Who couldn't take it no more.

They tried marches, and petitions
To stop the persecutions.
They tried voting
But these things brung more problems
Than solutions.

So the sistas, and bros,
Continued looking for answers.
They studied Nat Turner
Harriet T., and the Panthers.

By looking at their lives
For knowledge, and truth.
It became so clear
What they must do.

Chorus
So in a place called Springfield
A criminal operation
In 1987 we continued our liberation.

It didn't come from the hilltop
It didn't come from the college
It didn't come from the middle class
They were busy buying knowledge.

It came from the projects
Where they put us all to die.
Where they treated all of us like dogs
We call it genocide.

Break

Verse
So in T.R.A.
A vote was taken.
The question was would they
Start a radio station.

A radio station!
The people said.
If the pigs find out
We'll all be dead.

The S.H.A., the S.P.D., I.D.P.A., I.D.O.C. *
A radio station we know that's heavy.
But like Huey Newton said
They're killing us already.

From the very young
To the very old.
They're waging war against us
And it must be told.

So when the vote was over
And the count was made.
It was yes! for the station
Now they needed a place.

So Dia, and Mbanna said
We got to be free.
We will raise that station
With Our Family

Chorus
So in a place called Springfield
A criminal operation

---

* Springfield Housing Authority, Springfield Police Department, Illinois Department
of Public Assistance and Illinois Department of Corrections

From the sista's living room
We continued our liberation.

It didn't come from the hilltop.
It didn't come from the college.
It didn't come from the middle class
They were busy buying knowledge.

It came from the projects
Where they put us all to die.
Where they treated all of us like dogs
We call it genocide.

Break

Verse
So the people came to the station
And said talk about how we live.
And you can't have that discussion
Without talking about those pigs.

They abuse us in the morning
They abuse us in the night.
and they do all this abusing
To deny our human rights.

Now the beast he got riled up
And he rose up out the cave.
And the word got to his henchmen
He was tired of T.R.A.

So he cussed, and fussed
And fussed, and cussed.
The beast he couldn't sleep
So he picked up the phone
In a frightful rage
And called the F.C.C.

Chorus

From a place they call Chicago
A criminal operation.
Came Willfred Gray with his black face
And gave them a citation.

He did come from the hilltop
He did come from the college.
He did come from the middle class
And tried to use on us his knowledge.

But the people from the projects
Who were put in there to die.
Went off the air for 11 days
Then took it back to the sky.

Break

Verse
So they emptied out the projects
Well we know that they were crowded.
But they didn't do it just in Springfield
They were carrying out Global 2000.

By waging a so called war on drugs
Which really was war on us.
But that low watt radio station
Kept reporting on all that stuff.

The pigs shot in the window
They took Dia, and her son to jail.
Though they threatened us with starvation
The broadcast it did not fail.

They say the revolution won't be televised
They said this not long ago.
But if you're ever in the place called Springfield
You can see it on the radio.

Chorus
So in a place called Springfield
A criminal operation.
In 1987 we continued our liberation.

It didn't come from the hilltop
It didn't come from the college.
It didn't come from the middle class
they were busy buying knowledge.

It came from the projects
Where they put us all to die.
Though they tore them down in every town
We're still fighting genocide.

— December 31, 1996

"A NEW DRUM FOR OUR PEOPLE"

An Interview With Napoleon Williams (Black Liberation Radio)

Stephen Dunifer and Carol Denney, with Pat Hall (Free Radio Berkeley)

Stephen Dunifer (SD): Welcome to Free Radio Berkeley. Tell us about the crackdown by the authorities on Black Liberation Radio in Decatur?

Napoleon Williams (NW): Just about everything that you could think of has been thrown at me. I've been depicted as a child molester. When that didn't work, I was accused of being a cop killer and a friend of drug dealers. I've been thrown into the penitentiary for supposedly beating the police up while handcuffed behind my back. My wife is a convicted child abductor because she abducted her own child that they had taken from her. They sent out a signal that if I quit broadcasting my life could go back to being normal, but we simply refuse to give in. We feel it's more important that we use Black Liberation Radio in Decatur, Illinois as the new drum for our people. We feel that we are obligated to assist in our development as a people through liberation. To me, radio is a very cheap form of communication. Homeless people have radios. Anybody can have a radio. It's an inexpensive way of offering liberating information.

SD: What's been the reaction in the community?

NW: At first, Decatur was in a whole different economic fix. People felt that they had it alright and they refused to look at the rest of the country as a telltale sign of what was going to happen to Decatur. They thought they were pretty well off. Jobs were plentiful. Then, all of a sudden we had downsizing and overseas

*Photo of Napoleon Williams by Stephen Warmowski/*Herald & Review, *www. herald-review.com*

companies buying out local companies. Unions in Decatur who went on strike at companies such as Wagner Casting Company and Caterpiller were confronted with, 'Hey, we got people out here that want your job.' For the state of Illinois, Decatur now has the number one highest unemployment rate. While at the same time, we got the number one criminals in America at Archer Daniels Midland who just recently settled a one hundred million dollar fine for wrongdoing.

Yet, Decatur is a town that seems to want to stay in denial about its problems. When I issued a call to not accept this situation, a lot of people said, 'I've been here all my life. Ain't nothing that you can do about Decatur. Decatur is bad, and it's going to always be bad.' We had a lot of people say, 'Oh, we hope you win, I sure support you in that thing,' but their support came through just saying it. They said, 'We're on your side,' but wasn't nobody there when the judicial system and the good ole boy network ran rampant through me and my family's lives. Both me and my wife have been to the penitentiary. Our kids were taken. We lost our home and our cars. We lost everything. When I was released from the penitentiary on January 6 of 1995, and told to go home, I had no home to go to. My kids were in foster care.

Yet, I knew when I came out that the only way I could fight these people was to use the same weapon that had caused them to come against me in the first place and that was Black Liberation Radio. I put it back on the air a second time in an altogether different neighborhood. In other words, we went from being on the air around elitist people who didn't really want us there and snubbed their nose at us, to being around people who were suffering the conditions that Black Liberation Radio was talking about in the first place. These people could more easily relate to us. So, the response this time, after the penitentiary, is totally different, from before. I went to the penitentiary in 1994 and was released in 1995. In the time that I was in there, Decatur saw Staley workers and their families pepper sprayed right at the factory gates with CNN watching. People could remember Napoleon saying on the radio, 'You think your police force is here to protect you. You think they are your friends. Let big business give them an order and see what they do.' So all of a sudden, instead of being just some crazy person on the radio, Napoleon started looking like a prophet, somebody able to predict the future, and people started taking me a little more serious.

Now Black Liberation Radio has actually become the voice of the community of Decatur. We have drawn people who two years ago would have never listened to me on the radio as daily listeners. They will call in. They will support us now. We've been effective in the way that we've used radio simply by letting the community know that we are a voice. If you are depressed you might just call in for a simple conversation which is what you need at just that moment. No other station in Decatur is that accessible. The people feel that it is their station, which it is. They built it. They bought the transmitters and everything. Without them, I'm nothing. As I said, everything that we've done at Black Liberation Radio we've done with a commitment for our own development and growth. We're not in it to make celebrities out of each other or to put anybody down, but to simply let people make a decision based on the information that's given to them. At Black Liberation Radio we've done that, although we still remain under the hand of our persecutors who simply refuse to admit that they've been caught.

We've got a situation where I've got two daughters in foster care who come home every Friday from five in the evening 'til Sunday evening at five o'clock. They're with us all weekend, but at five o'clock we must do what the State of Illinois says because they refuse to admit that a low-powered radio station has really whupped them into submitting. Sooner or later they will have to explain to somebody, how children are at risk with their parents during the week, but you can put the kids with their parents every Friday 'til Sunday. It's like weekend furloughs and they are the youngest political prisoners in this country.

Carol Denney (CD): Your story is just amazing. I'm really glad that you're here tonight to give people a chance to see how your entire family is being treated.

NW: Earlier tonight I was telling my story on a college campus and after I told my story a sister come up to me and told me about how her kids were taken. You know the child protection services of our country are slowly getting out of control. You know they don't need a reason to take your kids no more. I refuse to give in and let them give me my kids back by me going to a parenting class. Nobody took my kids because I was a bad parent. People took my kids because I went on the radio and refused to bow. My kids get up in the morning on Saturday and Sunday and they can be on the radio with me. My kids were abused today. My kids were traumatized today. They got put in a car and taken away from their mother. Nobody has ever said we did anything. Nothing has ever happened to our kids. We are asking people to join us in simply demanding from Governor Jim Edgar and the state of Illinois a reason why we don't have our kids.

All we're asking is for people to join us in demanding a break to the black-out on this story. A radio station is a danger in a town such as Decatur, Illinois where everything is so controlled. When you are involved in a struggle, what people do to you no longer surprises you. It ain't like Napoleon Williams had his daughter taken, then he was on the radio. Napoleon was already involved in a struggle fighting police brutality; talking about the relationship between social service agencies and the destruction of our families; crack being introduced into the community … I came on the radio to discuss those things. People got mad and then started showing me what they can do to put me in my place. I'm a man that can't get my day in court. They'll try to keep my kids in foster care limbo 'til their 18 rather than move to terminate my parental rights which they can't make a case for doing. We can't afford a lawyer. When they put me in the penitentiary, I didn't walk the yard or train. I learned juvenile law. My public defender has already told me that if I want to straighten this out, I need a lawyer. So, even my lawyer done told me I need a lawyer! The public defender has told me that everybody in the city of Decatur knows that my kids are nothing but pawns in a game played by a man that we stood up against.

CD: Your public defender said that?

NW: Yes, so you know he can't do nothing. You got a Macon County State's Attorney that has told people, 'I hate Napoleon Williams and hope that the ground he stands on would burn up and blow away.' I know he hates me because I'm standing up against these types of people. I never thought I would be endeared to these people. I didn't think they would love me, but Decatur is a town where we're just unorganized and everybody's so filled with fear that nobody seems to be doing anything. It's nice that this visit out here would come along at this time because I've seen things that I can take back to Decatur. I'm better ready to fight. Critical Mass, the bike thing, has given me an idea. Let's just circle the State's Attorney's office and a make it damn near impossible for anybody to pass. These methods that I'm seeing out here in Berkeley in your papers and at the radio conference make it seem like you all got a protest going on everyday.

CD: Well, that's true.

NW: You know somebody said, 'We got too many protests.' I can't see it that way. You got to find what impacts you the most, and that's what you got to stand up to. If their protest is on Tuesday, yours might be on Wednesday. If I can take that same kind of spirit back to Decatur, Illinois, then everything I've gone through is worth it. I put the radio station on the air in Decatur, Illinois because Decatur was a mess of a town. Decatur is totally corrupt. It's Decatur's tax dollars that's going to take care of my kids. If I had my kids getting as much money from the State as the State is paying for other people to take care of my kids, everybody in Illinois would be on me. Yet for some reason through this new form of slavery called foster care, my kids have been turned into a business. These people ain't just volunteers, they got their State job. Now why would somebody have a job taking care of two kids that could be with their parents.

CD: That's wild! I think we have a caller. Caller are you there? You have a question …

Caller: Yes, I have a question for Mr. Williams. He was very inspirational when I heard him speak on Friday night. I'm just wondering to what extent the labor struggle with the Staley workers has been covered on his radio station and I'll take my answer on the air?

NW: We were on the air when they first put the Staley workers out. I think it was about June 10th of '93 that they locked the Staley workers out. Just the night before while listening to the police scanner I had heard Staley officials say, 'Get the police out to the factory because we are going to lock them out and we don't want any problems.' They called the police and the police locked the Staley workers out.

Before they got locked out the same workers who thought they were secure in their jobs had turned their back on us totally. We have told Staley workers over and over again we feel they lost their struggle because they refused to take advantage of Black Liberation Radio. They thought that since they didn't help me before their struggle came along, and I had predicted their struggle, that I wouldn't be of assistance to them. That's not the case. We issue a plea to everybody in Decatur. We are a community radio station. We are there for the community. You can actually give me a ninety minute tape where you're condemning me, you're condemning the way I bring my messages across on the radio, and, as I tell people, I will play the tape. I'm more than capable of defending myself. We don't hide from truth.

During the lockout, you had people saying, 'Well, that's an unlicensed station.' OK, but that's not stopping people from listening in their house. Union leaders can benefit from what we trying to do. They missed an opportunity. The Staley workers' story was not really told to the city of Decatur simply because they refused to use the same means to get the story out that I did. You know it's one thing to pass leaflets from door to door, but a lot of people can't read and a lot of them can read but can't comprehend what they read. So, sometimes you have to take advantage of other things that you have at hand, and they refused to do it. I sympathize with the Staley workers. I'm pro labor, pro-union, and to just see them be crushed was awful. I saw the police force spray women and kids with pepper mace and then heard the workers say, 'We never thought they'd do anything like that.' Well, they just didn't believe me when I was telling them about how they sprayed me in my face. Now they see the police spraying their kids, and all of a sudden they're these dogs, and they can't understand.

SD: It's apparent to me that the obvious reason the agents of what I call the therapeutic police state are trying to take your kids is the same reason that the Staley workers were pepper sprayed by the cops. It is the fact that you're out there speaking truth to power. What do you see in terms of the development of the microradio movement, in terms of it's potential for other communities like Decatur where it's really going to make even more of a difference than in Berkeley?

NW: This is not just about Napoleon Williams and his kids. It's about a movement of us having a new drum in our community. We are the drum players and the people can understand our drums.

CD: Are you doing your station out of your home then?

NW: Yes, my station has always been in the house. We have never had it anywhere else. It used to be around the dining room table, so it got a lot of use. You know you're effective when you have young gang banging guys step up to your house and you see them straighten their hat out before they come in. We've brought together guys of different factions and there is no confusion, there is no killing, and there is no arguing. You actually got people that are threatened by that. They feel that if people who don't have power come together, we become the ones that's powerful.

CD: So you're the only micropower station right now in Decatur?

NW: Yeah. We might be micropower but we're very big in listenership. You've got to understand what's in Decatur is just homogenized all-sound-alike radio stations all directed at white males between the age of thirty-five and fifty. It's just so fake that people have simply woke up and realized that's not what they want. They don't feel any connection to it. We have radio stations such as WSOY. They had a morning talk show where they would get people like the State's Attorney and the Mayor. Every time they'd get on the radio I'd be right there on the phone to confront them. They cut out that whole program. The local radio station is nothing but a station that's hooked up to a satellite where you got computers that tell you what to do. You ain't even got a live person at the station no more. So, you've even got people that worked at the radio station two or three years ago that's dissatisfied with the way the radio station went.

SD: What do they do during spontaneous disasters like tornadoes?

NW: In 1996, Decatur had two nights of tornadoes back to back. We had a tornado on the 19th of April and a tornado on the 20th of April. We got a radio station in Decatur that said they had eighty five percent of the people tune in to their station for tornado information. They're proud that they opened the station up to telephone calls. Why aren't they always on like this? If it's such a success, why do we need to wait for a tornado? In other words, when the tornadoes hit, the main radio stations became Black Liberation Radio. Our format all of a sudden became the format that they wanted to use ... 'If anyone is worried about somebody getting hurt, give us a call out here at WSOY. How are people doing up North?' ... Yet hours before the big boys, you had people already calling us.

If something happened to you in Decatur, Illinois, first thing they tell you is you ought to get on the radio and they're not talking about mainstream radio. Go to Napoleon. It's my house, but it's the radio station too, so I guess you could say it's a community center. You will have people knock on my door four or five o'clock in the morning wanting to get on the radio right then and there. So whatever I'm doing, I get up and let them get on the air. It's the perfect example of community radio. Everybody is willing to participate, little kids on up to the older people.

We are in a town where for a long time we never had a voice. We never had anything that we controlled on the radio. None of us were on the radio. It was just dedicated to big businesses and advertising. They were a money-making machine. Even the little college stations were so limited by what they could do that nobody listened to them. When we put Black Liberation Radio on the air we didn't have an immediate effect, but by hearing what we were going through, people were able to relate it to something that they were going through and began to participate. I have no doubt in my mind that we are going to be like Berkeley. We might have two or three radio stations on the air because I see now that they are needed. If we got one on every block, and they not interfering with each other, they are needed. We need to form a network. We need to get the word out that there is something on the scene that can make you get out of that feeling that you can't do nothing. For those of you all sitting out there thinking you can't do nothing, put a radio station on the air. That's a good start. [Laughter] It's better to make a mistake than do nothing.

SD: I think there's a related saying that it's easier to ask for forgiveness than for permission.

NW: After prison, I chose to go back to Decatur, chose to sleep in vacant cars, with my number one mission being to get the radio station back on the air as quickly as possible. Through getting the radio station back on the air we have proved what was said to us, truth crushed to earth shall rise again. Truth is what's making Black Liberation Radio as powerful as it is in Decatur, Illinois.

Truth has made us the number one station in the city of Decatur, Illinois. No fancy jingles, no big old promotions where you come and get four tickets for the price of one. None of that. Truth, and truth alone has made us as popular as we are in Decatur, Illinois, and I'm proud of that. I heard that Free Radio Berkeley has over a hundred volunteers. There's no telling how many volunteers we have at Black Liberation Radio that are simply not being used right. We're in a battle and we've got to learn how to run that battle. I've been looking for a general or somebody to lead us in the battle simply because I didn't know what to do. I'm sitting up here in California and I've never flown on an airplane before. The closest I'd ever been to California was the West Side of Decatur, Illinois [Laughter], but I've learned many things in the last few days from the soldiers that I met at the radio conference here.

I met a brother that talks about how in his struggle for radio he's been carrying a transmitter up where there ain't no roads, so he's got to put the transmitter on a mule's back and sometimes on his own back, to lug it up a mountain because the information is important enough for him to do it. So if these people are going through that type of thing to get the word out, I'm wondering how we could be so messed up in this country that we lay back as if we have the option of doing nothing. Anytime you concede to the rules of your oppressor then you can't stand around and say you don't know why you're being oppressed. What's happening to us in Decatur, Illinois is happening simply because we sit back and allow it to happen. We won't stand up.

SD: As a Wobbly, or member of the IWW, we have an old slogan that says, 'Direct action get the goods.'

NW: Right, direct action. Mainstream media don't want to let people know how easy it is to get radio. So, they have simply decided to leave the story alone.

SD: What do you see as the potential for a lot of stations primarily aimed at, and run by, youth?

NW: We are passing up the chance of a lifetime. We are instructing our kids to go to the Internet, but all that it would take is for something to happen to the telephone wires one day and the Internet is 'interout.' I don't know why we are not taking technology that's at our disposal and running classes to teach our kids to read schematics. Give your child some kind of electronic intelligence. You got to realize that technology exists to create a radio station almost on a matchbook, and our kids would be fascinated by that if we would direct them toward it. We used to give out walkie talkies every Christmas. Somebody got a pair of walkie talkies on the block. People don't even buy that no more. With the invention of the computer game, we simply quit talking to each other. Our best friend became the t.v. I think that we would serve our kids better if we taught them to pick up the soldering gun instead of picking up an AK-47 or UZI. We could get our kids fascinated by simply putting together something where his friend down the street can hear him speak or he can just play a tape. We need to get our kids interested in things that are going to offer them a way to fight to better their future.

I don't know why people of all ages are not creating organizations and getting them a radio. Why keep on trying this old system of getting people to the meeting instead of taking the meeting to the people. Radio takes the meeting to them.

SD: That's very well said. I think that really sums up what our work is all about.

CD: What we're trying to do ...

SD: What we're trying to say is that things are coming down and if you don't act, if you don't find and speak your voice now, you might not be able to later.

NW: You had a Million Man March go to Washington in 1995. I didn't go. I waited on the million men to come back. You see I became a man in 1990 when I put Black Liberation Radio on the air. I had already atoned for all of my bad ways and stood up by saying that I was going to create a voice for my people. This radio conference in Berkeley is proving to people in Decatur, Illinois, we don't have to be afraid to stand up because there are others that will come to our aid. There are other fighters. So when I get back to Decatur and play tapes of what people are doing out here in Berkeley, when I tell them what I saw, we can decide what we can do.

You got a lot of people saying, 'Napoleon, what do you want me to do.' Free people come up with things to do. A free person thinks freely. A free person never says there is nothing I can do. A free person will go crazy trying to always figure out a way to get theirselves out of a problem. Stephen, I'd like to thank you for being free, brother. I feel hopeful from this excursion that I will be more of a fighter than I ever was simply because of what I come out here and witnessed. Sometimes they say in a person's life there is an experience that changed them. This wasn't a pleasure vacation. I have learned well in the art of civil disobedience and I plan to take some of that civil disobedience back to Decatur, Illinois. I salute what you're doing. You all are going to be on my mind back in Decatur.

SD: Watch out Decatur!

CD: Watch out Decatur.

Pat Hall: Before you wrap it up, I wrote a poem for you Napoleon and I'd like to read it over the air. This is for you, I was really inspired by your talk Friday night. I sat down this morning, and here it is.

Oh Mister Williams ...
People should try to love and trust us
not go around to beat us
and bust us.

What they can't understand
is that they take too much for granted.
Their way of thinking
is lousy and stinking
much worse than a man out drinking.
Napoleon is just a man
doing what he can.
His words speak true
and the cops
and the law
don't know what to do.
He has the power
when he's on the air.
Telling the truth
the giver of a hell of a scare.
They have beat him
and jailed him
and still don't know
what to do with him.
They think they're going to do
something great
but they're not.
They should just sitback
and wait.
He has a message
that's loud and clear
but they're afraid
that everyone will hear.
The truth hurts many people
in many ways
but that's the power
that stays.

Good luck with your struggle in truth.

NW: Thanks a lot man!

CD: Thanks for that spontaneous tribute Pat. We've been talking with Napoleon Williams, the founder of Black Liberation Radio in Decatur.

NW: Thank you all for giving me the opportunity to tell my story.

— November 10, 1996

ATTACK ON BLACK LIBERATION RADIO

Lorenzo Komboa Ervin

One of the limitations of the present day black revolutionary movement is its inability to reach a mass audience. Owning or having no access to mass media in our own communities is a significant barrier that we can now act to remedy. How? Start your own community-based radio station, which can be done for little money [$250-1,000], but allows your organization to present black ideals and world news to a community which is starving for it. These stations are an important organizing tool, allowing the people and activists alike to impact local affairs. They are effectively the 1990s equivalent of the "underground press" of the 1960s. Clearly the white government recognizes the serious importance of BLR even if our forces still don't. The Radio Police [aka FCC] are brutal in their attempts to repress the stations which have come on air.

Black Liberation Radio, and all so-called "free radio stations," started with the work of Mbanna Kantako in a housing project in Springfield, Illinois. On November 25, 1987, Kantako, a legally blind project resident of the John Hay Homes began broadcasting on a one-watt FM transmitter to the inner city community. The station, called WTRA originally, was ignored by the city's white

Illustration by Curt Neitzke

political establishment and the FCC, until it began to expose police brutality against black city residents over the air. This earned him not only a $750 fine from the FCC, but a racist cop purportedly shot a pistol bullet into his house in an act of intimidation. The FCC also ordered him off the air, but he refused and continued to broadcast. He was threatened with eviction from his project apartment and cops even arrested his nine year old son to pressure him to cease broadcasting. Rather than frightening him off the air, however, the repression made him more determined to continue broadcasting, and even earned him more listeners and critical community support to oppose government censorship. Though he no longer broadcasts from the now demolished projects, his new station, called Human Rights Radio, broadcasts 24 hours a day in Springfield with his tapes played all over the world. Inspired by Kantako, other stations all over the country have gone on the air, managed by black activists.

But there is not yet a happy ending to this story. Although the feds have not decided to attack Kantako because of his base of support in the black community, they have been able to successfully attack others and even close them down. Zoom Black Magic Radio of Contra Costa, California was founded in or around 1989, and has been harassed incessantly by local cops and FCC agents. Although they continue to broadcast, the ZBMR collective have been threatened with arrest by cops, been subjected to police surveillance, lost jobs in retaliatory firings, and had their equipment seized several times by police and FCC agents.

Around 1993 Black Liberation Radio in Richmond, Virginia came on air to serve the black community. For almost a year, they were let alone, but finally because of their support of the 1995 Million Man March, they were raided by local cops, the FBI and FCC, who not only hauled off broadcast equipment, but also broke furniture, and dragged off computers and office equipment, and the resident's personal property. This intimidation by government thugs completely shut down BLR-Richmond, and to this day there is no further attempt at a broadcast.

One of the most egregious cases of political repression against free radio happened against Napoleon Williams of BLR in Decatur, in central Illinois. In order to silence his voice, Williams has been arrested, jailed on trumped up charges, seen his kids snatched by the Department of Child and Family Services (DCFS) goon squad and put into foster care and their mother imprisoned; all on account of dubious child abuse charges related to the illegality of the station and Napoleon's use of profanity on the air.

On January 9, 1997, police seized his broadcast equipment along with his personal files and computer. Most recently, on April 8, 1997, he had his station raided again by the Decatur police SWAT team and representatives of the Illinois State Attorney General after being indicted by a grand jury on spurious "felony eavesdropping" charge by three DCFS social workers he recorded for airplay purposes. Bail was set at $20,000. At this writing Napoleon — who had gone underground — was captured upon his return to the air on May 10, 1997 in a military-style SWAT team operations. Black Liberation Radio remains on the air 24 hours a day as a result of strong community support.

Williams and Jones need your help: they particularly need legal assistance. There are people like them all over this country. This is a story which needs to be told: We need to break the blackout on what's really going on in America ...

WHAT CAN WE DO?

Hundreds of micropower stations have come on the air in the last ten years, but the first thing one notices is how the government deals with the white radicals running a station like Free Radio Berkeley in California, as opposed to the life threatening repression of the BLR stations. Really the most that Stephen Dunifer, the other major figure in microradio, has had to suffer is threats of fines and other legal action. His home or offices have not been raided, nor has his inventory of radio transmitters been seized from his business, and neither he nor members of his family have been jailed at any time in retaliation for his broadcasts. Clearly we know the reason why. This is government racism and violent repression of the black community stations. The black stations are deemed to be more of a threat, but also having less community support, so the police (goaded on by the FCC) feel free to use as much force as they like. So they seize, destroy and intimidate. Now they have kidnapped a child to pressure the parents to give up broadcasting. Yet, this did not stop Mbanna and it has not stopped Napoleon and Mildred. But we got to create a stink to make them give the children back to the rightful parents!

Black Autonomy and all segments of the African freedom movement must support the Black Liberation Radio movement. We should not allow the white government to crush this very important incipient movement. We should in fact join this conspiracy to expose government repression and put even more stations on the air. They can't jail us all!

Here is what I suggest we do to ensure our right to broadcast and beat back the government:

1) Have a series of mass demonstrations in Berkeley and other cities while the hearings are going on in federal court based on the government's lawsuit to close down Free Radio Berkeley. We need to mobilize all those interested in human rights, especially the right to broadcast freely, as well as all those who listen to these stations. We have got to make this into more of a mass, activist issue or we will be stamped out by the state.

2) Create a legal and educational defense fund to raise money to support any harassed broadcaster and the lawsuits by the FCC. This also includes defense against criminal charges brought by the government and police which grow out of their broadcasting.

3) Start a campaign to get human rights organizations in North America and other parts of the world to support the rights of BLRs and other microbroadcasters. The seizure of the children of an activist and police raids of stations are routine in police states, now we need to expose it to our people when it happens in a "liberal democratic" state like America. If Amnesty International, the UN and other respected organizations object to the repression, which is in violation of both U.S. and international law, this would be a powerful weapon to isolate the U.S. government and its FCC.

4) Popularize the issue so that the masses of our people will support the rights of broadcasters. We must get all segments of our movement to support this issue, but more importantly we must get our individual communities to support this issue. The best way to do that is to start a station in your community or neighborhood — now!

5) Create an actual broadcast network of stations for shared programming, news, local experiences, legal defense, and other functions.

6) A key component of this entire proposal is that we must get the international radio support group AMARC to lead a worldwide campaign on behalf of the BLRs and microbroadcasters generally. It is also important that we get all organizations interested in protecting the rights of broadcasters to denounce the repression of the Black Liberation Radio stations.

This is not all that can be done, but it is a start. So let us all vow to set up a station next year where we live and counter-program all the government/corporate/media propaganda. Then the people in our communities can all say: "I finally got the news!"

"WE HAVE TO MAKE SURE THAT THE VOICELESS HAVE A VOICE"

An Interview With Kiilu Nyasha (San Francisco Liberation Radio)

Sheila Nopper

Sheila Nopper (SN): Tell me a little bit about your history and how it led you to get involved in the micropower radio movement?

Kiilu Nyasha (KN): Well I joined the Black Panther party in 1969. That automatically got me involved in the struggle. I didn't get involved with radio until around 1983 and that was kind of a fluke. I had not been long out of the hospital. My daughter and I still had a social worker keeping tabs on us, and she and I became friends. We used to talk a lot, and she discovered that I had a little information under my hat. So, she called me up one day and said that a group of disabled people were meeting and would I like to join them either to be interviewed or to do something on the radio. I did and I met with them at *Youth News* in Oakland which was wheelchair accessible at the time. Before I knew it I was on the air at Pacifica's KPFA. I had a microphone in my face and then off I went.

Photo of Kiilu Nyasha courtesy of Kiilu Nyasha

I started doing commentaries, and then worked my way into doing other things like 'Freedom is a Constant Struggle' which used to be on every Saturday hosted by different people. I got the second Saturday slot. That was a half hour slot that used to turn into an hour because the programmer after me never came in. So, I would always have plan B for the extra half hour, and often open up the live lines for call-ins. I also used to do specials. I did Black August specials for about three years running beginning in 1993.

SN: When you say specials, what do you mean?

KN: The first one was a four hour special which I called 'Black August.' In the black community we observe Black August, originally in memory of Jonathan and George Jackson and the August 7th and August 21st incidents, and then it just kept expanding because the MOVE Nine were busted in August, on August 8th, 1978. I think Nat Turner did his thing in August, and we discovered there were a whole host of August dates in our history that we needed to commemorate. So Black August kind of became a tradition. I was doing that kind of special programming every August up until '95. In '95, I was actually doing part of Black August from Philadelphia because I went to see about Mumia Abu Jamal who was scheduled to be executed on August 17th as you may recall. On that date, I was broadcasting live from Philly about what was happening. Thank goodness it was good news, but I had gone intending that, if they even thought about executing him, I was going to be there to raise as much hell as I could. That's how the whole radio thing got started.

As to my involvement with the microradio movement, you may be aware that Pacifica started making a lot of changes. They were disingenuous with me throughout this process. I was actually solicited to be a volunteer to attend these meetings about the changes they were contemplating. My input was solicited, and I certainly gave it, but they never gave me a clue that 'Freedom' was going to be cancelled, and that they were going to be throwing out practically all the black and radical programmers. So, I was pretty pissed off because it was two-faced and they were. ...

SN: It sounds like they used you ...

KN: Yeah, I felt used that's exactly the right word. I think they wanted to lend some kind of credibility to their stuff with me because I had a reputation of being radical and straightforward. I've never been one to bite my tongue. So, they gave us all this bureaucratic stuff where we were supposed to fill out all these forms to make proposals, and I was so angry at it that I didn't bother. I had worked with them for thirteen years and I thought it was a lousy way to treat people who have been giving their time and energy, to just unceremoniously drop them like a hot potato.

SN: Especially, still claiming publicly that they're upholding the original mandate of the station ...

KN: Oh, they're not at all! They're worse than ever. They just had a series of forums. I attended the one in San Francisco and it was so contrived and law-and-ordered that it was unbelievable. It was just awful. They're just pretending that they're getting community input when they've already made up their minds that they're going to expand Jerry Brown and they're going to give another guy a talk show. So, I put it on the Net. I said, 'That's just what KPFA needs, another white male hosted talk show.'

SN: So what's your take on their idea of market-driven radio?

KN: I think it's nonsense. It's a numbers game and it doesn't make any sense because what they're doing is actually diffusing the programming and watering it down. I don't buy into that. I think that if you're going to pursue the mission, which is to be an alternative radio station, then you should really be an alternative radio station. They've replaced all the evening talk shows with music, and it's not even particularly good music or music that I would be interested in listening to. Except for maybe 'Democracy Now,' which has some good programming, and 'Flashpoint,' which they're getting ready to eliminate, for investigative reporting there's not much else to listen to on KPFA anymore. Maybe an occasional special, but I've just got used to tuning out because I don't find their programming very informative. I mean it doesn't give me anything I can't get somewhere else better. As far as appealing to a broader audience, that just puts you in the same league with ABC or NPR.

SN: There's plenty of that.

KN: If they were really concerned about listeners and audience, they should have organized some community events. The Bay Area is loaded with artists and musicians who would be glad to perform. They could've organized some terrific events that would have advertised the station, and, at the same time, would have been an uplifting kind of experience for people to go to and come together. They could have held some town meetings on the radio to get real input from people as to what changes they would like to see made. They could have done a lot of real creative things that would have at the same time reached out and involved the community in the process of making changes in the programming. Instead, they had secret meetings. They even violated their own rules as far as board meetings are concerned. So, they're just full of it.

SN: It seems to be a part of a conservative sweep going on across the nation, the continent really. What role does micropower radio play in this conservative climate?

KN: I see it as a true alternative to the so-called alternative public radio and mass media. We put stuff out that you're not going to hear anywhere else. We don't have to abide by the FCC rules and regulations. One of the main things that I find liberating in doing microradio is that we can advocate. You know the FCC rules don't allow you to advocate. On micropower radio, we can encourage people to go to demonstrations. We can encourage people to get actively involved, to join protests, to go to commission hearings, and protest police brutality. We can broadcast the commission hearings, the protests. We don't have to worry about language and all that. So, we really are an alternative in so far as encouraging people, especially poor people and immigrants, to defend against these draconian laws that are coming down and these budget cuts that are about to wipe people out. I feel that this can be a revolutionary tool of communication and propaganda. You know, educating to liberate, that's what I've been about for years now. This is almost a perfect medium for that. It's not perfect in that we only reach a limited group, but if enough stations spring up and we continue to share tapes as we have been we can have an impact. The two-hour interview that I did with Ramona and Carlos Africa wound up on radio stations all over the country. It got passed around so much. People really liked it. So it can be far reaching if people pass around the tapes. Of course it doesn't reach anywhere near the audience I would like it to reach.

Just recently, as part of a European tour I did with the STAND Theatre company whose play "One to Life" is based on the writings of Soledad Brother, George Jackson, I brought back interviews that I did in Belgium with three different Africans. One is with someone who escaped from prison in Sudan and applied for political asylum in Belgium, and is terrified that if he is sent back he will be killed. As a radio programmer, I was able to bring to bare the reality of what's going on in Europe with the immigrants and refugees over there, and at the same time call attention to the legacy of colonialism in Africa, and the fact that we are now living in a global village run by the multinationals at the expense of our neighbors and ourselves. I told audiences there about how micropower radio stations are springing up all over the country here because of the corporate takeover of the media. I feel so liberated in doing micropower radio because I don't have to self-censor. Whenever you're doing so-called public radio, you really have to self-censor a lot because you know what they're going to object to, and you know what's going to fly and what's not. You know somebody is going to come by and pull your plug if you go too far.

SN: I was just wondering if you would be willing to share a little bit about your friend Michael Taylor and what happened to him so that we could give some kind of tribute to him in the book.

KN: Well, we had worked together just recently in Philly on Mumia's case. The Panthers put on a youth summit in Oakland just a month before he was killed. We had discussed, then, the microradio movement. He was working on starting this Black Liberation Radio station in Los Angeles. Apparently he had inadvertently gotten involved with some rather unsavory characters who wanted to take it in another direction. They wanted to start making money, and Michael wanted to keep it a liberation station with good revolutionary politics on it. He had a whole different idea of what he wanted the radio station used for. He stuck to his guns. They were trying to make him give up the equipment because, without Michael, they couldn't go off on their own and do their own thing. He wouldn't give it up. So, they offed him.

SN: What is Michael Taylor's legacy? Is there any kind of follow-up statement you'd like to make?

KN: Yeah, I would encourage more people to get involved in the microradio movement and set up more radio stations. They can be set up for under a thousand dollars worth of equipment. Stephen Dunifer is very willing to share information on how to do it, and I think that more people should be encouraged to join the network of micropower stations. I think that this is a movement that should be taken very seriously because the times are getting worse, and they are getting worse fast. We have to make sure that the voiceless have a voice. That would be a fitting tribute to Michael Taylor.

— February 20, 1997

Illustration from San Francisco Liberation Radio

RADIO LATINO

Ricardo Omar Elizalde

Chucho Chilango answers the phone. His voice is quiet, almost a mumble. Wary the FCC might be listening and trying to shut down Radio Libre again, he said he'd rather not answer questions over the phone.

Three hours later the pirate radio DJ walks into a Mission District Cafe in the heart of this Latino Neighborhood in San Francisco. He's with a friend who's carrying a guitar. Chilango's ready to talk about his "Sacrichingo Show" on 103.3. At Radio Libre, Chilango says, "we sacrifice the demons of information," he says as he nods to his friend that it's OK to leave. Maybe it's just one last precaution before he begins to trust his interviewer. Despite his cautious behavior, Chilango refuses to think of Radio Libre as an illegal entity. "Just like a community has its newspapers and community centers, they should also have their own radio stations," he says while sipping hot apple cider.

His show is broadcast on Sundays between four-to-six in the back room of a grey Victorian in the heart of the Mission District. On the way back to the makeshift station, an odor in the kitchen hints of sour milk. Bike frames are strewn throughout the flat. This is Radio Libre's temporary home, but it's so

YOUR VOICE OF REBELLION

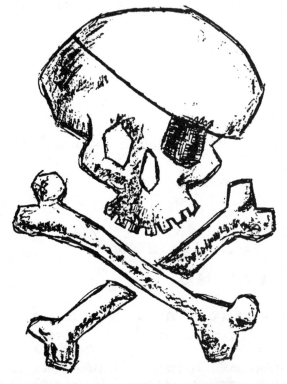

103.3FM

RADIO LIBRE

LIBERATING THE AIR WAVES OF THE MISSION & BEYOND
350- 7 TH AVE. #35, SAN FRANCISCO, CA 94118 (415)487-6308

packed it looks like the station's DJs have been here a lot longer. The room is crowded, littered with crates of records, speakers, a conga and a grey couch with a guitar case sitting on top of it. In the corner there's a blanket posing as a curtain in front of a broken window. Bits of glass fall to the ground below between conversations.

Chilango wears his long black hair in a ponytail and has skin the color of toasted clay. He's adorned with eight silver rings on his fingers and two earrings on each ear. His eyes are a deep black so he doesn't give away his thoughts. His speech is a monotone. "We offer an alternative, a different point of view than what you get in the mainstream media," says Chilango. On his show he tackles political and social themes, and information pertinent to the Latino community. He also plays music that provides social commentary. But on some Sundays, just for kicks, he plays mambos and the classic old jams that would have your *abuelita* dancing in her rocking chair.

Although Stephen Dunifer created the first station in the Bay Area, Latino voices were broadcasting in no time. From Watsonville to Sacramento, the list of the stations continues to grow. The station's names, Radio X, Radio Zapata, Radio Libre, hint at their status as mini radio revolutions. Radio Libre is a bilingual station broadcasting at thirty watts, which is the average wattage of a microbroadcaster. While the names connote the same sentiment as the stations in Latin America, that's where the similarities end. Those stations aided the revolutionary armies. Radio Rebelde in Cuba was instrumental in the overthrow of the Batista Regime. Fidel Castro used the radio to broadcast information about battles and give reports about soldiers who were injured or dead. Radio Venceremos of El Salvador transmitted from ditches in the mountains of Morazan. Today they still broadcast and are legal. These radio stations gave a voice to each revolution. They were not censored and they eluded capture.

Subcomandante Marcos, of the Zapatista Army of National Liberation, transmitting from the jungle through a clandestine radio station in 1994, let the people of Chiapas know exactly where they stood. "We are shadows of tender fury; our dark wings will cover the sky again, and their protective cloak will shelter the dispossessed and the good men and women who understand that justice and peace go hand in hand. If they deny us our rights, then our tender fury will enter those fine mansions. There will be no fence our shadows will not jump over; no door will be left unopened, no window left unbroken, no wall left standing. Our shadow will bring pain to those who call for war and death for our race; more tears and blood will flow before peace can sit down at our table with good will. FREEDOM! DEMOCRACY! JUSTICE!"

But while those radio stations served the oppressed of their countries they should not be confused with the stations here in the United States. "We are not clandestine or subversive at all. What we do is provide an alternative to the garbage that you hear on the mainstream press," says Lalo Rangal, who has a show on Free Radio Berkeley every Sunday. In the future, he would like to have a mobile radio station in the back of a van. He would take this station to the people and broadcast there, whether it be in the rural areas or in the urban areas. Rangal's a little disappointed with his show on the Berkeley station. He says there's only an eight percent Latino population and his show is in Spanish, so he doesn't have the numbers he'd like. His shows are a battle against the Latino stereotype. "We're not all Mexicans," says Rangal refuting the stereotype. "We're a very able and varied people." To contradict the mainstream radio stations, he plays music from the whole Latin American region, not just Mexico.

In October of 1996, amid heat from the FCC their nervous landlord evicted the station and four of its DJs from their Mission District home. It took the group four months to find another, albeit temporary home. The FCC tried to slap fines on four people who were in the house at the time and refused to let the agents of the FCC in. The FCC then wrote a letter to these people; it said they were in violation of the law and could be put in prison for up to a year or fined up to $100,000. It also accused the individuals of conspiracy.

"Where is the minority community gonna get access if it's not through micropowered radio," says Steven Dunifer of Free Radio Berkeley. "The media resources have dwindled down. The minority community is under-represented and can't fight back." Jennifer Navarro, who has traveled all the way down to El Salvador delivering and helping set up stations says, "That's what I like about pirate radio, we're not asking anyone for shit. We're doing it ourselves ... I see [micropowered radio] as a tool, a big responsibility." She would like to see a radio station that reflects the community, but it would be hard to say exactly what a Latino community looks like because it's so diverse. "I don't want to hear just activists. I want to see housewives, I want to see kids. If it's for the community, then it should reflect the community."

Jose Ibarra, of Radio Zapata in Salinas, has a station which reflects his community. The station goes on at the crack of dawn because it serves a migrant worker community. His DJs are seasonal because they are part of that community. Radio Zapata offers less programming at the end of Summer. This is when all the migrant workers follow the crops elsewhere or return home. Radio Zapata is one micropowered station where the FCC won't have to worry about profanity. "On mainstream radio they glorify drugs, gangs and sex because that's what sells," says Ibarra. "That culture no longer has any dignity. ... We don't play pop music. We play traditional, indigenous and revolutionary music that is popular to us." "We have felt that the *viejos* (elders) were being excluded from programming, our job is to keep their music alive ... It's a very important job we have," says Ibarra. But that's just the music they play.

Radio Zapata also offers a wide variety of news and views from a Zapatista point of view and also what's going on in the community around them. "A person has to be aware of their rights ... We have to know who's bothering us." Sometimes he uses a bit of comedy to get his point across. Ibarra tells of the person who doesn't want to worry about anything. "'O.K., O.K, but I don't want to think,'" he says. "But later they're worried about so and so on *la novela*, (*pobrecito*)." It's a criticism that his community would rather watch soap operas then deal with real issues. It's a little bit of sugar and a lot of truth.

In early 1997 Radio Zapata had to shut it's doors. A court order denied them access to their P.O. Box. Since it was Winter and their audience had moved either back to their countries or to follow the crops elsewhere, Radio Zapata made a conscious decision to close down its radio station and wait for its audience to come back in the Spring. "It wasn't much of a decision to close down ... Nobody would've responded for us, so we took that time to reorganize the people," Ibarra says, so that when their audience came back in the middle of March they would have a regenerated radio station. If they need to elude the FCC they are sure their audience will provide homes for them. An FM signal is easy to detect for the FCC, but it is also very mobile. He says they will bounce around from house to house in order to elude capture. Meanwhile they are saving their money for an AM transmitter, which is much harder for the FCC to detect. But also it is much heavier, thus harder to move around. Ibarra's criticism of his peers in the micropowered world of radio are that sometimes they tend to not serve their communities. "If the music is similar to that of a mainstream station, then it's just another station," Ibarra says. The mainstream is exactly what Radio Zapata is fighting against. "We are struggling for what is just," says Ibarra.

Another person who has bought a transmitter from Dunifer and will start a station in the near future is Robert Gandera c/s. He has experience working on micropowered radio. He used to do a show called "La Hora Sabrosa" on a station run by the Friends of the Nation. He plays strictly Salsa because up in Sacramento there are too many stations playing Banda said the man whose speech is littered with what you might call veteranoisms or *cholo* speak. He plans to start his station in late 1997, "I plan to call it 'La Tuya FCC,'" jokes the one time activist. For his radio station he would like organizations to come in and create their own shows. While some of the programs are messages to organize and fight back a lot of the music on the air is Hip-Hop.

Mykel and L.O.C. are young DJs practicing their routines to perform at the clubs where they spin their records. The radio station serves to get their names out into the neighborhood. Certainly nothing socially conscious about that, but the beats they play wouldn't normally be on the radio. "This is straight up underground flavor," says L.O.C. R. Love reads the news from the barrio while Myke1 and L.O.C. mix. Although she just recently realized it, Radio Libre serves as kind of an internship for the broadcasting degree she seeks from San Francisco State. R. Love stands at five three, her hair is long and straight. When she talks, she looks you right in the eye, as if trying to read your sincerity. She is 26 but looks about 19. She speaks fast and with a passion that only comes from doing something you love, something worthwhile. "I love doing pirate radio," she says with conviction. At Radio X in San Francisco Camila who refused to give her last name says it is very empowering to hear people like yourself on the radio. "Now we have access to means of communication ... we can talk about our community especially in a racist society ... We can talk about events that don't make it into the mainstream press."

What rings true for most of these people is that the mainstream sells us nothing but garbage and consumerism. They want to provide an alternative. An alternative that isn't driven by the advertisers search for the buck. In this decade of California's anti-immigration, anti-Affirmative Action backlash and the Federal Welfare Reform Act, this whole country needs a different point of view. Micropowered radio stations and their DJs have the guts to offer this different view. In this day and age where we're glutted with news shows, the community media outlets become a necessity. I think for Latinos it's a way to address the problems of their community and a way to fight back.

ON THE AIR

89.7	92.3	93.7	96.1	96.3	102.5	103.3	104.1	106.7	93.7	102.5	104.1
Que Pasa Radio	Free Radio Fresno	Radio Libre	Radio Watson	Free Radio Santa Cruz	Radio Califas	Radio Libre	Free Radio Mt. View	Radio Zapata	Liberation Radio	Radio X	Free Radio Berkeley
San Rafael	Fresno	San Jose	Watsonville	Santa Cruz	Berkeley	San Francisco	Mtn. View	Salinas	San Francisco	San Francisco	Berkeley
	Daily							Dawn to 11AM	evenings	4-5 shows per week	24 hours a day

COMMUNITY STRUGGLE AND THE SWEET MYSTERY OF RADIO

DJ Tashtego

1. YOU CAN'T TELL THE PLAYERS WITHOUT A SCORECARD

For the squatter community on New York's Lower East Side, the summer of 1995 kicked off with a bang, when a force comprising more than 400 NYPD riot police, a tactical assault unit, four helicopters and a tank, moved to evict five long-term squats on East 13th Street. Since the year before, the hundred-odd residents of the 13th Street squats had been waging a gutsy, aggressive court battle, spurred on by the City's announced plan to give their buildings to a federally-subsidized, controlled housing program — buildings which they had saved from dereliction, abandonment and burnout with their own work and direct action for more than ten years. Their legal strategy forced a long, in-depth hearing in New York State Supreme Court, parading the whole fabric of Lower East Side radical housing culture for the entire City to see, as more than a decade's worth of squatters, activists, priests, rabbis, artists and organizers took the stand to testify.

Clearly outmatched in court, and heading for a legal defeat, the City decided to act preemptively, settle some old scores, and tip the balance. They announced

Illustration by Eric Drooker

their intention, in the midst of three months of hearings, to evict the squatters on a building-safety pretext. Going into the Memorial Day weekend, the whole Lower East Side knew it was coming down. Squatters from the other twenty "houses" in the neighborhood rallied to defend 13th Street from the anticipated police raid, covering windows with plywood, building defensive structures, and turning out numbers of people committed to making the streets a scene of spectacular chaos.

I had lived in the squats on 13th Street for almost seven years when the morning finally arrived, and the cops came in force. After hours of street theater, skirmishes, clashes with riot cops and general confusion, they naturally prevailed. Around noon, black-uniformed ninja-cops finally reached my own barricaded door, which splintered under their battering ram, and I found myself up against the wall of my study, while four men in combat gear pointed locked-and-loaded machine guns at my head. Score one for New York's finest against the centuries-old defiance of property and its tyranny. Or something like that.

News coverage, for virtually the first time in New York squatter history, turned momentarily serious, if not exactly positive. A decade's worth of marginalizing stories in the papers and on television that never failed to characterize squatters as parasites, kooky artists or runaway street punks — without ever considering for a moment the direct action, threat-by-example posed by people seizing housing — grudgingly gave way now to a more measured, if still reactionary, consideration of the self-help housing movement and the disastrous City policies which had inspired it. Naturally, a real critique of the pyramid scam of rent-slavery could never come from the dominant media sources: no challenges to the economic order will ever come from the info-tainment establishment, those crown jewels of capitalism. ... Yet incrementally, through well-staged spectacles of resistance calculated to exploit the info-hegemony's own taste for lurid action, the squatters themselves changed the public's mediated knee-jerk perceptions, winning some converts where none had been before. And the judge was watching, too.

Our homes are gone now, and though we are still winning the legal strategy to this day, they have the buildings. Defeats cause growth, if you're desperate enough. And squatter tactics became sharper that summer, culminating in a brilliant re-occupation of the very same buildings, right under their noses, during the July 4th fireworks display — explosions and lights over the East River gave dozens of squatters the patriotic cover to go in and re-barricade. The ensuing late-night police-riot swept up hundreds of non-squatter neighborhood residents returning from the park, and embarrassed the cops who, once regaining the building, found no one inside. The local media savaged the NYPD, and the publicity coup rejuvenated organizers, low-income tenants and the squatter community alike. The rest of that summer passed in a blur of clashes with cops as 13th Street became an armed camp. The block was shut down and a mobile command center/arrest station was installed in front of our houses, where before we used to kick around the soccer ball. By September, the action had settled down a bit, as 13th Street turned into a fortress, the cops determined not to get caught napping again. Many of my evicted neighbors, including myself, were taken in as guests of other squats in the community, and local church and arts groups were lending a hand in the midst of a neighborhood occupation. It seemed like a good moment for a vacation, and a view from afar.

2. CALIFORNIA DREAMIN'

Taking a break from Loisaida, I travelled to California to get some thinking done. On the one hand, we'd lost a few buildings to the cops — homes encompassing years of passionate work and a dedication to housing free of rent slavery, and productive time free from wage slavery. Nearly 75 squatters were now scrambling for housing, and New York City mayoral strongman Rudolf Giuliani had declared us outlaws. On the other hand, for the first time in years of Loisaida's self-help housing movement, the public wasn't exactly buying the City's rhetoric anymore. We were finally telling our story, in our own way, and working the mainstream media skillfully. After all, capital and the real estate class work it all the time — why shouldn't we?

While in Berkeley, I met up with my old friend Jahnelle, and volunteered for a couple days helping him with East Bay Food Not Bombs. Driving around in the beat-up truck, making pickups of vegetables, we had Free Radio Berkeley's signal constantly tuned in. I had followed FRB's story in the national media for the past year or so, and knew of it. Moreover, Dunifer's status as the Johnny Appleseed of micropower radio was already legend in anarchist circles on the east coast. When Jahnelle offered to take me by their studio so I could see it in operation, an idea quickly formed in my mind — could this be something to take back to the Lower East Side, another tool for building on, or better still, for tearing down the alienation? Or just another big toy we could have some kicks with?

While as squatters, we had long had our own groups — Eviction Watch; the punk, painting and poetry center, ABC No Rio; and galleries like Bullet Space — a solid, activist bridge to the non-squatter community of Loisaida's fucked-over low-income tenants, struggling workers and homeless always seemed frustratingly elusive. While these groups should naturally have shared class-interests with anyone out to destroy the rent-slavery economy, the thorough atomization of the urban underclass by means of race, religion and reactionary politics effectively kept poor tenants and squatter-folk from uniting. But 1995's summer of spectacles, making direct resistance to big real estate and its NYPD goon-army manifest for anyone on the streets of Loisaida, had restimulated the idea of this bridge, and gave its construction a potent urgency.

The numbing effect of the corporate mediascape we all inhabit casts a long shadow over so much of the lived experience of the city — *their* economies, their architectures, their simulations and re-creations, their inculcating philosophies and their systems of control proliferate daily like one big social virus, increasingly unknowable, yet acting upon us in totalitarian fashion. Lacking any shared, identifiable culture but Consumerism, we are free to buy their products, services and ideology; beyond this, our freedom is mostly abstracted and notional. The very interpretation of Consumerism on a mass scale is ceded to those possessing the technologies of mass media — which is to say, those with the greatest stake in Consumerism's continued success.

To create spectacles which depend in part on the dissenters' ability to turn cleverly the media eye upon itself, or merely to add another enraged shout to their maelstrom, no longer seems like enough. After all, the avalanche of images and sounds that bury us in a kind of living death of over-stimulation and commodity choice permits only so much meaning to accumulate, most of it presented through their screens, before the receiver must purge, in preparation for the next binge. What's needed is a means to break the bulimia of info-consumption, and turn from passive consumers of images, words and culture into active makers. This is what the off-the-grid philosophy in all its manifestations practices: dropout homesteaders in Vermont generating all their energy from solar techniques and sensible living; 'zine culture and small-press distributors; the DIY emphasis of punk spreading outward in new DJ-as-expropriation-artist musical forms; Food Not Bombs' distribution system as moral imperative; and the squatter-recycler ethos, making homes out of the cast-off housing of the market economy. A real critique of the meaninglessness of work and the tenuousness of modern life will never come from those media that profit most from our meaninglessness. Just as squatting — a sprawling, inexact, messy social experiment — has endeavored here in New York and all over the world to create housing and community outside the bounds of the market economy so, too, does the micropower radio movement create media outside of capitalism. The answers lie somewhere out that direction. *Saddle up the horses, let's get going.*

3. Direct Actions Gets the Goods

Meanwhile, back in New York that fall, media merger fever had set off a new Gold Rush in corporate America, as Wall Street and Madison Avenue seemed to re-shuffle the deck of dwindling cards almost daily. Everything, from motion picture studios and distribution companies to local television chains, to paperback houses and sports franchises, to virtually every newspaper in the country, was now concentrated in the holdings of four or five transnational corporations — the inevitable culmination of the decades-long growth of what *The Nation* termed "The National Entertainment State." It's no longer easy to ignore the corporate world, and pretend to live in some parallel, "alternative" universe — to make that decision strikes me as a form of blinkered delusion at worst, and willful intellectual escapism at best — in either case, it seems urban people make this choice especially at their own peril. But what are working people to do, as Kulchur rushes headlong to a new *ironic* century awash in more information than ever before available, but signifying perhaps less than it ever has?

I came back to the Lower East Side on fire for a radio station — a community jungle drum we could all beat on together, a tool and a toy and a babble of shouts in the ether — that would complement and reinforce the already growing anti-culture of info-shops, anarchist book distributors, homemade housing and self-help. It took hardly any effort to organize a collective committed to getting on the air by Thanksgiving. The very idea of radio — a physical mystery so old and taken for granted in this techno-sexy age, it had almost been forgotten — excited people's imaginations, and drew enthusiastic support. Commercial radio in New York City has sucked for a very long time, and everyone knows it.

Shortly after our first meetings, Keith McHenry came through town with his "Rent is Theft" Tour, and he demonstrated at ABC No Rio one of Dunifer's five-watt packages. Squatter organizer Feedback Philtre, who had been a radio hobbyist as a kid in Queens, took on the technical aspects, while non-squatter Grace O'Malley concentrated on finding the start-up money, with additional technical assistance from an old friend of Dunifer's we found living in Manhattan, who got us answers (and the ever-rare #14 tinned buss wire) whenever we needed them. It was Grace who, in a stroke of genius, came up with our moniker — *Steal This Radio*. The name was golden: Abbie would've appreciated it, but it was much more than mere Yippie homage — it worked as an exhortation to everyone in earshot to throw down in the re-creation of community-based, new media. *Start your own station. Let a thousand transmitters bloom.* The collective grew quickly, with a varied mix of neighborhood folk, and we eventually opted to go with a five-watt unit combining locally-bought parts and some re-configured FRB kit elements. We found a seemingly clear point on the dial, researched its availability in the *Broadcaster's Annual*, and built a five-eighths ground-plane antenna out of plumbing supplies which, owing to its ungainly appearance, was christened "Sputnik."

New York City's Lower East Side presented special challenges and potential rewards that distinguished our task from what other micropower stations might have contended with before us. The physical density of the neighborhood, with a tight grid of six-story walkups and narrow streets, necessitated a strong signal centrally-located in the concrete-and-steel bowl formed by 14th Street and the Stuyvesant Town projects to the north, Delancey Street to the south, and the wall of Broadway to the west, with the projects on the East River hemming our signal in to the east. On the positive side of the ledger, a decent signal hitting most of this area would, by virtue of population concentration alone, reach 100,000 potential listeners. But again, we had to wonder if setting up shop in the belly of the beast, in Corporate Media's Babylon itself — where every point on the dial is treated as some holding company's private fiefdom — would draw quick heat. No one wanted to rely on the FCC's holding pattern, *vis à vis* their frustration in prosecuting Dunifer, to last forever. The collective decided the best insurance against trouble was a widely diversified, community-based programming, thinking that it's easy enough for authority to move against anarcho-squatter-troublemakers; but it's a different matter when the folks doing the broadcasting come from every aspect of the neighborhood, talking directly to their neighborhood, free from the alienation of mediation. This general aim for a maximum of community input would be coupled with a stalwart insistence that *we are doing nothing wrong*. The term "pirate" isn't used much around the station to this day — it cedes the legal and philosophical terms of the debate up front, and there's no reason to give them any edge. Raffishly glamorous as the pirate image may be, "micropower" gets to the simple philosophy much better, and insists on a positive self-definition, outside the authority of government regulatory strait-jacketing, declaring a new paradigm they can either get with now or try to oppose. On this point, it seems the barn door's been open for some time now — it's a bit too late for the state to close it up with new regulations.

4. Another Friday, Another Rooftop

In typical grandiose Lower East Side fashion, going on the air from a rooftop perch with a couple of Walkman tape-players and a microphone patched into the transmitter never appealed to us. For our first broadcast, we went for the full-console approach, with a hastily-gathered array of dumpster-dived tape decks, donated cd players and turntables, all patched into a cranky DJ mixer set up in the living room of a squatter apartment on a Friday night, with our first two DJs, Maxx and Chrome, mixing beats and neighborhood news. For our first few weeks, we moved to a different squat every Friday night show, solemnly vigilant against FCC-detection in a way I find charming and quaint now. Our weekly broadcasts quickly became the best floating house party on the Lower East Side, and as thirty or forty people would inevitably arrive at every broadcast location, we often asked ourselves if anyone was home listening to the show. A number of wildly successful, live broadcast-benefits from ABC No Rio's sacred punk basement were engineering marvels of low-tech willpower, with live bands, DJs, poets, and news reports alternating between our stage set and our control-room upstairs — crazy, all-night parties that came off every time like the Normandy Invasion in their technical coordination and *esprit de corps*.

But standing on the high top of an abandoned Matzoh factory elevator shaft in a stiff January wind, watching the snow swirl around the World Trade Center, skinning our frozen knuckles while Mr. Peabody bolted down Sputnik and Liverpool Steve held the mast upright, we figured these increasingly ambitious, mobile Friday nights were going to kill us. We needed a real studio, a fixed place to settle into and get down to the business of creating open programming for the whole community, where anyone with an itch to communicate with their neighbors could have a stake in the experiment — a party ain't nothing but a good time, after all, and we had always aimed for much more than that. Simultaneously, we knew how the neighborhood had voices that needed hearing, but who were unlikely to come to all-night parties — we felt a responsibility to make space for conceivably anyone who had an idea and the commitment to presenting it on the air: high school kids, older folks, radical church people, and so on.

To find a studio home, Steal This Radio reached out again to the squatter community, and presented its proposal at house meetings, until a building with an empty storefront in need of serious renovation invited the station in. Agreeing to perform the work strictly to building codes, STR's collective pitched in to demolish the old space and pour a new concrete floor, frame out walls, install soundproofing, plumbing and electricity. Finally at home in a space we could put to good use, STR quickly expanded its programming in the spring of 1996 to seven nights per week, starting at 6 p.m., and broadcasting until dawn, or as late as DJs want to go. The station upgraded its transmitter in stages as well, abandoning the old five-watt unit for a jerry-rigged ten watter, before moving its current half-watt PLL exciter into a twenty-watt amp stage that has powered us since moving into our new home. Now reaching the edges of the Williamsburg neighborhood of Brooklyn and as far uptown as United Nations Plaza (on a good day with bad weather!), the technical and physical tasks are mostly accomplished, leaving the hardest part of all — the social organizing — as an ongoing challenge.

To keep a station on the air and on a schedule, it's not enough to set up the equipment and turn it on — dedicated people are the key to any sustained micropower operation, and creating an organization to accommodate their dedication is inevitably the toughest part of the experience. There is no manual for this stuff. The philosophy comes first, informed by general principles of open access, anti-censorship, and community service. With these ideals in mind, the collective has had to reconcile practical considerations to them — operational ability, accountability to each other, and full participation. Just keeping the studio equipment working requires enormous organizational resources, and money is eternally in short supply. All community organizing needs many hands to make the work lighter for all — a radio project should be no different. In this respect, a maximum of access and participation makes things easier — the more voices on the air, representing more neighborhood elements, the greater the likelihood of success as a station. Even better, as an essentially democratic, community-focussed project, micropower radio's first and best moral *and* legal defenses are exactly those based on the free exercise of community autonomy.

5. "THE COPS ARE OUR BEST LISTENERS."

Steal This Radio has a good way to go before it becomes all the things it wants to be. Continually hamstrung by lack of money, we make do in the best improvised way we can — after all, squatting the airwaves is really a piece of cake after years of squatting real estate. Still, the unheated studio is cold in these winter months, and keeping up with the neighborhood is like chasing after a pack of wild horses. Yet programming is expanding rapidly, and as of this writing, it runs the gamut from neighborhood news to original, live radio plays, to all-night jungle and house mix shows to call-in talk radio on the studio phone line. DJs range in age from thirteen to sixty, and Spanish-language programming is growing rapidly — best of all, I still get a palpable thrill up my spine when, tuning in the station on some car radio, I hear a DJ rapping in Spanish over a free-style beat mix, and the sound is *different* from anything else on the band. And in a modest fulfillment of one of STR's original intentions, the station has been present and busy at several demonstrations and evictions in the neighborhood, including the cowardly demolition of the 5th Street squats in February, 1997, when the City's wrecking cranes almost killed squatters still inside their homes. Throughout the twenty-four hours of tense uncertainty about what to do, with squatters traumatized at the loss of their homes and all their possessions, the live phone lines stayed open, and functioned as a community meeting space for the expression of rage, grief, schemes for striking back — never further away than your radio or your phone. At times when the neighborhood is overrun with riot cops, and information is hard to come by, the power of community radio to get the word out has been nothing short of electrifying. And the excitement is contagious — as of this writing, two stations are going on the air in different neighborhoods of Brooklyn, with still more rumored in the Bronx and Queens. As we say at STR, "If you don't like what you hear on the radio, go out and start your own damn station."

Perhaps one of the greatest compliments we've had yet on our place in the neighborhood came during violent clashes in yet another round of squatter evictions last summer. Arrested activists, handcuffed in the police van and on their way to the Ninth Precinct station house, were surprised to hear their FM radio tuned-in to STR's nonstop live coverage of the demonstrations. Driving a moment behind an especially tall, massive building, the signal flagged a bit and static came up. "Heh, heh — guess a piece of tin foil blew in front of their antenna," cops joked. Then the signal came back strong and unsilenced. They didn't turn it off.

Illustration by Mac McGill

RADIACTIVE

Meme Sabon

Spun off and spat out of New York City on a number of nomadic wanderings, fortune and fate helped me to find my way to the "fringe," the ends of the roads, the places where the freaks and the travelers meet. Once "there," I found myself *everywhere*, overstepping geographically imagined boundaries, hopping from one place to another, discovering various temporary alternative spaces and places that exist in spite of, and often in the midst of, the torrent of "mainstream" society. Emanating forth from these shifting zones, is the vast communications network of the disenfranchised. Through it, utilizing various mediums including the mail, the web, the airwaves, and even, yes, via the dream world, we are able to stay in contact with one another, collectively (though often unintentionally) creating and sharing an indefinable subculture.

It was on one of my "wanderings" a few years ago that — after participating in a tipi raising — I found myself lost somewhere in Wisconsin, on a dirt road, in the middle of the night. Lost with me were a number of characters, including a road-doggie who now goes by the name of "DJ Chrome." Our "accidental" meeting resulted in a, well, you know, we're two of those people who just *keep* running into each other, like having long-term, intermittent deja vu's. We have a character trait in common which bonds us: wherever either of us land, we create something, something that didn't exist previously. As a way of providing ourselves with the outlets we need for our creativity and for our alternative views of reality.

Last winter DJ Chrome played a key role in the starting up of "Steal This Radio," a community Pirate Radio effort in NY's "Lower East Side." I heard about it from someone I'd met elsewhere on another one of my adventures, Kzurt. I saw Kzurt on the street in NY, and he invited me over to be on the "Audio Damage Laboratory" radio show. "Radio show? What radio show?" "*Our* radio show! On the Pirate Radio station that we got going." Of course I went, got to be on the radio show, and afterwards, crashed on *DJ Chrome's* sofa. You see? It's this "connection" business I was talking about! We connect, then multiply the possibilities of connections. That's how I found myself involved with "Steal This Radio" my first experience with "Pirate Radio."

I started going to the station on Wednesday nights and that night would be the best night of my week. I met poets there, rappers, singers. People who constantly amazed me with their abilities, their sounds, their words. My life was incredibly enriched by the experience. Through the people I met at those Wednesday night jam sessions, I got my own radio show which I've been doing for about nine months now. And I tell you, the entire experience has been one big lesson on the value of COMMUNITY EMPOWERMENT.

When I arrived for my first radio show I had absolutely no idea of what to do with any of the equipment. But they let me go on anyway. Station Manager Argo showed me the basics and then I was FREE to do whatever I wanted, including, make mistakes. The mistakes were part of the learning and that's what we were doing, learning, learning that we could communicate, learning a new way to communicate and experimenting with this very powerful new toy. Nobody told me what to do, and nobody told me what to say, and nobody said "You can't do that!" Wow. I knew I was out of the mainstream, had escaped society and all its restraints once again! This time, via radio waves.

I now know how to use all of the equipment that once seemed so daunting. I'm even figuring out how it all works. I didn't have to go to a school or pay a lot of money for some piece of paper to legitimize my knowledge, it's just naturally become a part of my *life*. And I'm feeling motivated because it seems to me that *more* people should have the opportunity that I have, so . . . . .not only can I work two turntables, two CD players, a tape deck and three mics at once, but I'm also learning the difference between a capacitor and a resistor. I'm figuring out how electricity works. I know what "Pf" stands for, and I'm *really hoping* to find out if we need a "transition line filter."

We now have a station in Brooklyn, just a shout over the bridge from the Lower East Side. It's been a frustrating struggle to get up. Communicating hasn't always been easy, especially when you're dealing with a lot of "free" people. Although there are many people involved with the stations we've been in contact with, only one or two people at any of them have technical knowledge. Getting to these people can be incredibly difficult because they've already spent so much time working on their own set ups, they don't have energy or time left over for anything else. There's also the element of secrecy to deal with, that counterculture element of fear, fear of being known, found out. And there's the issue of power. Some people don't want to share their knowledge, some people try to share knowledge they don't even have. Still, in spite of the frustrations, we did it. Because we NEED another outlet for expression, for creativity. One that's not commercial or Soho-ized, one that reflects the creative fringe constituency, as well as the interests of a racially mixed neighborhood in Brooklyn.

I've helped to organize creative projects in my Brooklyn neighborhood for years and watched an amazing and magical creative scene flourish and fade. As the police no longer tolerate large gatherings, a waterfront warehouse party scene has vanished. Due to rising real estate and rent costs and the new and conservative business community in our area, other creative outlets have disappeared. More and more artists are being forced to relocate to Brooklyn and Queens as a result of the Governor's overriding concern for making Manhattan a haven only for the wealthy elite. Yet in spite of the fact that there are more creative types than ever in my neighborhood, there is far less of the underground culture that drew many of us here originally.

A lot of people have given up on the neighborhood creative scene. "It's over," I keep hearing people say as we watch one uninspiring Manhattan-style-track-lit-gallery open after another. But I've been hearing people say that for years. They were saying that a couple of years ago when a group of artists proved everyone wrong by having an event called "Organism" and then running a warehouse, "Mustard" for a year following the initial event. Mustard engaged hundreds of artists during that period. And though the lure of possible fame and recognition has tempted a number of the talented away from the more romantic idea of an "underground," there are still many gifted people looking for something new to involve themselves with. Something, perhaps, outside of the established norms. Though renegade events and illegal performance spaces may currently seem impossible, creativity is a lot like the water of the river that forms our neighborhood's western boundary. When one outlet is dammed up, things that flow create diversions.

Starting a Brooklyn Pirate Radio station seemed like an ideal way to recognize the community's needs and provide it with a new creative vehicle. So we had ourselves a fund raiser, featuring local performers "Puss Pie," "Fresh Dave" and Stevie Craig's "Future Room," and made enough money to get the project started. That was four months ago. The interest generated by the project since then has been so substantial, we could easily program and staff two stations! It's definitely *not* "over," over here. Thanks to some of the guys from the local "Happy Hour" scene, where our technological difficulties are enthusiastically discussed by John-John and Snake Man over margaritas most Fridays at 6:00, we actually built the radio. We've got a transmitter, an amp, a power source, an antennae, coaxial cable, a mixer, a tape deck, a turntable, some mikes. We got parts for a low pass filter and the dummy load, too. We've got a name — **"RADIAC"** — after our favorite friendly neighborhood nuclear waste containment facility.

As for myself, Meme Sabon, I plan to do a radio series of mind-altering sound experiments, and then, pass the radio on. And then I think I'll go. By the time you read this, I plan to be traveling again. And maybe I won't come back. For my next project, I plan to create a new reality, to provide one of those alternative arenas for nomads to wander to, as we move around, redefining the idea of "community," connecting and reconnecting through time and space. I'll start another radio, wherever I end up. You may run into me there, somewhere, you know, at the end of the road, wherever the freaks and travelers meet. ...

Illustration by Peter Gowrfain and the Slingshot Crew

"THERE IS NO IDEAL LISTENER"

An Interview With Geov Parrish (Seattle Liberation Radio)

Captain Fred (Radio Califa)

Captain Fred (CF): Could you talk about the limits of free speech, and how you deal with it at Seattle Liberation Radio?

Geov Parrish (GP): Seattle Liberation Radio is a rotating collective of people. Then there's a larger community of people who come in and do programming. Even before we went on the air we went through a very long and involved, and, for those of us who aren't fond of meetings; tedious, procedure of deciding what we wanted on the air and how we were going to go about that. On the one hand, obviously we wanted to champion free speech. We wanted an open forum for the public. On the other hand, there were things that we were not comfortable broadcasting. We didn't want somebody from the Klan, to pick an extreme example, coming in and saying, 'Well, this is an open microphone for anybody in the community to come in — here I am.' We did not want SLR to be a cable access forum of the radio airwaves. What we wound up with was

essentially a series of what we call value statements that simply said we didn't want hate speech on the air. We did not want things that were offensive to various communities and we went through and listed them. We did not want programming that was usually heard on licensed radio stations. The other thing we said at the same time was, 'If you're coming to us, and you have something that you'd like to do on the air, and we don't feel it would be appropriate for *our* station; start your own.'

CF: I was looking at this SLR handout sheet that you brought with you and I was wondering if you could read some selections from it to our Radio Califa audience?

GP: OK, here goes:

'Seattle Liberation Radio is a not-for-profit collective of political, cultural, and media activists who — just like you — can't afford to buy a radio station. So we decided to start one of our own. It's run by the community, for the community, and everyone is welcome to join in and help out.

SLR is part of a new movement of microradio media activism that's taken hold in Seattle and across the country. As fewer corporations own more of our media, and as government policy (as in the 1996 Communications Act) gives more of our publicly owned radio and television stations to these enormous corporations, there remains almost no chance for our voices to be heard.

Low-power, community-based stations like SLR are a chance to get our foot in the door before the economic elite slam it shut. SLR is not about selling things — products, image, or lifestyle. We're about people talking, exchanging news, playing music, performing audio art, and communicating with each other about what's real in our daily lives. You may not be used to hearing voices on the radio that sound like you — but it's habit forming. It's exhilarating. It may even inspire you to want to broadcast, too. And that's what we want to see happen.

Our mission is to build community in the Capitol Hill district of Seattle and to encourage other independent radio ventures throughout the city, state, and country. To that end, we provide an avenue for voices otherwise unrepresented in the mainstream press to be heard — on our radio station. We will be broadcasting at 103.1FM in the Capitol Hill area.

The FCC has a mandate to shut down those operating without a license, citing the chaos that would surely commence if people were to start broadcasting on their own. But, with the excellent signal quality that can be achieved with low-cost transmitters, we see the true motives of the FCC. The real issues are not technical — they are political. It's about auctioning off freedom exclusively to those who can afford it.

We can use your help, whether you live locally or anywhere else. Help us by sending us programming of any sort — news, commentary, arts, entertainment, educational, anything. Anyone with technical knowledge of this sort could also lend a hand in engineering. Of course, we can always use financial support. And others involved in similar ventures should get in touch as well. We can be contacted at PO Box 85541, Seattle, Washington, 98145; email: slr@scn.org.'

If you'd like to start your own station, get in touch with us and we'll show you how.

CF: What is your vision of the ideal SLR *listener* ...?

GP: There is no ideal listener. What we ask for people to do when they get behind a microphone is exactly what we're doing here, which is to have one-on-one conversations with whoever's listening. It's not about projecting image. It's not about being perfect and coming back and doing a second take when you fuck things up or use inappropriate language, because the FCC will come down on your fuckin' head. It is about being real and having the same sort of conversations that you would have over the fence or through the wall with your apartment neighbor. These are the same sorts of interactions with other people in the community that are becoming increasingly rare in our lives. It's about communicating with one another and, for that reason, the ideal listener is whoever you want to talk with.

We encourage our people to think *not* in terms of the commercial radio approach where we want music that will appeal to "females 25-44 who live in Walnut Creek and make between $65-95,000 a year and have a boat." That's not what this kind of broadcasting is about, and it is such a fundamentally different way of using the technology that I think it's eye-opening for people to really consider what the possibilities are. Most people haven't been exposed to the idea that this kind of medium — or that *any* kind of medium, not just radio but television or newspapers or whatever — can be used by people to communicate with each other, as opposed to being a very one-way, top-down communication that is used to promote a corporate agenda of consumption, materialism and buying things and the powerlessness which goes with that role. We are about trying to empower people, trying to convince people that their own voices are important, both the people who are on the air and the people who are listening. And if the people who are listening want to be on the air, well, come on down!

CF: We had a really excellent meeting of micropower broadcasters on April 6th in San Jose. Over a hundred people from *all* kinds of radio stations made it to this event. It really gave us a sense of belonging and a sense of power to realize there are a lot of people out there who support what we're doing and want to get their own radio stations going. We all need to be working together and to support each other because if each of us just acts as one little isolated voice with no connection to anybody else, we'll just be silenced. The federal authorities will come down on our necks. Our equipment will be confiscated, smashed. In fact, that is the normal way the FCC deals with people who violate their regulations and it's only through some sort of miracle that Free Radio Berkeley got a judge that was somewhat sympathetic to the cause. Somehow FRB has been allowed to keep going as it has for so many months now, 24 hours a day, seven days a week of in-your-face radio. Also, we're finding out that other stations are getting a chance to thrive for the same reason because the FCC is not really going to make a move on either FRB or a lot of other stations until this case is finally resolved. So somehow we have this little window of opportunity here, and it really is quite wonderful.

GP: It's not entirely luck though. I think a large part of it with FRB as with some of the stations back east that were on the air *before* FRB, has to do with community support. The FCC is more reluctant to go after stations that are highly visible, that have a strong base in the community and where the random and arbitrary enforcement of their rules is going to become a political issue. That is what has happened in the East Bay. That is what has happened in San Francisco. It's not just luck ...

— June, 1996

REFABRICATING COMMUNITY

An Interview With
Charlie Goodman (Excellent Radio)

Stephen Dunifer

Charlie Goodman (CG): You're on Excellent Radio here in Grover Beach, California ...

Stephen Dunifer (SD): Charlie, what are the overall goals you're trying to accomplish with Excellent Radio; and, how are you going about accomplishing them?

CG: Well, we took our queue from what you were doing at Free Radio Berkeley and we wanted to take it another step by actually showing how a micropower radio station could be a tool to refabricate the community. We sprung off of a show called "Father of Lies Versus the Mother of Invention."

SD: You may want to explain that one a little bit.

CG: The "Father of Lies" was a fictitious planet that was ruled by a television. We saw micropower radio as the answer to the social breakdown caused by the "Father of Lies."

SD: In terms of re-fabrication, perhaps you could give us examples of things that happened here on the station that have helped re-fabricate the community and bring it together to explore issues and find some sort of common ground.

CG: The first thing that micropower radio does is evens the playing field. We are right here on Grand Avenue and the door is always open so that we can just draw anybody in off the street. Indeed, that's how the radio station really got going. Very quickly we realized the quickest way we could be valuable was to look for the problems in our particular town and try to figure out how a micropower radio station could solve them. One big problem we have around here is getting a school bond passed. The local high school has about three times more people than it can stand, but we watched a school bond issue get defeated over and over. It was necessary really to hear from the kids and their parents as to the impact of that vote. We asked people what was wrong with the town, and how could a micropower radio station help. We then made an offer to the city to broadcast their city council meetings. We are particularly lucky here in that there was a feeling by the city council that they wanted their meetings more public and they wanted participation, so ...

SD: I understand there was a rather humorous moment where they actually asked for the opinion of the city attorney because of the station not being licensed by the FCC.

CG: They wanted to know about their liability, yeah.

SD: Right and what did the attorney say?

CG: He seemed to feel it might even be illegal *not* to accept an offer to broadcast the meetings and that the issue of whether or not they were violating the law was moot.

SD: I understand there was also a problem between skateboarders and the city government that the station helped resolve in an excellent way.

CG: I think we are still resolving that issue. It was the first time that young people and old people alike started to actually talk about what their needs were in the community. I think it kind of turned some heads around a little bit in that there were eloquent people on skateboards. Up to that point, I think it was looked at as just a youth sport rather than as a social activity having some thirty or forty years of history. So, they formed a task force and a group to raise money and consciousness about skateboarding, and to look at recreation, and how skate parks could be money well spent.

SD: Perhaps you could describe briefly the type of programming that you present to the community and, what the process is for people coming on the air. How do people find you and become part of that process?

CG: Initially, it seemed like my wife and I spent thirty-six hours a day here even though we were only on from noon until nine or ten o'clock at night. At first we were doing the programming to attract attention. We made sure we played absolutely nothing that the other radio stations were playing. Sometimes I would play the same song over and over for three hours because it gave me energy, and it attracted people here after they realized that this wasn't just another commercial

photo of Charlie Goodman by Stephen Dunifer

station. My old friends from my National Public Radio days, when I did reggae, African, and avant garde shows, started coming out of the woodwork again to share a diversity of culture and music. Then some of the other folks that I knew who had an interest in the environment started to come together. Then, the talk shows and the nutritional shows started to build.

Right now we have a pretty hot line up full of old time DJs that are known the world over. They are real musicologists, who share what they have with no reluctance whatsoever. It's not an ego thing. It's much more of a giving thing. Now they're teaching young people. I'm really proud of the musical line-up that we have here. I'm also very proud of the fact that the Spanish-speaking community has come forth and really turned the station around. Alex and Maria come in with the best of salsa tropical and cumbia every weekday morning from seven 'til twelve. They started out with a Thursday slot that was only a three hour show and they were always asking me, 'When are we going to get some more hours.' At that point we had all our nights taken care of and they said, 'Give us the mornings.' Every single morning the phones are ringing off the hooks and they are doing dedications. I've had so many people come up to me that I don't even know and say, 'Your station plays great music.'

SD: What about news and public affairs, what are you doing in that direction?

CG: We are able to rebroadcast alternative radio tapes from up in the Bay Area. That really helps us to stay more relevant, and it helps to back up many of the local shows that have the same concerns. We also have been bringing on people from the air and water quality boards. You notice that we are surrounded by pollution from UNICAL and some of the biggest spills in history are underneath ...

SD: I saw one of UNICAL's "green washing" ads in one of the local weeklies ...

CG: Yeah, it's pretty sad, more corporate bread and circuses rather than facing their responsibilities. This station has had the effect that the good people on the public boards now feel like they have the ear and the backing of the community. So they are taking those extra steps and really holding polluters to the law. It is much easier to do that if more people become informed about something like methylbromide. We actually had an interesting little case where we were on the air talking to somebody from the air quality control board and in comes a guy, I believe from up around Richmond, where they had just had a release that caused a fire. Are you somewhat familiar with that?

SD: Oh yeah!

CG: And the community, rather than take the word of those government officials for what was coming down wind, bought their own machine to do some testing this summer on our own methylbromide situation. It all just happened spontaneously. He was in here looking for one of the hosts while on the radio we had somebody from the air quality board. They started talking and he offered to show them how to use this machine which was cost effective because you don't need lab work done and you don't need manpower hours. They got together and did a demonstration later. Evidently UNICAL was listening and they had actually bought a machine that they didn't know how to use. They ended up paying this guy to show them how to use it [Laughter]. Ultimately, he showed that there was large overspray down further south in Ventura county. Locally here, we were starting to find out just how many residential areas were actually in this overspray area. So, you never know who might show up here or what kind of effect that person might have.

SD: Right.

CG: We're doing the work that journalism used to do. So much of that is excluded now that it's pretty easy for us to have a big effect by comparison.

SD: When you mention the job journalism used to do, I think of the CIA-Contra/cocaine/ crack expose where the *San Jose Mercury* is the only paper that's really trying to do an investigation. All the 'trained dogs' of the Establishment are just barking on command, that is the *Washington Post, L.A. Times,* and the *New York Times.* There is a major gap in any sort of investigative or advocacy journalism. There is so much that is kept below the surface and instead we just get essentially tabloid journalism whether it's in print or broadcast media. Do you feel that you are able to counter that with what you are doing here?

CG: Oh, absolutely! This Friday we ran a show that was called 'Violence: Reflections of a Voiceless Community'. It's pretty obvious that if you don't have a voice on the radio or in the press, the only way to get attention is to blow up buildings and release a statement. We didn't really want that to start happening in our community, and I think it was inevitable watching how the Telecommunications Bill was squeezing us all out of a voice. So, we started that show with the idea of diffusing anger and giving people an opportunity to peacefully solve problems. We found ourselves discussing the parallels between our situation and that of Germany and the rise of fascism where scapegoating was used to play people off against one another. Sometimes, we'd get so bummed out by our own discussions that we had to take a break and just watch cars go down the street and comment on them. After a while, we had to figure out how we could, as individuals and as a community, empower ourselves if we were just civil to one another. That would be the beginning of it. Then to understand that we are all in the same pile of people no matter who we were IDed as; and, we needed to get along because those that were taking the power from us were not about to reverse that situation.

SD: What plans do you have for the future of the station? Where are you going from here?

CG: I gather a lot of hope from some of things you are telling me that are available technologically. We have access to the Internet here. With as many other people doing micropower radio, we feel like our work is not in vain and is exploding in many different areas all at once. Our hope is to inspire people to recognize what a great tool radio can be. I don't think we ever thought we'd be on over a year and a half now. We got our letter from the FCC within a month and I don't think any of us really thought that this station would be here today. We just hoped we could pass on the idea that radio can be a great tool, and that communities with limited budgets should be looking at it as a pragmatic way to restructure for the future.

SD: You did also receive a visit from the FCC as I understand it, correct?

CG: Yeah, we did and it is strange how that worked out. We filed a Freedom of Information Act afterwards which filled in the questions we had about the complaint. What we found was that the complaint itself was a year old and that nobody had actually checked it out. Supposedly, we were blocking communications with Search and Rescue, which was pretty bogus. We checked it out with Search and Rescue to see if this was really true and nobody would respond. There wasn't any real complaint from them. We found it was about radio phones within this one block residential area where they are certainly not going to be doing much Search and Rescue. We might have broken into the communications of somebody's mobile communicator or something. So, we sent back east for a particular filter that would take care of this and we went off the air after we did the last city council meeting to show that we were more than willing to comply like any other radio station. We put in the filter which cleaned up the problem and then we went back on the air. When the inspector from the FCC came, he wasn't impolite at all. We had a good discussion, but he told us, 'Hey, buddy, you know they're selling off the air waves and that's a fact of life and you better get used to it.' We tried to explain that the Disney Corporation didn't actually live here, and that as a matter of principle that we were going to have to stay on the air. We've been broadcasting ever since.

SD: No further interaction with the FCC?

CG: No, other than the report from the FCC agent that he had come here and what little analysis he had done. It was strange because he didn't actually run a test to see if we were interfering with anything; and, the tests that he did make were without the new filter or even without the filter that came with the unit in the first place. We made a response to the letter through our attorney, Alan Korn, part of the National Lawyers Guild, saying we wanted to wait until the test case with Free Radio Berkeley had gone through the courts.

SD: It's not going to be resolved for the foreseeable time that's for sure and I think this is really giving all of us a breathing space to continue to grow and develop these stations and put more on the air. What is really critical in this whole thing is to reach a certain point where there are so many people on the air doing all kinds of creative things and these things become so much a part of the community that it's going to be hard for the FCC to extract them. Do you think the community would stand up to support and defend the station if the FCC really acted in a heavy manner?

CG: I know they care about the station. As to whether people would get off their butts and actually take a stand, I don't know. Certainly, there would be a recognizable void in the community if we weren't broadcasting. Micropower radio is better than a third political party when it comes right down to it because the programming is not just a matter of sound bites. It's way beyond putting another icon out there in front of us to vote for and us not taking responsibility for our own lives. So, I couldn't predict what might happen, but, it seems to me there would be an outcry.

PEOPLE HAVE NO IDEA HOW POWERFUL THEY COULD BE

An Interview With Carol Denney (Free Radio Berkeley)

Sheila Nopper

Sheila Nopper (SN): Why micropower and not community radio?
Carol Denney (CD): Gosh, I just wish it didn't tear my heart to answer that question. This is the birthplace of Lou Hill's vision of community radio, KPFA. KPFA is what we used to call our community radio station, and it was the flag-ship station of Pacifica. Its charter originally said that its prime commitment was to give a voice to the voiceless and progressive community-based politics, but that has all changed. Now, they are kind of on an NPR-track. They are still predominantly a listener supported station, but it's fairly clear from the pro-grams that they've axed recently, and the volunteer programmers that they've not only axed but blacklisted, that they want a kind of middle of the road station. They see that as more lucrative. It's all about demographics now. So, in a way we see ourselves as the opposite of that, being free of a profit orientation, and

that is what defines our politics. We have no obligation to sell anything. The truth is not always popular, and we can tell it the way we see it. In a town like Berkeley there is a lot of truth that people will pay a lot of money not to have told. Those of us who are committed to speaking these truths are a minority, and we know better than to knock on the door of KPFA anymore.

SN: Why not?

CD: Here is a good way to explain the contrast. Back in '64 when the free speech movement was at its height on campus, KPFA went into Sproul Hall with its live mike and broadcast from the sit-in. You would never have that happen today at KPFA. On the other hand, at Free Radio Berkeley, we've aired the jailhouse calls of arrested protesters. We have complete freedom. People have in a sense defined their own formats as they've come on the station. They'll say they want to do women's issues or they want to do labor issues or they want to do free form music or they want to do music from a particular country. They're free to do that. They are also free to completely suspend that format on occasion which is something that is extremely unusual if not unique in this nation.

SN: So a programmer might do a show for a number of months and then one week come in and want to do something different, and they would just do that?

CD: That's right. They might want to take calls from jail because in the community something is happening and the importance of the immediate issue might predominate for that week. What I'm trying to illustrate is the flexibility that I think makes this micropower concept unique.

SN: When did you start getting involved in micropower, and how did that come about?

CD: It was possibly a year after Stephen Dunifer started the Berkeley Hills broadcast which he was doing on a fairly regular basis on Sunday nights. He would take the equipment up to the hills where he would get a five to ten mile radius of opportunity for people to listen, but he was limited to broadcasting only as long as he could stand the cold or to as much programming as he had available there with him. I'd known Stephen since '91. I began working with him in the transmitter workshop and helping with correspondence on a part time basis in the summer and fall of '94. At that point, we were headed towards a court confrontation with the FCC. After they were denied an injunction, we found a location and went on the air twenty four hours. I think it has helped illuminate for people that micropower can be more than an exotic toy. I think it's made a difference that people can actually hear it.

SN: Was it the FCC that brought the station to the forefront?

CD: I think you're right. I think the FCC deserves a lot of credit here. The FCC, by trying to suppress micropower as an option for people, really put it on the map. The FCC decided to contend that we were anarchy and chaos on the

photo of Carol Denney and Stephen Dunifer by Phyllis Christopher

airwaves doing irreparable harm. I think we have an opportunity as we grow to really prove ourselves useful to this community, even if only by providing a party line for people to hear each other without the horror of having to schedule a meeting. [Laughter] I would like to thank the FCC for providing us with such a wonderful spotlight and I would also like to thank the vacuous nature of commercial programming, whether it's TV or radio, for driving people into our arms. There is really very little else that you can stand to listen to.

SN: When did the Jolly Roger Comedy Troupe come about?

CD: It came about before my presence on the scene as a broadcaster. I began by doing soldering in the shop, and I've done correspondence work trying to help with inquiries, mailing kits out and pulling parts for kits. I started by doing field broadcasts at demonstrations, in front of the Federal Building for instance, so that anybody driving by could tune in and find out what the demonstration was about. I have helped in every way I knew how because I really think micro-power radio is an important concept. When I saw what the Jolly Roger Comedy Troupe were doing, I just began to write scripts. I had been writing political satire for a long time for a variety of outlets. I'd done some theater. So I thought it would be perfect to just help them. My dream is to someday have an arrangement set up so that we could produce shows more swiftly, and every week be able to satirize the City Council meeting so that there would be the City Council meeting on Tuesday and that Sunday night you could listen to the complete satire and the real dope behind the politics of that meeting. We're not at that point yet. We don't have the facilities, and most of us are wage workers, so we don't have the time, but that's what I would like to see someday. I think that just about all of the mainstream media's political satire is either so watered down that it's not really instructive or else it's so national that nobody is really focused on local politics.

SN: Why local politics?

CD: People just don't realize how much of the corruption of the current political administration, whether it's Bay Area or municipal, is only because of the apathy of people who have no idea how powerful they could be by just walking into the room and being a part of the debate. First of all, there are very few people who want to get into the politics of, for instance: real estate, planning and zoning, but that's where the real dirt goes down and that's where the real money is made in this town. I see myself as useful in the sense that I can peruse these two thousand page plans and turn it into comedy and put it on the air. Actually, I'm hoping to make politics more friendly, more fun, more interesting and less frightening to people here who may not realize a lot of what's going on until it's badly written up in the real estate developer-biased local newspaper.

SN: Can you tell me about the *Celebrity Fat By-Products* show?

CD: I'm going to give Stephen credit for that concept. We were on the road doing some errands and driving along behind a truck that said something like 'Universal Rendering'. I said to him, 'What is rendering?' I had taken drawing classes where rendering mean sketching and drawing and filling in the details. He said that's fat by-products probably from animals. We just got to talking about it because it was so horrible. It was this vat of stuff going down the road. Then I went home and wrote up this script thinking about all of the fat sucked out of the thighs of local women celebrities and I thought that would be a big selling point to the yuppie crowd. [Laughter]

SN: What is the ratio of male and female involved on the station?

CD: Well, it's dismal, and it's improving. In the beginning it was really dismal, and what's happened is a combination of things. First, a little bit of raised awareness. I'm not going to give full flying colors to that yet. We've had an open policy, a policy in which we really wanted everyone, including people who might have a mental disability or might have an extreme disadvantage like living on the street, to be welcome on the station. In the beginning we started with a chalkboard. What one did was write one's name on an unoccupied square. My hat's off to beginning that way. I hope I will hang up my hat if we have to have a thousand dollar deposit before one can join this project. I can't call it a collective because it really is not at this point, but I like the idea of erring in favor of an open policy. However, that creates problems when you end up with people who are disrespectful of the station's mission. We came up with a mission statement after six months, maybe a year, as a consequence of a man who went on the air and willfully and determinedly used racist, sexist, homophobic material and felt that this was an important exercise of his free speech rights. I'm thankful that a majority of the group tried to explain to him and to others that while we accepted that it was his free speech right to be racist, homophobic, or misogynist, it was not part of our mission to promote those values. How do you come in after a misogynist show and do your lesbian hour? For a lot of people, the Mission Statement was our only defense mechanism against turning into everything else you hear on the air.

It was a very painful process, but we finally evicted that programmer from the air. We had a similar incident this summer with exactly the same set up. Again, all I want to say is I'm glad we err consistently in favor of inclusion, and I'm glad that we've given people a chance to sort these things out. I strongly believe in free speech rights. I believe our fight is about free speech, but it's not our best move to promote the values that other commercial stations are out there promoting if we want to shine as an alternative of some kind. It has also helped us to finally disassociate the station from a private residence. I think that's a really important thing for people setting up stations to know. Our initial location was in a residential setting. With twenty four hour programming, residents at that location were constantly sleep deprived or uneasy about their privacy or their belongings. It was very rough. Now we are much more likely to have a peaceful basis upon which to build a community station. There were times when the people in the house just wanted to shut the door. [Laughter] and I couldn't blame them.

SN: Getting back to women, have you been to any of the micropower radio conferences? What is your sense of women's participation in micropower radio?
CD: I was at the one in San Jose, the initial national micropower conference. It's funny because there was a woman there who was the MC, and she was writing down workshop topics, but she didn't write anything having to do with women. Then a woman just went up there and wrote 'Women's Issues' or something like that. She must have been looking for this kind of connection, and as it happened a lot of other women were too! [Laughter] We sat in a circle and were very fortunate to have with us the woman who started the women's department at KPFA. What became clear was that there was a strong need to discuss women's issues, and that there was an extreme amount of sexism that women were experiencing within the groups with which they were working. People had many interesting suggestions, and it was clear that there was an enormous amount of work to do. I really hope there can be more focus on such issues in the future. In terms of meetings in general, one of the problems we have had, is that the meetings in the past often have become sort of a cock fighting scene. What tends to happen is the women leave, and they're robbed of the opportunity to use the

meetings for any productive purpose. Instead of trying to cure the meetings, maybe we could have our own women's network and then have a representative bring to the meeting what the women have decided is a good idea. I think that's a great concept because for a lot of women it is partly the atmosphere and the style of the meeting that's the problem. For me it's just the time. I've put up with a lot of strange behavior in my life. I'm old enough now that I feel like I've seen it all. But, it is hard to do a three hour show Sunday night, spend four hours at a meeting Sunday afternoon, and get the material written somehow in the meantime. It's too much. I hope we'll straighten out our meetings soon.

We do our best, but I think that our station has a long way to go. Here is part of what I see happening. Men teach men easily. Men don't teach women easily. They might be thinking about something else. They might be making a problem for women who want to come in and participate in some way. It's not just because of youth, and it's not because people aren't intelligent. I think there's something sort of horribly natural about it. Unless there's a focus on it and an awareness, I think that mechanism is going to go on and on. Access to information is crucial, and until sexism is untangled from those mechanisms we are going to be stuck with a mainly male scene. I want to say though that a lot of the men working with Free Radio Berkeley are aware of this problem and doing everything they know how to do — although sometimes it's not enough — to try to change it. Stephen is a good example. He wants to work with women, appreciates what women bring to the project, and appreciates women's voices. I think there is at least a core of awareness that we can brag about right now. I know we will get better. Right now we don't have all the answers. So, it's going to be something that evolves over time.

SN: I think when you're talking about teaching, women have a different way of learning and men need more patience. Plus that sort of sexual stuff that comes into it really gets it all distorted.

CD: I think there's a whole different framework around how women define themselves and their egos and how men define themselves and their egos. Being stuck in gender roles is a part of the problem, and, as everybody frees themselves from that, I think we'll really have something else. At Free Radio Berkeley, it's very hard since you don't see all the DJs at once and our participants change constantly, but I think that it might be fair to say that it's only about ten percent female. One thing though is that whatever it is, there are more women than there used to be. There are more older people than we used to have, and there is certainly less of the initial confusion that we had about what the station is for. Some people honestly thought the best expression of free speech would simply be profanity, and it's hard for me to talk to those people.

So, we just keep trying. It's hard because there are several different components that all make up this micropower project. There is the workshop, selling the kits, and trying to assist people who wish to go on the air. It's not easy even to follow the schematics for most people, and unless they have technical assistance the likelihood is that they're going to burn their unit right out by not really believing that they need a fan or something like that. Then there's the station itself, trying to keep interesting programs on the air twenty four hours a day and get the rent paid. Then there's the lawsuit. Then there are related projects: fundraising projects, educational projects, and the micropower conventions.

SN: How *do* you pay the rent?

CD: We actually did raise some money at the convention, but it's so much work that I wouldn't suggest that as a fundraising base for anybody. The kits are partly a fund-raiser, but there's a reason why they're low cost. They're low cost so as to increase the availability for just about anybody. No matter how poor you are if you pool your money with your neighbors for a year the likelihood is you can come up with enough to go on the air. With all due respect to the lawyers who are defending us, I think our safety is in our numbers as micropower stations. When just about every community has one I think the FCC will quietly stop trying to criminalize something that's such an obvious fact of community life.

SN: Beyond having more stations, where would you like to see the micropower radio movement going? Could you expand on that a bit?

CD: I'd love to! Here would be my dream. The Bay Area has very crowded air space, but there's plenty of room for lots of micropower stations. I always love how the FCC tries to argue that the more powerful the station, the more watts that are broadcast, the larger the number of people are reached and served. However, if instead of that one powerful station, you had twenty-five or fifty-five stations specific to groups that the big powerful station isn't even trying to reach, that might serve people too. What I would love to see is every high school have its own micropower station. All they'd have to be is five miles apart and they could all use the same frequency. I'd love to see the Mung community, the Cambodian and Vietnamese communities, each have their own station. It will never be profitable to have a Vietnamese station, but they don't have to be profitable if micropower is available to them. I'd love to see the all poetry station. I'd love to see the all original song station. I'd love to see the kids' station where under twelve would be your cut-off, and the kids would figure out what they wanted to do, the music they wanted to play or whatever they wanted to read. I'd love to see people focus on children's programming, as has been done at Free Radio Berkeley and San Francisco Liberation Radio, that wasn't based on trying to sell you a Dalmation or some other Disney product.

For me it's kind of endless. I'd love to see politically focused shows that were really local, so that you could get your own city council member to explain their vote from last Tuesday. I think that once it is that local, people's interest in politics will be a lot higher. They don't realize that, as fascinating as it is to know about Madonna's sex life, it's equally fascinating to know just how your district representative broke down and caved in to the developer. It's just as good a story. It's just a story that nobody is telling or nobody is telling well. That's where I see myself coming in, I dedicate a lot of my time to going to these extremely tedious, excruciatingly boring city meetings. I could reformulate it, either into a completely comic format or else just talk about it and let people know. The city of Berkeley, for all the reputation it has as so politically aware and radical, is not even trying to communicate anymore, and that's a vacuum I'd like to see us fill. Underground newspapers are important too, but they have the difficulty of having to make enough money for the print run. With radio, once you have the initial equipment, all you have to do is the research. It doesn't cost any money. You don't have to send it in the mail. You don't have to lick the stamp. I'd also love to see prison related projects broadcasting straight into the prisons. That's a project that cries to be done. Then, in a town like this, it would be great to have a real campus radio station, as opposed to the kind of constricted one they have right now that is towing a more acceptable line these days.

SN: What about the technical end of it?

CD: I envision a micropower radio technology that would become increasingly simple to use. I think some women are intimidated by the technology, but, hey, a lot of men are too. At Free Radio Berkeley, we're at the point now where all you have to do is to not touch the buttons when you come in. You can move the faders around, but hopefully you won't screw around with the compressor and mess things up. So that it's a lot less of a problem than it would be if people were being expected to crawl up the hill by themselves and actually set up the station from scratch. In my dreams, we will create schematics so simple and kits so foolproof that the beauty of the design will create much less opportunity for people to end up discouraged along the way. You will be able to get part A, and part B, clap them together and be on the air.

— December 28, 1996

SOAPBOXING THE AIRWAVES

An Interview With Internal eXile (Free Radio Berkeley)

Salvatore Salerno

The Industrial Workers of the World (IWW), popularly known as Wobblies, have a long tradition of soapboxing which dates back to the beginning of the century. Wobblies used soapboxing in a variety of ways, but basically as an organizing tool. Towns and cities frequently passed ordinances to prohibit Wobblies from using the streets to organize workers. In these early free speech fights, Wobblies challenged these ordinances by affirming their constitutional right to free speech. As part of their tactic to repeal these ordinances, Wobblies continued to mount the soapbox and would soon fill the jails in small cities and towns beyond their capacities. In many states this tactic was successful in forcing the ordinances to be rescinded. Wobblies in various cities across the country are once again battling with authorities around the issue of free speech, but this time on the airwaves. I interviewed Internal eXile,

collage by Carol Petrucci

a Wobbly deejay on Berkeley's pirate radio station Free Radio Berkeley.
He talked about some of the ways he and other Wobblies use pirate
radio as an organizing tool.

Salvatore Salerno (SS): Tell me about the Wobbly Radio project with which
you were involved?

Internal eXile (IX): Well, it was loosely IWW programming. It was more of a
labor and ecology show. Now I'm doing a graveyard shift music show. I am one
of about sixteen Bay Area Wobblies doing a show on Free Radio Berkeley. A
number of people joined the Wobblies who were Free Radio Berkeley deejays
through contact with Wobbly organizers. So, though I'm no longer doing the
original show, it's not as though Wobbly programming is not happening anymore. Stephen Dunifer himself is a Wobbly, so it's not as though we're unrepresented at the radio station.

SS: Your idea was to do a show on labor and ecology?

IX: Well I could give you a little background on how my show began. I had been
volunteering at the station doing various odd tasks, but not being a deejay. Then
finally I had a graveyard shift from 2:30 to 6 a.m. just playing music. Then a
prime time slot opened on Free Radio. When the show opened up I asked for it
and the rest of the members of the radio station said it was okay. Stephen Dunifer

asked me to take the show on the condition that I would try to do a night time labor show since working folks couldn't always listen during the day. I said great, but I also wanted to include ecology as well. I had been doing work with Earth First! and much of what I had done for the radio up until that point had entailed going up north and involving myself in Headwaters and Sugar Loaf to cover those Earth First! actions for Free Radio Berkeley. So, everyone agreed that it would be a show that was about speaking truth to power.

For a year, I consistently did shows on local organizing campaigns but sometimes more regional ones like the Headwaters Campaign. There was always an attempt to focus on the perspective of what it's like being a worker in post-industrial society. It's not the same as it was at the turn of the century when there was mass industrialization going on. I gave the perspective of anybody like myself who is a former college student, now turned working class simply because there are no meaningful jobs available. Every week I'd try to cover something that was happening locally like the ongoing organizing campaign in the Bay Area by an AFL-CIO union, Local 2850, in a hotel in the well-to-do suburb of Lafayette.

SS: What is that about?

IX: Well, that is a situation where workers tried to organize with a union. The boss used union busting tactics to intimidate them and openly to fire them which is of course illegal. The added twist to this particular campaign is that the workers that were trying to organize a union were all Latino or Chicano and mostly women so there was an added element of racism and anti-immigrant hysteria thrown in because of Proposition 187. I had already been doing a lot of solidarity picketing, donating my time and going out to their picket line. So I figured what I would do in addition to that is to start covering it for the radio station. I had hoped to interview some of the organizers, but the timing was too late and other Wobbly deejays wound up interviewing them on their radio shows. So in a sense I laid the groundwork, but others followed. Other campaigns that I focused a great deal of energy on in that one year period were organizing efforts that the SEIU health workers were doing in San Francisco and in Oakland. I would record sounds of the demonstrations and talk with some of the workers involved with that struggle. Then there was Judy Bari's ongoing case against the FBI and her work in organizing people up north to fight to save Headwaters and other areas of redwood forest. I chose her in particular because of the working class perspective she brought to Earth First!

SS: Have you done any work around Muni fare increases?

IX: Yeah, there were various times where I got involved with that as well. I did some stuff about the racism that BART workers were facing , and I would have liked to do even more.

SS: Are there other examples of how pirate radio can be used as a good organizing tool?

IX: In one way free radio adds the element of listener participation. Listeners can call in and talk about things which are going on right now unlike your standard station where you call in, get an operator, and you *might* get on. Free radio is uncensored, so anybody can call up and talk about things which are going on right at that moment. Where IWWs have had organizing drives going on, like the campaign against Borders Books, they've called the radio station and, for example, said, 'Call the boss of Borders and complain about their union-busting activity.' ... This was in June when the organizing was just getting underway. As a result Borders got quite a few calls. In fact somebody called the radio station and said, 'Yeah, I called Borders and the boss there said they had gotten tons of calls already and they keep saying they heard about it on the radio.'

There's another thing that we've been able to do. We have a portable transmitter which we take to demonstrations and set up just for that particular occasion. We set up a little station with maybe a six mile radius and then we have people carrying signs that say tune in to our frequency. Then people driving by tune in, and they get a sense of what's going on instead of just seeing some people on the street with picket signs or doing guerilla theater.

SS: Any other examples?

IX: We've had live call-ins from activists in the forest. Once four Free Radio Berkeley deejays took a trip up to Sacramento where the state was doing an environmental hearing on Ward Valley [proposed site for toxic waste on Native land in the Mojave Desert]. The mainstream media had been ignoring what was going on. They were saying things like, 'There are a bunch of people standing on the road protesting.' People driving by heard only that sound bite on their car radios. It's like, ho hum, another protest, big deal.

So what happened is that one Free Radio Berkeley deejay got out a tape recorder and started interviewing Bradley Angel of Greenpeace. Then I walked up to him and just held my mike out. Both of our tape recorders had the word 'PRESS' written on them. All of a sudden mainstream reporters started coming out of nowhere and started interviewing him as well. One AM radio station reporter even stepped out of the bushes and started interviewing him. I guess it was just the effect of people standing around the guy with the tape recorders and then reporters started thinking, gosh this must be a story, so they headed over there. We felt what happened at that point was like a catalyst for agitation. It got the mainstream media to actually sit up and pay attention. Now whether or not they played what was recorded uncensored or not I don't know, but, if they didn't, at least we played it live and uncensored on free radio.

SS: How about other programming?

IX: Well the thing about free radio is that since it's not licensed by the FCC, we don't get hit up with these stupid rules on format. So music is pretty much free form. Often times lots of music that you will obviously not hear at other radio stations gets played, including songs by local working class bands and activists. We play music by activists from Earth First! as well. ... We play a lot of genres that you don't hear on mainstream radio. There's a lot more punk and hip hop played on free radio.

SS: Have there been problems with the FCC?

IX: The FCC has left Free Radio Berkeley alone, partly because of the court case. They realize if they do anything now, it's not going to help their case. They have on occasion harassed other stations, particularly ones which are Latino-based, and they've threatened people with deportation as well. Two Latino radio stations got visits from the FCC and those two stations had to shut down. One of them shut down permanently. We did what we could to help the other one get up and running again. What happened in the case of the San Francisco station was that they had to shut down because their landlord threw them out after the FCC came and visited them.

Let me actually back up just a bit and point out that it's not just having a strong collective organization that guarantees people being on the air. It's also the will of the individuals involved to say we're going to fight for our freedom of speech. This is our freedom and if we have to fight for it, we will. If the FCC's going to harass us, we're not going to let it get to us because they can't do anything without a warrant, number one, and, number two, the legality of their actions is tied up in the courts.

You have to admire a person like Napoleon Williams from Decatur or Mbanna Kantako from Springfield, Illinois, who have just simply said, 'We don't care if it's legal or illegal. We consider the system to be illegitimate because they have done nothing for us as black men, or as black people, or as people in general; and we're just not going to take it any more. The only way we have found that we're going to get our freedom is if we take it ourselves. Our attitude is if they won't give us any spots on the air waves, we'll just do it ourselves.'

SS: Is Wobbly radio a version of the free speech fight.

IX: Yeah, that's the analogy that Stephen Dunifer likes to use. He brought that up at the last free radio conference in Oakland by comparing our struggle to the free speech fights of the past by Wobblies in Centralia and Everett, Washington. This is a modern version of the free speech fight. Utah Phillips in fact has been a constant guest and supporter in our court cases saying, 'Hey it's a free speech fight.' What would a free speech fight be without old-time Wobblies hanging around?

SS: And so Wobbly deejays are in a sense soapboxers.

IX: Yeah, Stephen Dunifer likes to call it the leaflet of the Nineties.

SS: Soapboxing the air waves.

IX: Yeah, exactly.

SS: How is the IWW involved?

IX: Well, actually the IWW's very much involved. The people doing a lot of the work, particularly with Free Radio Berkeley and Free Radio Santa Cruz, are Wobblies. I don't know if it just happened to turn out that way or if there's something about the level of organizing ability that Wobblies have, but two of the people in the workshop building transmitters are Wobblies. As I said before, Stephen Dunifer who started this station is a Wobbly. Many of the people who are involved in the scheduling committee at Free Radio Berkeley are Wobblies. Free Radio Santa Cruz is run by Wobblies. There's been talk about forming an industrial union of micropowered radio stations. It would be part of a communications industrial union. In the Bay Area there is an industrial union around the administration of the Internet. The IWW Internet server was built and is maintained by Wobblies. Then there is a collective of telephone switching called Integrated Switching and Networks. This is all part of one small local which is starting to look toward organizing bigger industrial unions.

There's talk about inviting the radio stations into this as well. I think that's a good idea because the technological revolution is largely in the hands of capitalists right now. In order for this technological revolution to serve the masses it has to be far more democratic. Free radio is one of the few alternatives that there is in this change in telecommunications which is going on because of the globalization of capital. The Telecommunications Act centralizes communications into the hands of a few rich, powerful elites who are strongly involved with the government. If there's going to be any alternative it's going to have to be working class and community-based, and the IWW seems to be one of the few organizations playing even a minor role in this organizing right now.

SS: Why haven't other unions been involved in micropower radio?

IX: Well, first of all I have to say that some of them actually have. In the Bay Area Local 2850, which has been organizing the Lafayette Park Hotel, has expressed very strong support for free radio. They have been on our station and they have called us up and let us know when their pickets are happening. They send us material, and they are strong supporters of this station mainly because we have given them lots of air time and solidarity. They hosted the last micropower radio gathering in their union hall. Also the Oil, Chemical, and Atomic Workers Union in Los Angeles have expressed interest in getting their own station which would be part of the Labor Party chapter down there.

Other than that, I think the main reason why other unions have been reluctant to support micropower radio is that a lot of unions, especially the AFL-CIO unions, are hamstrung by their internal bureaucracies which are very conservative. The American labor movement has mostly had a silent if not open partnership with capital since the end of World War II. A lot of workers are dissatisfied with the way things are. They're very unhappy with both the government and the bosses. Yet a lot of workers unfortunately take very reactionary political stances because they've been coerced or confused into scapegoating people who are not really their enemies. The rank and file militants in these unions would certainly love to do something like micropower radio, but getting information to them is hard because they don't necessarily have access to leaflets or the Internet which are places where you find these things out. As far as locals doing it, they are either bureaucratically vested in the system and therefore not willing to take the plunge, or just afraid. It's a big step to do this because it's not exactly legal. You run the risk of being slapped with a notice of apparent liability and a $10,000 fine, and that could be your whole strike fund right there, so it's not like there's going to be a lot of help coming from any International.

SS: Right, it also crosses the line into direct action.

IX: Indeed. Direct action is something that's being *talked about* now by the AFL-CIO, but *real* direct action is still something that they haven't *done*. Rarely do you ever see direct action advocated, much less carried out, by the local union bureaucrats. Free radio, on the other hand, is definitely about being proactive.

SS: Does Wobbly radio give voice to perspectives that are working class?

IX.: Yeah, it does. I do have to insert a bit of a caveat though. Many of the people who organized the free radio movement are not necessarily what you'd call traditional working class, but rather post-industrialist working class. The Food Not Bombs kind of situationist/anarchist perspective is more prevalent in free radio, and that's fine. I count myself as being an anarchist, but I am somewhat disappointed about the lack of class consciousness that some deejays have. They tend to support labor unions in principle, but they're not necessarily out there agitating themselves. It'd be nice to see more of that, but I attribute it more to just the American mindset than anything else. It just shows how much microradio is needed to offer more exposure to working class perspectives. As Stephen Dunifer says, we need not just one of these stations, or even 100; we need 10,000. One in every community if possible. There's even talk of an IWW-specific radio station, starting in the Bay Area in the near future. It's just a matter of organizing!

— January, 1997

Micro Power Broadcasting
Breaking the Media
Blockage

Illustration by Keith McHenry

IF YOU CAN'T COMMUNICATE, YOU CAN'T ORGANIZE, AND IF YOU CAN'T ORGANIZE, YOU CAN'T FIGHT BACK

A Composite Interview With Stephen Dunifer (Free Radio Berkeley)

Ron Sakolsky

Ron Sakolsky (RS): Stephen, you've taken two trips to Haiti. Could you explain what brought you there?

Stephen Dunifer (SD): As part of a developing international aspect to the micropower broadcasting movement we are now taking an active part not only in Haiti but in Mexico, in Guatemala, Canada and some other countries as well. What we have underway is a project that we're calling International Radio Action Training in Education (IRATE). Everyone who should be is pissed off about the global corporate state/new world order. I went to Haiti to check out the situation as far as community radio is concerned, and to try to meet with as many people as I could who might be doing this type of development work.

Part of my work there was to try to network with people to see if we could develop some form of working coalition made up of radio people, some of whom hadn't been really aware of each other up to the time I started bouncing around and started talking to people. I compiled a list of various people who are working in it and got that around to everyone concerned. Haiti presents a very good opportunity for this type of grassroots democratic form of communications.

RS: Why is that?

SD: For one, because the predominant language in Haiti is Creole and most of the media in Haiti is not in Creole but in French, particularly the written media is almost strictly in French with the exception of one publication, *Libete*, which was started several years ago just prior to the coup in 1991. Basically the elite speak French but for everyone else their native tongue is Creole. Given that and given the fact that 80 percent of the people in Haiti are illiterate, radio seems like a perfect medium at this time for the Haitian people.

RS: What exists in terms of community-based radio at the moment?

SD: I'd say it's in the very beginning stages. There are several community radio stations. Through micropower technology they're using the same power levels that we're using here: 15, 30, 75 watts or something like that. Of course they're being charged a fair amount for the equipment. What we hope to do is to train people there in Haiti to build transmitters on site, from kits that we supply. By doing that we'll reduce their cost tremendously, and also they'll get training in electronics and can start production of other electronic devices that might be needed within Haiti itself. Our efforts are based on a model of self determination that's being expressed at the grassroots community level. This is all part of a surge of movement around the party that Aristide began, the Lavalas Party. They use a logo of people seated around a table. They say they don't want a situation where just a few people are sitting at the table and everyone else is sitting on the floor beneath the table. They want everything equally distributed around the table. Needless to say this causes concern within the ruling elite both in Haiti and in the United States, of equal distribution of wealth and resources. What a concept! Concomitant with this movement, it would seem that there is a growing use of micropower community radio as a tool for grassroots democracy.

RS: If it's a tool for grassroots democracy, to what extent can it be free of government control? How can it also be critical of Aristide and Lavalas when need be?

SD: That's part of what we're working on. I actually spoke with former President Aristide. On my first trip, I had a meeting with him on the very day I was leaving. Basically, we talked very briefly about protection of community radio in Haiti. We didn't get into any details, but we worked on a model that was developed by the National Lawyers Guild's Committee on Democratic Communications of which I am a member. The committee worked on developing some model legislation for the South African government, for the ANC, to essentially create three classes of radio: commercial radio, public radio (meaning government radio) and community radio. We want to create the same model in Haiti where it reserves 50 percent or more of the spectrum for either public or community radio.

RS: Community radio would be autonomous then?

SD: Right, it would be autonomous. There would be frequency spectrum management done by the government, but there would be protections built in against interference of content and analysis. Free speech would be absolutely guaranteed in this medium. The government party seems very supportive of the concept and I don't think there'll be any trouble getting it passed through the Haitian legislative bodies and then we'll have it locked in for at least as long as the Lavalas Party remains in power. Actually, the emphasis on grassroots radio is a form of coup insurance. Somewhere in the manual of overthrowing a government, perhaps on the first page, it says, seize the radio station. The fact that most of the radio stations in Haiti are presently in Port au Prince makes it easy to shut them down. But if you have dozens to hundreds, of small stations operating throughout the entire country that are portable (something that essentially can be placed in a backpack), and where people are trained in how to build the transmitters, maintain them, set them up and if necessary move them around; then it'll be impossible for any sort of occupation forces to deal with them all.

RS: Now is micropower radio mostly seen as a rural thing or is it both rural and urban?

SD: It is to be used in both rural and urban areas. For example, we're sending equipment in for the establishment of a small station in a rural community which is up in the hills about 30 miles from Port au Prince, and the other project is at a facility called "La famille c'est la vie," which was actually begun by Aristide to provide education, a place to live, and medical care for some of the urban street youth — young boys and men. There's an estimated 50-100,00 street kids in Port au Prince alone, with an estimated 200,000 all across Haiti. Aristide has a vision of having radio stations for young people all across the island and/or having a national station for youth alone.

We're looking at a country that has been raped by the forces of colonialism. As one person I talked to put it, at this point, they want to go from a state of destitution to a poverty with dignity. In the north, the land has been almost denuded in cases because of it being stripped for resources. The people cook with charcoal. This, of course, causes an immense amount of deforestation. Because of our contacts, not only in the radio community but within other communities as well, we hope to create a larger material and technical assistance program to Haiti that goes well beyond radio. For example, a group of us are working with the commercial production of hemp as a fuel, as a source of fodder for building materials and for oil. Hemp can serve to produce and also reforest the country at the same time because it sends down deep roots and stabilizes the soil.

RS: As you say, one of the things that Haiti has had to deal with is imperialism, and U.S. occupation at various times. New president Rene Preval, though a long time ally of Aristide, is faced with an economy that is in shambles, an unemployment rate that is upward of 80 percent, a hostile U.S. Congress, very lukewarm support from Clinton, a World Bank demanding increasing privatization, and an entrenched mulatto elite and armed right at home. His compliance with IMF austerity measures has recently caused a rift between himself and Aristide and the democratic popular movement itself which opposes the neoliberal solutions of both men. Is your impression that a divided Lavalas will be able to make radical kinds of changes without interference from the U.S. government or reactionary Haitian groups?

SD: I think, given the popular tide of opinion and the fact that we have a whole grassroots democracy movement that has woken up and is developing, it's going to be very difficult for the course to be reversed by the U.S. outside of full scale military intervention. There will be a basic continuity of the same programs that are in process now unless something drastically alters the political landscape.

RS: What about the sensational stories about Aristide that have appeared in the U.S. press?

SD: They're all based on total fabrication, that he was psychotic, unstable, blah, blah, blah. He's one of the most stable, sane people I've seen.

RS: Now one of the things you mentioned was the Creole language as a culturally significant thing that radio can address. What about the neo-African religion of Vodou? To what extent can that be incorporated as a cultural entity in radio programming?

SD: It's all up to the communities involved. To me it's just providing them with the enabling technology.

RS: So in a sense then, whatever the cultural interests of the community are would be the ones that they could bring to the station?

SD: Absolutely. We don't want to impose any particular gestalt on the situation. We want them to develop as they wish and how they see fit. We can help provide the tools, technical training and support but there should be really no attachments to any sort of agenda.

RS: Transmitters have found their way to Chiapas as well. People there are in a situation where there is a popular uprising, while in Haiti, they're attempting to consolidate people's power. What are the different ways that people use the tool that you're bringing them in those situations?

SD: First off, we actually did provide transmitters to Haiti prior to Aristide's reentry. We supplied transmitters after the coup clandestinely. Secondly, it's easy to say that in Haiti the movement's consolidated and in Chiapas it's an uprising. Yet it's still kind of an uprising in Haiti. It is an uprising movement towards grassroots democracy. It just happens that the government is on the side of the people whereas in Mexico you have a government which is decidedly in the hands of the ruling class and the world corporate state. As to the situation in Chiapas, it is not monolithic. You have the Zapatistas, which are an insurgent movement, and you also have the autonomous movement, which is the non-armed civil society movement. Both are pushing for autonomous regions and essentially self-determination and self-government. So there's quite a parallel in my mind between Chiapas and Haiti. You have the same desire on the part of both peoples for a political, economic and social structures that is on the side of the people and not on their backs.

RS: Are you saying then that the uses of radio are pretty much the same in both situations or do they use it differently at all?

SD: I would say the applications would be quite similar. You've got the same levels of poverty, same types of disease, same atrocious conditions, particularly in the rural areas. Radio can be used to tell people how to make water potable. It can be a tool for education. It's all part of a struggle of the people to develop a greater sense of self, to build autonomy, and to create a better life for them-selves. So I don't really see much difference. In fact, we talked about the possi-bility of setting up an exchange program, that is bringing a couple of people from peasant communities in Chiapas to Haiti and vice versa so as to promote this idea of unity of struggle. The conditions they're dealing with are not that vastly different. Under the international trade agreements that are part of the New World Order, farmers in Chiapas are being devastated by the importation of cheap corn from the U.S., while in Haiti, cheap U.S. rice is devastating two million small farmers.

RS: At the same time the New World Order is happening and consolidating that way, there's this sort of undercurrent of people who are resisting it. This seems to be one of the ways of doing that.

SD: I think radio can play an extremely vital role. Without radio I think it would be much more difficult for people to organize against GATT and NAFTA.

RS: If we're going to do that, let's add North America to the mix. We're talking about not only Chiapas and Haiti, but you've just been telling me about a station that is up and running in Watsonville, California.

SD: Right. Watsonville is on line. So is Salinas. In Watsonville and Salinas we're dealing with an exploited community of people; a Mexicano/Chicano commu-nity of immigrant workers who are now finding a voice. We have to work on our program to ensure that all these communities of people who never had a voice before get a voice through the free radio movement.

RS: And I assume that part of that would be to make the connections between those groups as well?

SD: By the nature of being in touch with all three groups, we can inform them of each other's presence, so they can network and form even greater webs of solidarity both on a national basis and an international basis as we evolve this into the Internet as well.

RS: How would you do that?

SD: We could provide them with computers and access to information/telecommunication systems. That way people can be aware of each other all around the world. They can act within the geopolitical boundaries of their community, but they can also be aware of all the other struggles people are involved in around the world which are not too vastly dissimilar. They are all struggles for greater self-identity, self-worth, self-determination and basic grassroots democracy; and can act in concert. It could build to the point where let's say the striking newspaper workers in Detroit had their own station. We'd get unions and others on line as people become aware of these other struggles and news reports shared through the Internet or tape exchanges. We're looking at recording programs and putting them on the Internet in a digital file format so people around the world can download these sound files of news stories through the computer to cassette and play them on the air. There is incredibly revolutionary potential within this idea.

RS: Who are the people working on this right now?

SD: These situations are coming out of our work here with Free Radio Berkeley and the Free Communications Coalition, and Keith McHenry of Food Not Bombs has toured 47 cities around the country with a transmitter exposing people to micropower radio. What we're going to see is much more of this happening both inside and outside the U.S. Major changes will occur.

RS: You are a self-proclaimed anarchist. How would those changes move us more in an anarchist direction?

SD: This current crew in Washington, I think, have done more to discredit government than any group of anarchists could ever hope to do, so they've done some of the work for us already. To me the whole point is to develop local community autonomy. Through a community radio forum, people can become better aware of each other, and share their ideas, music and knowledge and whatever else they have to offer. That gives people a better sense of their community. Plus, on top of that, it provides an effective organizing medium for getting info out about an event, about struggles that are going on locally and nationally so people have a more cohesive picture of what's going on.

For example, to me one of the best uses of this was on June 26th of this year (1995). There was a major march in San Francisco in support of Mumia Abu Jamal. It turned out to be a torch light march. A few of the people in the march decided to burn a couple of dumpsters in front of the Mission police station. It kind of pissed off the cops. They didn't do anything for awhile. Then they followed the march and managed to cordon it off on a side street. It all ended up in a mass arrest of almost 250 people. It was an amazing scene.

In solidarity with the protesters, the residents in the neighborhood actually opened up their doors so that people could run through their apartments out the back door and over the fence. On top of that quite a number of people who had shows on Free Radio Berkeley were among the arrestees. They shouted out the studio line number of Free Radio Berkeley. One of the adjoining apartments was that of our attorney on the National Lawyers Guild Committee On Democratic Communication. Within five minutes of this bust occurring, a phone call went into the studio line and was put on the air. Someone else reported from a second story window overlooking the scene giving a blow by blow description. This went on for quite a while and you could hear the shouts of people in the background, giving listeners the immediacy of the whole situation.

A lot of people in the East Bay community here are covered by the Free Radio Berkeley signal. Their friends were being arrested on totally bogus charges. Collect phone calls came in from the jail to the studio because the station number had been written on the wall, like the Wobblies used to do in their free speech fights. The station also orchestrated a phone campaign to bombard the DA and any other appropriate offices, with phone calls demanding that people be let go. Needless to say the DA and the mayor's office received lots of phone calls. It was actually an international effort. Word went out on the Internet so people were mobilized rather quickly. What it did was give people a greater sense of themselves as a community. It really tied things together in a way that had a very long lasting effect.

RS: Talking about activism, what are the connections, as you see them, between your work in the Free Radio Movement and your other activist endeavors like the September 15, 1996 Headwaters forest action or the radical unionism of the Wobblies, just to name two. How do you see radio connected to those things and how are they all integrated into your own personal politics?

SD: Radio to me is an integral key to the whole process. To be effective in what we're doing, we need our own means of communication. The slogan I have for that is, 'If you can't communicate, you can't organize, and if you can't organize, you can't fight back.' I think that really permeates a lot of what we're doing in that we're developing more effective means of communication within our communities. It's a very integral part of my life, which has really been pretty much dedicated to one form of activism or another. To me it's all part of what we want to do in building our own alternatives. It's something that grew, in myself, out of the movements of the Sixties. I've always had a focus on building alternatives, on creating viable infrastructures such as food coops and community cultural centers. I've worked in all those areas, as well as doing anti-intervention work in relation to the Vietnam war, El Salvador, etc. It's all about trying to prevent atrocities from occurring, and, at the same time, trying to build alternatives.

Given my skills as a self-taught electronics computer systems engineer, I feel that there are many ways that technology or science can be used in a liberating fashion. Unfortunately the Left seems to rather bereft of people with technical skills. I think it's a shortcoming that has to be addressed one way or another. In the Free Radio Movement, particularly with the link provided by the Internet, we're seeing people setting up little garage operations. For example, one person has now gone into business building antennas. Other people are setting up to do production. There are people who are buying our kits, assembling them and sending them out to other people. We're seeing more networking on a technical basis than ever before.

My activism could be placed on a continuum of things that I do and in which I choose to be involved, but I try to focus mostly on the radio work right now so that I can put my energy where I feel it can be best directed. For example, for the Headwaters rally, I didn't feel that doing civil disobedience and chaining myself to a tree with Earth First! was where I could be most effective, though I support that action. I don't have the time to spend in jail right now. So, being an organizer, what I did instead was to help organize a tabling operation which was able to raise somewhere close to $800 in a matter of a few weeks to help support the base camp. I also went to a number of different rallies and taped them and put them on the air. So basically I plug in where I can when something is needed. Being an activist my whole adult life I can look at a situation and figure out what needs to be done, and if I can do some aspect of that, then I will.

RS: One final question. Could you tell us about the international conference of micropower broadcasters that was held in Oakland in the Fall of 1996? What came out of that gathering from your perspective?

SD: There was a lot of sharing of ideas and information informally between people. There were workshops that were held and information was given out. Some people have formed a working group to plan the next conference and moves are underfoot to link different stations with some sort of newsletter and, through the Internet, really build communications between the stations. We had an attendance of about 125-to-150 people, including representatives from Amsterdam, Chiapas and Canada. It was publicized mostly through the Internet, email and personal contacts because we did not have the financial resources to do a mailing to everyone on our contact list of about 4,000 people. I'm looking forward to the next conference that's organized because the movement is really growing every day. It's no longer just isolated stations but a grassroots movement that will continue to get stronger. I'm really not sure what the government can do to stop it now....

— December 1995 and January 1997

ASSOCIATION OF MICROPOWER BROADCASTERS CONTACT NETWORK

Paul Griffin

The Association of Micropower Broadcasters is a collective of small stations scattered all over the world. We operate without government or corporate control and do not care about Arbitron. We are free-form, low-power stations operating on the FM band for the most part, but there are plans to start on AM and television stations too. The AMPB REPORT is our publication and it comes out six times a year. There is also an audio version of the report featuring music and news. Our community is spread far apart and it's not easy to share information sometimes. These are some of the projects we are working on right now:

Organization of Efforts. One plan is to have audio information available on the world wide web for stations to share with each other. Eventually, we want to have a real network with people uploading news stories and time-critical information. The AMPB is helping to coordinate these efforts and keep folks updated on the progress. We're also planning to have micropower radio organizing conferences on a regular basis. This effort requires a lot of coordination and input from everybody to be successful.

Tape Swapping. We will swap "pirate radio" tapes with you on a one-for-one exchange. Pick from our catalog — send us tapes of your broadcasts.

Record Charting. Some record companies don't care if we are FCC authorized or not. These companies will get our report which tells them how their records are doing. Radio stations that give us playlist information will receive promo copies of records as they become available.

Friend of the Court Brief. As you may know, the National Lawyers Guild is challenging the FCC in federal court. The AMPB is jumping in to fight on behalf of radio rebels. Tell us about your encounters with the FCC and especially any harassment that has come your way.

For confidential information, send a self addressed stamped envelope to:

AMPB
2018 Shattuck Ave. #22
Berkeley, CA 94704
or email: Paul_W._Griffin@bmug.org

Illustration by Keith McHenry

PART III

SETTING
TECHNOLOGY
FREE

Illustration by Johann Humyn Being

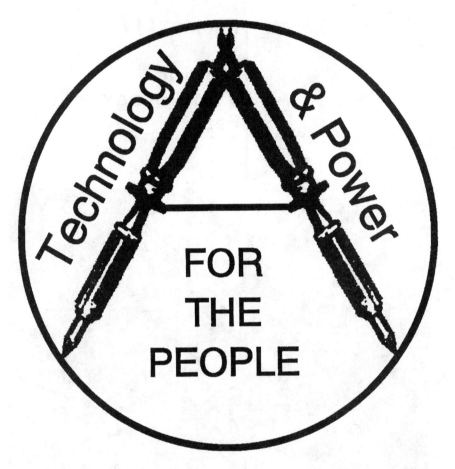

Illustration by Stephen Dunifer

MICROPOWER BROADCASTING

A Technical Primer

Stephen Dunifer

Many people still assume that an FM broadcast station consists of rooms full of equipment costing tens of thousands of dollars. The Micropower Broadcasting, Free Radio, Movement has shown this to be untrue. Micropower broadcasting uses FM transmitters whose power output is in the range of 1/2 to 40 watts. Such transmitters have a physical size that is not greater than that of your average brick. These transmitters combined with other equipment including inexpensive audio mixers, consumer audio gear, a power supply, filter and antenna enable any community to put its own voice on the air at an average cost of $1000–$1500. This is far more affordable than the tens or hundreds of thousands required by the current FCC regulatory structure.

All of the technical aspects of putting together a micropower broadcasting station are covered in the following material. It is important to note that the main argument the FCC uses against micropower broadcasting is the issue of interference with other broadcast services. Interference is a valid concern. By using equipment that is frequency stable and properly fitted with harmonic suppression filters along with good operating procedures and standards, the FCC's argument can be effectively neutralized.

Further, the technical aspects of micropower broadcasting require some basic knowledge in the areas of electronics and broadcast practices. Hopefully, this primer will be able to convey some of this knowledge to you. If you are unsure of your abilities try to find someone who has the technical experience to help you. It is hoped that as this movement grows a network of people with the required technical skills will be formed to assist in the process of empowering every community with its own voice. If you are a person with engineering or technical experience, please contact Free Radio Berkeley to become part of this network.

FINDING A FREQUENCY

Before you can proceed any further you must determine if there are any available frequencies in your area. Due to frequency congestion in the large urban metroplexes such as Chicago, Boston, Los Angeles, New York, etc. this may be a bit difficult. You will need several items to do a frequency search: a, listing of all the FM radio stations within a 50–70 mile radius of your area; and a digitally tuned radio. There are two online databases on the world wide web which can be searched for FM radio stations in any given area — www.jagunet.com/~kodis/station.html and www.airwaves. com/fccdb.html.

Channel separation is the biggest problem. FM broadcast frequencies are assigned a frequency channel 200 kilohertz wide. Good broadcasting practice requires that at least one channel of separation must exist on either side of the frequency you intend to use. In other words, if you have picked out 90.5 as a possible frequency then 90.3 and 90.7 should be clear of any receivable signals. This is why a digital receiver is an important item for the frequency search.

Once you have a complete listing of all the FM radio stations look for possible frequencies with the appropriate channel spacing. Depending on topography, distance and the output power of the other stations certain "used" frequencies may in fact be open. Compile a list of the possible frequencies. Then, using a digital FM receiver with an external antenna, scan and check these frequencies. Do this from a number of locations and at varied times within the area you propose to cover. In most cases weak, intermittent, or static filled signals can be ignored and counted as either usable or providing the necessary channel separation. Hopefully you will find at least one or two usable frequencies. If you live in a more rural area or some distance from a large urban area, finding a usable frequency should not be very difficult. 87.9 can be used as a frequency under two conditions: 1) if there is not an existing station on 88.1; and 2) if there is not a TV Channel 6 being used in your area.

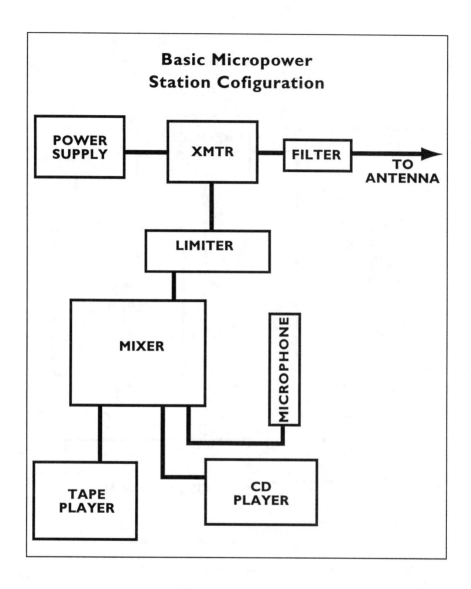

Basic Micropower
Station Cofiguration

POWER SUPPLY

XMTR

FILTER

TO ANTENNA

LIMITER

MIXER

MICROPHONE

TAPE PLAYER

CD PLAYER

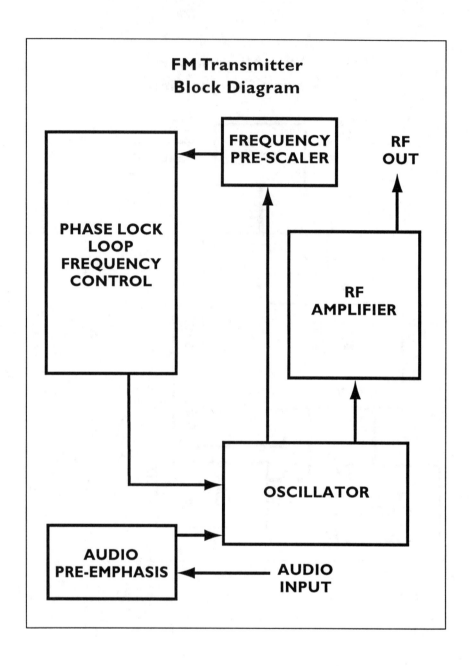

FM Transmitter
Block Diagram

FREQUENCY
PRE-SCALER

RF
OUT

PHASE LOCK
LOOP
FREQUENCY
CONTROL

RF
AMPLIFIER

OSCILLATOR

AUDIO
PRE-EMPHASIS

AUDIO
INPUT

After compiling your list of possible frequencies have your friends check them out on their receivers or radios as well. It is helpful to do this since a variety of different receivers will more accurately reflect the listening conditions in your area. After all of this you should have a workable list of frequencies to use.

LOCATION OF STUDIO AND TRANSMITTER

Before you set up the station an adequate location must be found. Since the antenna will be there as well a site with adequate elevation is required. Ideally the top of a hill or a spot somewhere on the side of hill overlooking the area of coverage is best. FM transmission is "line of sight" the transmitting antenna and receiving antenna must be able to "see" each other. Therefore, any large obstructions will have a tendency to block the signal path. Keep this in mind when choosing your location. If your site is a one-to-three story building, a 30 foot push up style mast attached and guyed to the roof or a TV antenna style tower bracketed to the side of the building will be needed to provide adequate height for the antenna. At the very least you need to have the antenna at least 40-50 feet above the ground. In some areas a building permit may be needed to attach a mast or tower to a building.

It is good practice to keep the transmitter some distance from the audio studio since the radio frequency emissions from the transmitter can get into the audio equipment and cause noise and hum. Your transmitter should be set up in another room, attic space, etc. as close to the antenna as possible. Keep the distance from the transmitter to antenna as short as possible to minimize signal loss in the coaxial cable feeding the antenna.

These are some of the basic issues regarding site selection. Landlords, roommates, leases etc. are your problem.

FM TRANSMITTERS

FM is an abbreviation for Frequency Modulation. Modulation is how information is imparted to a radio frequency signal. In the case of FM the audio signal modulates what is called the carrier frequency (which is the frequency of the broadcast signal) by causing it to shift up and down ever so slightly in response to the level of the audio signal. An FM radio receives this signal and extracts the audio information from the radio frequency carrier by a process called demodulation.

Modulation of the signal takes place within the FM broadcast transmitter. The transmitter consists of several different sections: the oscillator, phase locked loop, and gain stages. Generation of the broadcast carrier frequency is the responsibility of the oscillator section. Tuning (as distinct from modulation) or changing the frequency of the oscillator section is either done electronically or manually. For a practical radio station that will be operated for more than a few minutes, it is almost essential to have the tuning done under electronic control since free running or manually tuned oscillators will drift in frequency due to temperature and inherent design limitations. This is an important consideration is selecting a transmitter. Since one of the goals is to deprive the FCC of technical objections to micropower broadcasting it is critical to have transmitters that stay on frequency and do not drift. This, of course, rules out using transmitters based on free running oscillators.

Frequency control brings us to the next section. Oscillator frequency drift is corrected by a circuit known as a phase lock loop (PLL) controller. In essence, it compares the output frequency of the oscillator to a reference frequency. When the frequency starts to drift it applies a correction voltage to the oscillator which is voltage tuned, keeping it locked to the desired frequency. In a PLL circuit the frequency is selected by setting a series of small switches either on or off according to the frequency setting chart that comes with the transmitter. In some cases the switch array may be replaced by four dial-up switches that show a number for the FM frequency of transmission, i.e. 100.1 for 100.1 MHz. Even simpler, some units have a display like a digital radio with up and down buttons for changing frequency.

One part of the oscillator section, the voltage tuning circuit, serves a dual purpose. As described above it allows the oscillator to be electronically tuned. In addition, it is the means by which the broadcast carrier frequency is modulated by an audio signal. When the audio signal is applied to this section the variations in the audio signal voltage will cause the frequency of the oscillator to shift up and down. Frequency shifts brought about by audio modulation are ignored by the PLL controller due to the inherent nature of the circuit design. It is important not to over modulate the transmitter by applying an audio signal whose level is too great. Many transmitters are equipped with an input level control which allows one to adjust the degree of modulation. Further control of the audio level is provided by a compressor/limiter which is discussed in the studio section.

As the modulation level increases the amount of space occupied by the FM signal grows as well. It must be kept within a certain boundary or interference with adjacent FM broadcast channels will result. FCC regulations stipulate a maximum spread of plus or minus 75,000 cycles centered about the carrier frequency. Each FM channel is 200,000 cycles wide. Over modulation — the spreading of the broadcast signal beyond these boundaries — is known as splatter and must be avoided by controlling the modulation level. As a result the signal will be distorted and interference with adjacent channels will take place.

Following the oscillator section are a series of gain stages which buffer and amplify the signal, bringing it to a sufficient strength for FM broadcast purposes. In most cases this will be 1/2 to 1 watt of output power. This level is sufficient for a broadcast radius of one-to-two miles depending on circumstances. For increased power a separate amplifier or series of amplifiers are used to raise the power level even higher. Amplifiers are covered in the next part of this primer.

Transmitters are available in kit form from a number of different U.S. sources including Free Radio Berkeley, Progressive Concepts, Panaxis and Ramsey Electronics, though the latter is rather debatable in terms of broadcast quality. An English firm Veronica makes some rather nice kits as well. Assembly requires a fair degree of technical skill and knowledge in most cases. Free Radio Berkeley offers an almost fully assembled 1/2 watt PLL transmitter kit requiring a minimal amount of assembly.

AMPLIFIERS

Although 1/2 to 1 watt may be perfectly adequate for very localized neighborhood radio coverage, higher power will be required to cover larger areas such as a town or a portion of a large urban area. In order to increase the output power of a low-power FM exciter or transmitter an amplifier or series of amplifiers are connected to the output of the transmitter. Amplifiers are also referred to as amps, and should not be confused with the unit of current also called amps.

Amplifiers are much simpler in design and construction than a transmitter. Most of the amplifiers used in micropower broadcasting employ only one active device, an RF power transistor, per stage of amplification. By convention most broadcast amplifiers have an input and output impedance of 50 ohms. This is similar to audio speakers having an impedance between 4 and 8 ohms. When an RF amplifier with a 50 ohm input impedance is attached to the 50 ohm output impedance of a transmitter this matching of impedances assures a maximum flow of electrical energy or power between the two units.

A mismatch between any elements in the chain from transmitter to amplifier to filter to antenna will reduce the efficiency of the entire system and may result in damage if the difference is rather large. Imagine the results if a high pressure water pipe 4 inches in diameter is forced to feed into a 1/2" water pipe with no decrease in the action of the pump feeding the 4 inch pipe. In an RF amplifier the RF power transistor will heat up and self-destruct under analogous conditions.

An RF power amplifier consists of an RF power transistor and a handful of passive components, usually capacitors and inductors which are connected in a particular topology that transforms the 50 ohm input and output impedances of the amplifier to the much lower input and output impedances of the RF power transistor. Detailed circuit theory of this interaction between the components is not covered in this primer.

Amplifiers can be categorized as either narrow band or broad band. Narrow band amplifiers are tuned to one specific frequency. Broad band amplifiers are able to work over a specified range of frequencies without tuning. Most of the amplifiers that have been used in micropower broadcasting are of the first type. A tunable amplifier can be a bit of a problem for those without much experience. In a typical tuned stage amplifier there will be two tuning capacitors in the input stage and two more in the output stage. If not correctly adjusted the transistor can produce unwanted sideband spurs at other frequencies both within and outside of the FM band.

To make set up easier for the average micropower broadcaster a broad band amplifier is preferable or one with a minimal amount of tuning stages. Several designs are available. One rather popular one is a 20-24 watt amplifier using a Phillips BGY33 broad band power amplifier module. It is a rather rugged device that requires no tuning and produces a full 20-24 watts output for 250 milliwatts of drive from the transmitter. Free Radio Berkeley has a kit based on this device. This kit includes an output filter as well which other vendors may not include in their kits. Regardless of the source, the BGY33 is not the most efficient device and requires a good sized heat sink for proper dissipation of heat, and the use of a cooling fan is strongly suggested as well.

If you buy a kit or transmitter package based on this device be certain to determine from the manufacturer that the BGY33 is mounted directly to the heat sink, not to a chassis panel with a heat sink on the other side of the chassis panel. It must directly contact the heat sink with a layer of heat sink heat compound between the module mounting flange and the heat sink surface.

Broad band designs are not as a common due to the degree of design experience required to create a functional unit. It seems a number of kit providers are content not to optimize and improve their amplifier designs. Free Radio Berkeley is now offering amplifiers that are either no tune or minimal tune designs in several different ranges of power. Certain broad band designs may be too wide in their range of frequency coverage and will amplify the harmonics equally well. For FM broadcast purposes the width of frequency coverage should be for only the FM band, about 20-25 Megahertz wide.

Selecting the right amount of power is rather important since you should only use enough power to cover the desired area. Unfortunately there is not an easy answer to the question of how much area a certain amount of power covers. Antenna height is very critical, five watts at 50 feet will not go as far as five watts at 500 feet. Assuming you do not have a 10-story building or a convenient 500 foot hill to site your antenna and transmitter on, experience in urban environ-

50 Ohm Dummy Load Design

Use for tuning and testing transmitters and amplifiers. Do not operate either without a load, damage will result. This design can be used with the 30 watt amplifiers for a short period of time; do not let the resistors overheat.

10 - 510 ohm carbon compostion or film, 2 watt resistors. Solder one end to the isolated strip and the other end to the ground portion of the circuit board.

Isolate a 3/4-to-1 inch wide strip in the middle of a piece of copper circuit board material, use a dremel tool or sharp xacto knife to cut away the copper

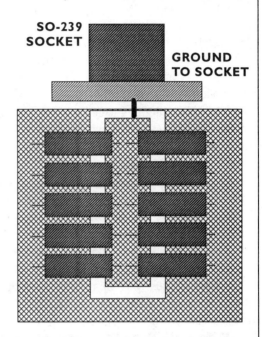

SO-239 SOCKET

GROUND TO SOCKET

Mount resistors 1/4 inch above the board

Attaching the S0239 socket to the board: Bolt the two ground lugs to the S0239 socket with 4-40 nuts and bolts. Attach to the side with the solder pin on it. Be sure the lugs are on opposite to each other, not diagonal. They should point straight down when held above the circuit board. Bend the solder lugs up at a 90 degree angle, the bend point should be flush with the edge of the S0239. Solder the lugs to the ground side of the circuit board, straddling the center strip. Use a piece of jumper wire to connect from the center pin to the center strip of the circuit board.

ments has yielded the following rough guidelines. With an antenna approximately 50 feet above the ground. 1/2 to 1 watt will yield an effective range of one-to-three miles, five-to-six watts will cover out to about one-to-five miles, 10-15 watts will cover up to 8 miles, 20-24 watts will cover up to 10-12 miles and 30-40 watts will cover up to 15 miles. Coverage will vary depending on terrain, obstructions, type of antenna, etc. If your antenna is very high above average terrain you will be able to go much further than the figures given above. Quality of the radios receiving your signal will be a determining factor as well. Since the power levels are rather low in comparison to other stations an external antenna on the receiver is highly suggested, especially an outdoor one.

It is very important to provide adequate cooling for RF amplifiers. This means using a properly sized heat sink and an external cooling fan. Heat sinks have heat dissipating fins which must be placed in an upward pointing direction. Overheating will cause premature failure of the transistor. A cooling fan, usually a four-to-five inch square box fan, will offer extra insurance. It should be placed so that the air flows over the fins of the heat sink.

Under no circumstances should an amplifier/transmitter be operated without a proper load attached to the output. Failure to do so can destroy the output transistor. When testing and tuning, a dummy load is used to present a load of 50 ohms to the transmitter/amplifier. It is very bad practice to tune a unit with an antenna attached. Use a dummy load of proper wattage rating to match the transmitter output wattage.

An output filter must be used between the transmitter/amplifier and the antenna. Some amplifier kits come with a filter included, such as the 20 watt FRB amplifier. These do not need an additional filter. More on this in the filter section.

Heavy gauge (12-16 AWG) insulated stranded wire is used to connect the amplifier to the power supply. Observe correct polarity when making the connection. Reversing the polarity will result in catastrophic failure of the transmitter. Red is positive and black is negative or ground.

POWER SUPPLIES

Most of the transmitters and amplifiers used in micro broadcasting require an input voltage of 12-to-14 volts DC. Higher power amplifiers (above 40 watts) require 24-28 volts DC. In a fixed location the voltage is provided by a power supply which transforms the house voltage of 110 volts AC to the proper DC voltage.

Power supplies are not only measured in terms of their voltage but current as well. A higher power amplifier is going to require a greater amount of input power as compared to a lower power amplifier. Output current is measured and specified as amps. A power supply is selected on the basis of its continuous current output which should be higher than the actual requirements of the amplifier. Power supplies operated at their fully rated output will have a tendency to overheat under continuous operation. An amplifier which requires eight amps will need a power supply with a 10-to-12 amp continuous capacity. In most cases the following ratings are suggested for transmitters requiring 13.8 volts.

1-5 Watt Transmitter	2-3 Amps
10-15 Watt Transmitter	5-6 Amps
20-24 BGY33 Based Unit	10 Amps
40 Watt Transmitter	12 Amps

Any power supply you use must have a regulated voltage output along with protection circuitry. Some reasonably priced brands include Pyramid, Triplite and Astron. Do not use any of the wall transformer type of power supplies. Such units are not adequate for this application. Higher power transmitters require power supplies with an output voltage of 28 volts. Astron is the best manufacturer of this type of power supply. A 75 watt transmitter will require a power supply with a current rating of six-to-eight amps and 28 volts.

For mobile applications voltage can be fed from the cigarette lighter socket of a car with the correct plug and heavy gauge wiring. This may not work well in some newer vehicles with are reported to have some sort of current limit protection on the lighter socket. Check with an auto mechanic about this if you are in doubt. Electrical systems on newer vehicles are rather sensitive and can be damaged if not properly understood.

Another problem with mobile operation is battery drain. A 20-40 watt transmitter running for four-to-five hours can deplete the battery to the point where the vehicle may not start. It is better to have a separate battery running parallel to the charging system with an isolator. Isolators are available from recreational vehicle accessory suppliers. Use a high capacity deep discharge type of battery.

Lead acid batteries are not very benign. Acid can leak and spill on people, clothing and equipment. It is best to keep the battery in a plastic battery box. Vapors from the battery are explosive in confined areas. Keep this in mind for mobile vehicle operations. You might consider using a gel cell type of battery which is sealed and can not leak. These are a bit pricey but have far fewer problems. A good quality gel charger must be used to ensure battery longevity.

Smaller gel cell batteries work really well for setting up a low power (six watts or less) transmitter on a street corner as a public demonstration of micropower radio. In Berkeley a 6 watt micropower station is set up at the local flea market as a community demonstration on weekends. It is called Flea Radio Berkeley. Transmitters can be set up at demonstrations and rallies so motorists can tune their radios to the frequency which is displayed on large banners near the streets and listen in on what is happening. This has worked very well. Use your imagination to show how micropower broadcasting can be brought into the community.

FILTERS

Although it is rather simple in design and construction a filter is one of the most important elements in broadcasting. No matter what, a proper filter must be used between the transmitter and antenna. Use of a filter will help deprive the FCC of one of its main arguments against micropower broadcasting — interference with other broadcast services.

A proper filter reduces or eliminates harmonics from your broadcast signal. Harmonics are produced by the transmitter and are multiples of the fundamental frequency you are tuned for. For example, if you broadcast at 104.1, you may produce a harmonic at 208.2, and (less likely) 312.6 and so on. Most filter designs are of the low pass type. They let frequencies below a certain frequency pass through unaffected. As the frequency increases and goes beyond that point the filter begins to attenuate any frequency that is higher than the set point. The degree of attenuation increases with the frequency. By the time the frequency of the first harmonic is reached it will be severely attenuated. This is very important since the first harmonic from an FM transmitter falls in the high VHF TV band. Failure to reduce this harmonic will cause interference to neighboring TV sets.

You do not want to generate complaints from folks who engage in the odious habit of watching TV. Noble sentiments, such as telling them to smash their TV if they have a problem will not suffice. Use a filter. Complaints increase the possibility of the FCC showing up at your door. One needs to be good broadcast neighbor and an asset to the community

Harmonics further up the scale can cause interference to other mobile and emergency radio services — not desirable either.

Transmitters with output power ratings of less than 25 watts will need at least a seven pole design. Higher power units will need a nine pole design. An increase in number of poles increase the degree of attenuation. Representative designs are shown. If you build one of these put it in a metal, well-shielded enclosure.

Not really related to filters but an important side issue is the use of FM frequencies at the bottom and top ends of the band. Do not use 87.9 to 88.3 or so if their is a channel 6 TV frequency being used in your local area. Television sets have notoriously poor selectivity and your signal might end up coming in on the sound carrier of the TV if channel six is being used. At the top end of the band do not go any higher than 106 MHz if the transmitter is near an airport. In fact, do everything possible not be too close — at least several miles and away from the flight path(s). Even though interference possibilities are minimal there is not any point in taking chances since the FCC has claimed airplanes will fall from the sky if micropower broadcasting is given free reign. However, corner cutting corporate airline maintenance polices most likely pose a greater danger to public safety than micropower broadcasting.

ANTENNAS

An antenna's primary purpose is to radiate the FM broadcast signal from the transmitter to surrounding FM radio receivers. In order to do this several conditions must be met. First, the antenna must be tuned to the frequency being transmitted. Secondly, it must be sited and oriented properly.

At FM frequencies the radio waves travel in a straight line until an obstacle is met. This is known as line of sight transmission. If the receiving antenna and transmitting antenna can "see" each other and the path distance is not too great to attenuate the signal, then the broadcast signal can be received. Radio signal strength is based on the inverse square law. Double the distance and the signal strength will be 1/4 of what it was.

Since FM broadcast transmissions are line of sight, the height of the antenna is very important. Increasing the height is more effective than doubling or tripling the power. Due to the curvature of the earth the higher the antenna the greater the distance to the horizon. Increased height will place the antenna above obstructions which otherwise would block the signal. Your antenna should be at least 40-50 feet above the ground. Count yourself lucky if you can site the antenna on a hill or a ten story building.

An antenna is rough tuned by adjusting the length of the radiating element(s). Many antenna designs are based on or derived from what is called a dipole, two radiating elements whose length is roughly equivalent to 1/4 of the wavelength of the desired frequency of transmission. Wavelength in inches is determined by dividing 11811 by the frequency in megahertz. The result is either divided by four or multiplied by .25 to yield the 1/4 wavelength. A correction factor of .9 to .95, depending on the diameter of the element, is multiplied times the 1/4 wavelength resulting in the approximate length of each element.

Fine tuning the antenna requires the use of an SWR power meter. SWR is an abbreviation for standing wave ratio which is the ratio between power going into the antenna and the power being reflected back by the antenna. A properly tuned antenna is going to reflect very little power back. Correct use of an SWR meter is described a bit further down in this section. If you can afford $100, get a dual needle meter which shows both reflected and forward power at the same time. A good brand is Daiwa.

A dipole with tuning stubs is one of the easiest antennas to make and tune. Two dipoles can be combined on a ten foot mast if they are spaced 3/4 of a wavelength from center to center with the elements vertical and fed with a phasing harness. A phasing harness consists of two 1.25 wavelength pieces of 75 ohm coaxial cable (RG11) cut to a length that is the product of the 1.25 wavelength times the velocity factor (supplied by the manufacturer) of the cable. A PL259 plug is attached to the end of each cable. These are connected to a 259 T adapter with the center socket being the connection for the feed cable coming from the transmitter. The other ends go respectively to each dipole. Such an arrangement will increase the power going into the antenna by a factor of two.

Besides the dipole a number of other antenna designs are employed in micropower broadcasting. Each one has a characteristic pattern of coverage. Antennas can be broken down into two basic types — omnidirectional and directional. Under most circumstances the omni is the antenna of choice for micropower broadcasting. Polarization is another aspect to consider but does not play that big of a role in most cases. Antennas can be vertical, horizontal or circular in polarization. Most micro broadcast antennas are vertically polarized. In theory a vertically oriented receiving antenna will receive better if the transmitting antenna is vertically oriented as well. Obstructions in the receiving environment will have a tendency to bounce the signal around so that the signal will not be exactly vertically polarized when it hits the receiving antenna, particularly in a car that is moving. Commercial broadcasters employ circular polarization which yields both vertical and horizontal components to the signal. It is said that this is best for car radios. This may be true given the dependence of commercial broadcasters on "drive time" as a peak listening period.

A single radiating element vertically oriented will have a rather high angle of radiation where a good portion of the signal is going up to the sky at an angle of around 35 degrees or more. When you combine two vertical elements such as two dipoles you reduce the angle of radiation to a point where the signal is more concentrated in the horizontal plane. This is what accounts for the apparent doubling of radiated power when you use two dipoles phased together. Power output from the antenna or antenna array is known as effective radiated power (ERP) and is usually equal to or greater than the input power.

Several vertical element antenna designs have a lower angle of radiation even though they only use one element. These are the J-Pole and the Slim Jim designs. Having a signal pattern that is more compressed into the horizontal plane makes the Slim Jim ideal for urban environments. Both can be easily constructed from 1/2" copper pipe and fittings. Plans are available from FRB directly or the FRB web site: www.freeradio.org.

Tunable Dipole Antenna

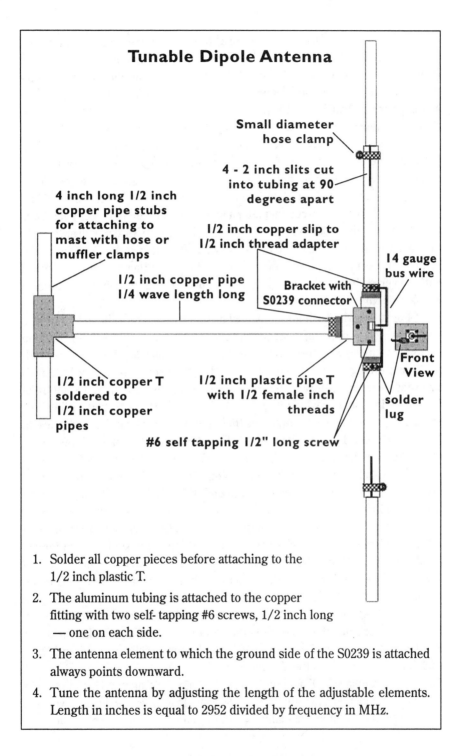

Small diameter hose clamp

4 - 2 inch slits cut into tubing at 90 degrees apart

4 inch long 1/2 inch copper pipe stubs for attaching to mast with hose or muffler clamps

1/2 inch copper slip to 1/2 inch thread adapter

1/2 inch copper pipe 1/4 wave length long

14 gauge bus wire

Bracket with S0239 connector

1/2 inch copper T soldered to 1/2 inch copper pipes

1/2 inch plastic pipe T with 1/2 female inch threads

Front View

solder lug

#6 self tapping 1/2" long screw

1. Solder all copper pieces before attaching to the 1/2 inch plastic T.

2. The aluminum tubing is attached to the copper fitting with two self-tapping #6 screws, 1/2 inch long — one on each side.

3. The antenna element to which the ground side of the S0239 is attached always points downward.

4. Tune the antenna by adjusting the length of the adjustable elements. Length in inches is equal to 2952 divided by frequency in MHz.

Another class of antennas are the 1/4 and 5/8 wave ground plane antennas. A commercially manufactured 5/8 ground plane for FM broadcast purposes is available for around $100. It is an ideal antenna for those who want an easy-to-tune-and-assemble antenna. Set up time is less than 15 minutes. Plans for these antennas are available from FRB.

Directional antennas are not usually required for micropower broadcasting. If the area you wish to cover lies in one particular direction you might consider the use of such an antenna. An easy way to do this is to put a reflecting screen 1/4 of a wavelength behind a vertical dipole. The screen will need to be a bit taller than the total length of the elements and about two-to-three feet wide. This will yield a nice directional pattern with a fair amount of power gain. Your pattern will be about 60-70 degrees wide. Another type of directional antenna is the yagi which has a basic dipole as the radiating element but additional elements as reflectors and directors. A yagi can be a bit difficult to build for those not well versed in antenna design and construction. Your best choice is a dipole with a reflector.

For those who wish for a practical design that can be built and put to use the following is a basic dipole antenna which can be constructed from common hardware store items. It uses 1/2 inch copper water pipe and fittings along with aluminum tubing. A half inch plastic threaded T is used with a copper 1/2 inch threaded to 1/2 inch slip adapters at all three points. An aluminum tube 9/16 of inch or so in diameter will fit into this slip adapter and is attached with two #6 self-tapping sheet metal screws. This tubing is 20 inches long. Another piece of aluminum tubing 15 inches long with a diameter small enough to slip inside the other tubing is used as the adjustable tuning element. Four slots 90 degrees apart and 1–1/2 inches long are cut into one end of the larger tubing. A small diameter hose clamp is slipped over that end. With the smaller tubing inserted inside, the hose clamp is tightened to hold it in place. This is repeated for the second element. A copper half inch thread to slip adapter is soldered to one end of a 36 inch piece of 1/2 inch copper tubing which is the support arm for the dipole. A copper T is soldered to the other end. Then, two three-inch pieces of 1/2 inch copper tubing are soldered to the T fitting. This allows easy clamping to a mast. A solder lug is attached to each element using one of the self tapping screws holding the elements to the slip fittings. Your coaxial cable will be attached to these solder lugs. Center conductor to one, braid or shield to the other. You can get a little fancier and make an aluminum bracket to hold an SO239 socket and attach this to the T connector.

Once you have it all put together as shown in the diagram it is time to tune it. Adjust the element lengths to the 1/4 wave length you arrived at with the above formula. Tighten the clamps so the tuning stubs can barely slide back and forth. Mark each stub where it enters the larger tubing. Using either hose clamps or U-clamps attach the antenna to the end of a mast piece ten feet long. The element to which the braid or shield of the coax is attached must be pointing down Support the mast so that it stands straight up with the antenna at the top. It is best to do this outside.

Set up your transmitter and connect an SWR/Power meter between the transmitter and the antenna. Adjust your meter to read SWR according to the directions that came with it. SWR is the ratio of power coming from the transmitter and the power reflected back from the antenna. A properly tuned antenna will reflect very little power back, resulting in a very low SWR ratio. Too much reflected power can damage the transmitter.

Turn on the transmitter and observe the SWR or amount of reflected power. Shut the transmitter off if the level is very high and check your connections. Rough tuning the antenna by measurements should have brought the readings down to a fairly low level. Turn off the transmitter and adjust each tubing stub up or down about 1/4 of an inch. Turn the transmitter back on and note the readings. If the reflected power and SWR ratio went lower you went the right direction in either increasing or decreasing the length of the stubs. Turn off the transmitter and continue another 1/4 inch in the same direction or the opposite direction if the SWR ratio and reflected power increased. Turn the transmitter on again. If the reading is lower continue to go in the same direction in 1/4 inch increments being sure to turn off the transmitter to make the adjustments. Continue to do this cycle until you have reached the lowest possible reading. At some point the readings will start to increase again. Stop there.

You can do this with two dipoles as mentioned earlier in this section. Each dipole is tuned by itself and then both are connected with a phasing harness when mounted to the mast section.

CONNECTORS AND CABLE

Radio frequency cables are referred to as coax as a generic term. It is short for coaxial. A coaxial cable consists of an inner conductor inside an insulating core. This is surrounded on the outside by a metal braid or foil, called the shield. This shield is in turn covered by an insulating jacket of plastic material. Coaxial cables are specified in terms of impedance which for most micropower broadcasting purposes is 50 ohms except for dipole phasing harnesses.

In the 50 ohm category there are a number of choices when selecting coaxial cable. The most important characteristic of coax is its level of signal attenuation. This depends on the length of the cable and its particular frequency response. RG58 coaxial cable has a high degree of attenuation and should only be used for short connections. RG8X or mini-eight works well for lengths under 50 feet and is suited for portable and mobile set ups since it is rather flexible. RG8 and its higher performance cousins such as 213 and Belden 9913 are the best for fixed installations. Belden 9913 has the lowest loss for any given length as compared to other variations of RG8. In fact, it has a loss figure at 100 MHz that compares well with commercial broadcast hard-line coax. It is rather stiff cable and must be installed correctly.

Coaxial cables do not take rough treatment very well, especially 9913. They must be carefully rolled up by hand, not wrapped between palm of hand and elbow like a rope. Kinks are to be avoided at all costs. When routing a cable keep the bends from being sharp and keep it away from circumstances where it can be pinched or slammed.

Three types of connectors are in general use — BNC, PL259 and N. Most micropower broadcasting equipment uses PL259 and its mating socket known as the SO239. Any connector will introduce some small degree of signal loss. N connectors are used where high performance and reliability are of most importance.

STUDIO SET UP

A typical broadcast studio consists of an audio mixer (DJ style works best), one or more CD players, one or more cassette tape decks, a turntable or two, several microphones, and a compressor/limiter. Optional items can include a cart machine and a phone patch.

Reasonable quality mixers start at $200 and go up in price from there. DJ styles are best since they have a large number of inputs available and support turntables without the need of external phono preamps. Any mixer you select should have least two or more microphone input channels. These should be low impedance inputs. Other features to look for include high visibility VU (level) meters, slide faders for each channel, switchable inputs for each channel, stereo or mono selection for the output signal, and an auxiliary output for an air check tape deck.

CD players and tape decks can be your average higher quality consumer audio gear. Day in and day out usage will eventually take their toll so pay for the extra warranty period when it is offered. When one wears out in six months or so just take it back under warranty for either repair or replacement.

DJ style turntables are the best choice for playing vinyl. Cheaper units just will not stand up to the wear and tear of daily usage. Select a heavy duty stylus as well.

Microphones should be fairly good quality vocal types. They can be either directional or omnidirectional. Directional microphones will pick up less ambient noise but need to be on axis with the person's mouth for best pick up. Since some folks do not pay attention to where the microphone is in relation to their mouth, an omnidirectional might be considered a better choice if this is the case. A distance of about four inches should be maintained between the microphone and mouth. Place a wind screen foam piece over each microphone. Some microphones have built-in shock and vibration isolation to keep bumps to the microphone from being audible. It is a good idea to use some sort of isolated holder for the DJ microphone. An old swing arm lamp can be adapted to hold a microphone.

For programmers who do a lot of reading of material on the air a headphone microphone is something to consider since it will maintain a uniform distance from mouth to microphone no matter where the head moves to. One drawback is that they tend to be a bit fragile in rough hands.

Headphones are essential for monitoring and cueing up program material. You can either opt for high quality rugged units that are a bit costly or plan on replacing an inexpensive set every few months.

A limiter/compressor is an essential part of the audio chain. It is used to keep the audio signal from exceeding a preset level. Without this the transmitter will be overmodulated resulting in signal splatter and distortion. Signal splatter will cause interference with adjacent stations and distortion will send your listeners elsewhere.

Common to most limiter/compressors are a set of controls — input level, output level, ratio, threshold, attack and decay. To properly set up the mixer, limiter/compressor and transmitter you start with a steady audio source (a signal generator plugged into the board or a test tone CD, tape or record). You adjust the input level and master output level controls so that the meters are reading zero dB. Master level should be at mid position. Audio output goes from the mixer to the limiter/compressor and from there to the transmitter. Do not turn the transmitter on at this time.

Most limiter/compressors have indicator lights or meters to show how much gain reduction is being applied and the output level. Set the ratio control to the infinity setting, as this enables hard limit function. Attack and decay can be set around mid position. Adjust the threshold and the input level until the gain reduction shows activity. Adjust the output level so that the indicator lights or meters show a 0 dB output level.

Turn the level input on the transmitter all the way down and power up the transmitter. Monitor the signal on good quality radio. Slowly turn the level control until you can hear the test tone. Compare the signal level to that of other stations. Your level should be slightly less since most other operations are using quite a bit of audio processing on their signal. You may have to make fine adjustments to the limiter/compressor to get things exactly right.

When everything is set up correctly any audio signals that exceed 0 dB on the board will be kept at that level by the compressor/limiter. You will need to listen carefully to the signal to make sure when a "hot" audio source exceeds this that the transmitted signal keeps an even level and does not distort or splatter. There will be some interplay between the output level and the threshold setting. Nor do you want a signal that is too low in level either since that will produce a weak sounding broadcast.

A very important consideration is to keep as much distance between the studio gear and the transmitter as possible. RF (radio frequency signals) will find their way into audio equipment and produce a hum or other types of noise. You can separate the two areas by using a low impedance cable between the limiter/compressor and the transmitter. This can be a long microphone cable with XLR connectors or a made up shielded two conductor cable with XLR connectors. You can have about 150 feet of cable maximum. A high impedance to low impedance transformer will be needed at one end or both depending on whether the limiter/compressor and transmitter have low or high impedance connections. These transformers usually have an XLR female connector on the low impedance side and a 1/4" phone plug on the high impedance side. If your transmitter has an RCA style input you will need the proper adapter to go from 1/4" phone plug to RCA plug.

Your studio should be arranged to provide easy access to all controls and equipment with plenty of table space. An L or horseshoe shape works well for the studio bench. An open area within the sight line of the operator should be provided so there will be a place for extra microphones and guests.

FINAL WORD

Although it seems like there is a lot to deal with in setting up a micropower station, it can be broken down into three areas — studio, transmitter and antenna. It should not be difficult to find someone with studio set-up experience to help with the project. Transmitters, particularly their construction and tuning, should be left to an experienced person. If such a person is not available there are a number of people who will assemble, test and tune your transmitter for whatever fee they have set. Stick to a commercial, easy to tune antenna such as the Comet if your skills are minimal. These can be purchased pre-tuned for an additional fee from FRB and L. D. Brewer. It is best to put most of the energy into organizing and setting up the station.

Experience has shown that once the technical operation is in place and running, it will require very little in the way of intervention except for routine maintenance (cleaning tape heads, dusting, etc.) and occasional replacement of a tape or CD player.

What requires most attention and "maintenance" is the human element, however. More time will be spent on this than any equipment. As a survival strategy it is best to involve as much of the community as possible in the radio station. The more diverse and greater number of voices the better. It is much easier for the FCC to shut down a "one man band" operation than something serving an entire community. Our focus is on empowering communities with their own collective voice, not creating vanity stations. Why imitate commercial radio ?

Before you commit to your first broadcast, it would be advisable to have an attorney available who is sympathetic to the cause. Even though they may not be familiar with this aspect of the law there is a legal web site which offers all of the material used in the Free Radio Berkeley case. There are enough briefs and other materials available to bring an attorney up to speed. That web address is: www.surf.com/~graham. A list server, nlgcdc@agora.rdrop.com, for the National Lawyers Guild Committee on Democratic Communications puts you in touch with the group that is doing a lot of the legal work on micropower broadcasting. Their contact address and phone are:

National Lawyers Guild Committee on Democratic Communications
368 Hayes Street (between Franklin and Gough)
San Francisco, CA 94102
(415) 575-3220
Fax (415) 575-3230

The following is a guide to what to do when the FCC knocks.

WHEN THE FCC KNOCKS ON YOUR DOOR

Note: The following discussion assumes that you are not a licensed broadcaster.

Q: If FCC agents knock on my door and say they want to talk with me, do I have to answer their questions?

A: No. You have a right to say that you want a lawyer present when and if you speak with them, and that if they will give you their names, you will be back in touch with them. Unless you have been licensed to broadcast, the FCC has no right to "inspect" your home.

Q: If they say they have a right to enter my house without a warrant to see if I have broadcasting equipment, do I have to let them in?

A: No. Under Section 303(n) of Title 47 U.S.C., the FCC has a right to inspect any transmitting devices that must be licensed under the Act. Nonetheless, they must have permission to enter your home, or some other basis for entering beyond their mere supervisorial powers. With proper notice, they do have a right to inspect your communications devices. If they have given you notice of a pending investigation, contact a lawyer immediately.

Q: If they have evidence that I am "illegally" broadcasting from my home, can they enter anyway, even without a warrant or without my permission?

A: They will have to go to court to obtain a warrant to enter your home. But, if they have probable cause to believe you are currently engaging in illegal activities of any sort, they, with the assistance of the local police, can enter your home without a warrant to prevent those activities from continuing. Basically, they need either a warrant, or probable cause to believe a crime is going on at the time they are entering your home.

Q: If I do not cooperate with their investigation, and they threaten to arrest me, or have me arrested, should I cooperate with them?

A: If they have a legal basis for arresting you, it is very likely that they will prosecute you regardless of what you say. Therefore, what you say will only assist them in making a stronger case against you. Do not speak to them without a lawyer there.

Q: If they have an arrest or a search warrant, should I let them in my house?

A: Yes. Give them your name and address, and tell them that you want to have your lawyer contacted immediately before you answer any more questions. If you are arrested, you have a right to make several telephone calls within 3 hours of booking.

Q: Other than an FCC fine for engaging in illegal transmissions, what other risks do I take in engaging in micro-radio broadcasts.

A: Section 501 of the Act provides that violations of the Act can result in the imposition of a $10,000 fine or by imprisonment for a term not exceeding one year, or both. A second conviction results in a potentially longer sentence. If you are prosecuted under this section of the Act, and you are indigent (unable to hire an attorney), the court will have to appoint one for you.

Q: Are there any other penalties that can be imposed upon me for "illegal broadcasts?"

A: Under Section 510 of the Act, the FCC can attempt to have your communicating equipment seized and forfeited for violation of the requirements set forth in the Act. Once again, if they attempt to do this, you will be given notice of action against you, and have an opportunity to appear in court to fight the FCC's proposed action. Realize, though, that they will try to keep your equipment and any other property they can justify retaining until the proceedings are completed. You have a right to seek return of your property from the court at any time.

Q: If the FCC agents ask me if I knew I was engaged in illegal activities, should I deny any knowledge of FCC laws or any illegal activities?

A: No. You will have plenty of time to answer their accusations after you have spoken with an attorney. It is a separate crime to lie to law enforcement officials about material facts. Remain silent.

Q: If I am considering broadcasting over micro-radio, is there anything I can do ahead of time to minimize the likelihood of prosecution?

A: Yes. Speak with an attorney before you are approached by law enforcement to discuss the different aspects of FCC law. Arrange ahead of time for someone to represent you when and if the situation arises, so that you will already have prepared a strategy of defense.

Q: What can I do if the FCC agents try to harass me by going to my landlord, or some other source to apply pressure on me?

A: So long as there is no proof that you have violated the law, you cannot be prosecuted or evicted. If there is evidence of misconduct, you might have to defend yourself in court. Depending upon what the FCC said or did, you might be able to raise a defense involving selective prosecution or other equivalent argument. If the conduct of the agents is clearly harassment, rather than a proper investigation, you can file a complaint with the FCC or possibly a civil action against them.

Q: If I want to legally pursue FCC licensing for a new FM station, what should I do?

A: It isn't the purpose of this question and answer guide to advocate or discourage non-licensed broadcast operations. A person cited by the FCC for illegal broadcasting will find it virtually impossible to later obtain permission to get a license. If you want to pursue the licensing procedure, see the procedures set forth in the Code of Federal Regulations, Title 47, Part 73. The application form (Form # 301 A) is extremely complicated, and requires a filing fee of $2,030.00. If you want to contact the FCC directly, call them at their Consumer Assistance and Small Business Division, Room 254, 1919 N St. NW, Washington, DC 20554, tel (202) 632-7260. Don't bother to try this without significant financial backing.

ABOUT THE CONTRIBUTORS

Lee Ballinger is a downsized steelworker who has been an associate editor at *Rock & Rap Confidential*, the muckraking music and politics monthly, since 1983. *Rock & Rap Confidential* has promoted microradio as a tool of empowerment for many years — Zoom Black Magic Radio founder, Black Rose, is on its staff. For a free sample copy, write: RRC, Box 341305, Los Angeles, CA, 90034.

Jon Bekken was an airshifter at WEFT-Champaign from 1986-1990 during which time he was on the Programming Committee. He is presently an Assistant Professor of Journalism at Suffolk University.

Stephen Dunifer is a longtime activist and founder of Free Radio Berkeley. He is currently engaged in the design, development and promotion of free radio stations on an international basis.

Ricardo Omar Elizalde currently writes for *Frontera* magazine, and is working towards his teaching credential. He is a journalism graduate from San Francisco State who lives happily in San Francisco with his wife Angela.

Lorenzo Komboa Ervin has been a member of the Student Nonviolent Coordinating Committee and the Black Panther Party. He was a political prisoner in the Marian Penitentiary. Since his release he has worked as a community organizer with Concerned Citizens for Justice in Chattenooga, TN, the Anarchist Black Cross, and is the founder and coordinator of the Black Liberation Radio Support Committee.

Charles Fairchild lives in Baltimore and has written extensively on the media in Canada and the United States. He is currently preparing a book on community radio in both countries.

Paul W. Griffin: After ten years at KALX, he went on the air with "Anarchy Radio" for some test broadcasts, and later had a show on San Francisco Liberation Radio. He's been on the air at Free Radio Berkeley since January 1995 and continues to broadcast every Saturday night. He started up the Association of Micropower Broadcasters (AMPB) in 1994 as an outreach vehicle.

Jerry M. Landay is an honors professor emeritus at the College of Communications at the University of Illinois at Urbana-Champaign. He has taught a course entitled "Issues in Television," and writes on telemedia and democracy issues. He was an ABC/CBS news correspondent in a former life.

Robert W. McChesney teaches journalism at the University of Wisconsin-Madison. He is the author of *Telecommunications, Mass Media and Democracy: The Battle for the Control of U.S. Broadcasting, 1928-1935* (Oxford University Press, 1993), *Corporate Media and the Threat to Democracy* (Seven Stories Press, 1997), and, with Edward S. Herman, *The Global Media: The New Missionaries of Corporate Capitalism* (Cassell, 1997).

Sheila Nopper is a cultural activist, and freelance journalist for such publications as *The Beat, Herizons* and *Illinois Times*. Before moving to Fools Paradise she was, for eight years, a CIUT community radio DJ and music documentary producer in Toronto, Canada.

Meme Sabon enjoys instigating and participating in creative, collaborative experiments, including the Brooklyn phenomenon "Organism" which evolved into "The Mustard Factory." She has performed in various incarnations at St. Marks Theatre, LaLaLandia, Experimental Arts Intermedia, The Synagogue, Nada, the 6th & B Garden, and most recently at W.O.W. Cafe. A sometime resident of Dreamtime Village, she hopes to one day be able to live as a hunter/gatherer. She has recently completed a book of photos and essays, *Against the Tyranny of the Square*, which will be hand-distributed to secretaries in Mid-town Manhattan.

Ron Sakolsky has long been a co-conspirator with Mbanna Kantako, whose Springfield station is the original catalyst for the micropower radio movement in the United States. He is a member of the Union for Democratic Communications and the IWW, and a national board member of the Alliance for Cultural Democracy. For more than two decades, he has taught courses on music, cultural activism, and workplace/community organizing for the University of Illinois at Springfield. His other books include: *Gone to Croatan: The Origins of Drop-Out Culture in North America* (co-edited with James Koehnline) and *Sounding Off!: Music as Subversion/Resistance/Revolution* (co-edited with Fred Ho).

Sal Salerno is the author or *Red November, Black November: Culture and Community in the IWW* and *Sabotage & Direct Action: the Early Pamphlets of the IWW.* He teaches at Metropolitan State University in St. Paul, MN.

DJ Tashtego has been a squatter on the Lower East Side of Manhattan for many years. You can contact **Steal This Radio**, 88.7 fm on the lower east side, at P.O. Box 20743, Tompkins Square Station, New York, NY 10009. Homepage: <www.panix.com/~blackout/str>

AND ALL THE INTERVIEWEES AND RADIO ACTIVISTS: **Antonio Coello** (Truth Radio); **Carol Denney** (Free Radio Berkeley); **Internal eXile** (Free Radio Berkeley); **Charlie Goodman** (Excellent Radio); **Louis Hiken** (National Lawyers Guild); **Mbanna Kantako** (Human Rights Radio); **Kiilu Nyasha** (San Francisco Liberation Radio); **Geov Parrish** (Seattle Liberation Radio); **Black Rose** (Zoom Black Magic Radio); **Liszet Squatter** (Radio Vrije Keizer); **Annie Voice** (San Francisco Liberation Radio) and; **Napoleon Williams** (Black Liberation Radio).

Contributing artists and photographers are: Freddie Baer; Phyllis Christopher; Guy Colwell; Tim Drescher; Eric Drooker; Stephen Dunifer; Carol Genetti; Peter Gowrfain; Johann Humyn Being; Dia Kantako; Scott Marshall; Frank Martin; Mac McGill; Keith McHenry; Curt Neitzke; Carol Petrucci; Ron Sakolsky; Meme Sabon; Michael Schwartz; Sean Vile; and Stephen Warmowski.

SOME RECENT TITLES FROM AK PRESS

NO GODS, NO MASTERS

This is the first English translation of Guérin's monumental anthology of anarchism, published here in two volumes. It details through a vast array of hitherto unpublished documents, letters, debates, manifestoes, reports, impassioned calls-to-arms and reasoned analysis, the history, organization and practice of the movement — its theorists, advocates and activists; the great names and the obscure, towering legends and unsung heroes. Edited, introduced and annotated by Guérin, this anthology presents anarchism as both a revolutionary end and  a means of achieving that end. It portrays anarchism as a sophisticated ideology whose nuances and complexities highlight the natural desire for freedom in all of us, and in these post-Marxist times, will re-establish anarchism as both an intellectual and practical force to be reckoned with. Daniel Guérin was a lifelong anarchist and gay activist, and a prolific author. His works previously translated into English include Anarchism: From Theory to Practice, Fascism and Big Business and Class Struggle in the First French Republic. Paul Sharkey, an accomplished translator, has almost single-handedly made

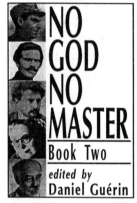

available a vast body of non-English language anarchist writings. His numerous translations include the works of Alexandre Skirda, Nestor Makhno, Osvaldo Bayer, José Peirats and Antonio Tellez.

No Gods, No Masters: Book One. ISBN 1-873176 64-3; 304 pp, three color cover, perfect bound 6x9; $15.95/£11.95. Book One includes the writings of Stirner, Proudhon, Bakunin, Guillaume, Nettlau, Kropotkin, Goldman and de Paepe among others — traversing *The Ego and Its Own, What Is Property, God and the State*, The International Revolutionary Society, the controversy with Marx and the First International, the Paris Committee, Workers' Self-Management, the Jura Federation and more.

No Gods, No Masters: Book Two. ISBN 1-873176 69-4; 288 pp, three color cover, perfect bound 6x9; $15.95/£11.95. Book Two includes work from the likes of Malatesta, Henri, Pouget, Souchy, Leval, Voline, Makhno, the Kronstadt sailors, Fabbri, Durruti and Goldman — covering such momentous events as the Anarchist International, French propaganda by the deed, the General Strike, Collectivization, the Russian Revolution, the Nabat, the insurgent peasant army of the Ukraine and the Spanish Revolution.

THE FRIENDS OF DURRUTI GROUP 1937-1939
by Agustin Guillamón; translated by Paul
Sharkey. ISBN 1-873176-54-6; 128pp, two color
cover, 6x9; $9.95/£7.95. This is the story of a
group of anarchists engaged in the most thor-
oughgoing social and economic revolution of
all time. Essentially street fighters with a long
pedigree of militant action, they used their
own experiences to arrive at the finest contemporary analysis of the Spanish revolution.
In doing so they laid down essential markers
for all future revolutionaries. This study —
drawing on interviews with participants and
synthesizing archival information — is the de-
finitive text on these unsung activists. "Revo-

lutions without theory fail to make progress.
We of the "Friends of Durruti" have outlined our thinking, which may be
amended as appropriate in great social upheavals but which hinges upon
two essential points which cannot be avoided. A program, and rifles." — *El
Amigo del Pueblo* No. 5, July 20, 1937

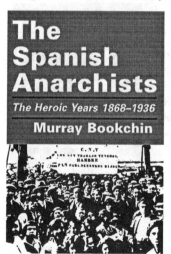

**THE SPANISH ANARCHISTS: THE HEROIC
YEARS 1868–1936**
by Murray Bookchin. ISBN 1-873176 04-X;
336 pp, two color cover, perfect bound 6 x 9;
$19.95/£13.95. A long-awaited new edition of
this seminal history of Spanish Anarchism.
Hailed as a masterpiece, it includes a new
prefatory essay by the author. This popular,
well-researched book opens with the Italian
Anarchist Fanelli's stirring visit to Spain in
1868 and traces the movement's checkered
but steady growth for the next 70 years. Inti-
mate portraits are vividly juxtaposed with
striking descriptions of events: peasant re-
volts, labor unrest, the saintly Fermin
Salvochea, official repression, the terrorists
and the evolution of exciting organizational forms. Bookchin weaves his way
geographically through the whole of Spain, revealing the shadings and subtle-
ties of each small section. From the peasants of Andalusia to the factory
workers of Barcelona, the Spanish people — and their exuberant belief in
and struggles for freedom and self-determination — come alive. *"I've learned
a great deal from this book. It is a rich and fascinating account.... Most important, it has a wonderful spirit of revolutionary optimism that connects the Spanish Anarchists with our own time."* — Howard Zinn.

MORE BOOKS FROM AK PRESS

TO REMEMBER SPAIN: THE ANARCHIST AND SYNDICALIST REVOLUTION OF 1936
by Murray Bookchin; ISBN 1 873176 87 2; 80pp two color cover, perfect bound 5-1/2 x 8-1/2; $6.00/ £4.50. In these essays, Bookchin places the Spanish Anarchist and anarchosyndicalist movements of the 1930s in the context of the revolutionary workers' movements of the pre-World War II era. These articles describe, analyze, and evaluate the last of the great proletarian revolutions of the past two centuries. They form indispensable supplements to Bookchin's larger 1977 history, *The Spanish Anarchists: The Heroic Years, 1868–1936* (now reprinted by AK Press). Read together, these works constitute a highly informative and theoretically significant assessment of the anarchist and anarchosyndicalist movements in Spain. They are invaluable for any reader concerned with the place of the Spanish Revolution in history and with the accomplishments, insights, and failings of the anarchosyndicalist movement.

I COULDN'T PAINT GOLDEN ANGELS: SIXTY YEARS OF COMMONPLACE LIFE AND ANARCHIST AGITATION by Albert Meltzer. ISBN 1-873176 93 7; 400pp, two color cover, perfect bound 210mm x 245mm; $19.95/£12.95. Albert Meltzer (1920-1996) had been involved actively in class struggles since the age of 15; exceptionally for his generation in having been a convinced Anarchist from the start, without any family background in such activity. *I Couldn't Paint Golden Angels* is a lively, witty account of what he claimed would have been the commonplace life of a worker but for the fact that he spent sixty years in anarchist activism. As a result

it is a unique recounting of many struggles otherwise distorted or unrecorded, including the history of the contemporary development of anarchism in Britain and other countries where he was involved, notably Spain. His story tells of many struggles, including for the first time, the Anglo-Spanish co-operation in the post-War anti-Franco resistance and provides interesting sidelights on, amongst others, the printers' and miners' strikes, fighting Blackshirts and the battle of Cable Street, the so-called Angry Brigade activities, the Anarchist Black Cross, the Cairo Mutiny and wartime German anti-Nazi resistance, the New Left of the 60s, the rise of squatting — and through individuals as varied as Kenyata, Emma Goldman, George Orwell, Guy Aldred and Frank Ridley — all of which have crowded out not only his story, but his life too. *"If I can't have a revolution, what is there to dance about?"* — Albert Meltzer

TALES FROM THE CLIT: A FEMALE EXPERIENCE OF PORNOGRAPHY

Edited by Cherie Matrix. ISBN 1-873176 09-0; 160 pp, two color cover, perfect bound 5-1/2 x 8-1/2; $10.95/ £7.95. Get wet with the wildest group of feminists yet!! True stories by some of the world's most pro-sex feminists, these women have provided intimate, anti-censorship essays to re-establish the idea that equality of the sexes doesn't have to mean no sex. From intimate sexual experiences and physical perception through to the academic arena, this groundbreaking volume documents women's positive thoughts, uses and desires for, with and about pornography. Essays include such diverse topics as how various authors discovered porn, what porn means to a blind and deaf woman, running a sex magazine, starting a sex shop, and what the contributors would actually like to see. Contributors include: Deborah Ryder, Annie Sprinkle, Tuppy Owens, Carol Queen, Avedon Carol, Jan Grossman, Sue Raye, and Caroline Bottomley.

SCUM MANIFESTO

by Valerie Solanas. ISBN 1-873176 44-9; 64 pp, two color cover, perfect bound 5-1/2 x 8-1/2; $5.00/ £3.50. This is the definitive edition of the SCUM Manifesto with an afterword detailing the life and death of Valerie Solanas. "Life in this society being, at best, an utter bore and no aspect of society being at all relevant to women, there remains to civic-minded, responsible, thrill-seeking females only to overthrow the government, eliminate the money system, institute complete automation and destroy the male sex. . . . On the shooting of Andy Warhol: I consider that a moral act. And I consider it immoral that I missed. I should have done target practice." —Valerie Solanas

REBEL MOON: ANARCHIST RANTS AND POEMS

by Norman Nawrocki; ISBN 1 873176 08 2; perfect bound; two color cover; 112 pages; $9.95/£7.95. The greatest hits of the writings and songs of the main man behind Rhythm Activism. Norman Nawrocki riotous new book, Rebel Moon, allows this international caberet artist and activist to let loose a collection of dangerous poems and forbidden words on paper.

THE FRIENDS OF AK PRESS

In the last 12 months, AK Press published around 15 new titles. In the next 12 months we should be able to publish roughly the same, including a collection of essays and interviews by Murray Bookchin, the first book from Jello Biafra, three books from members of Crass, a stunning new cyberpunk novel, and the animal rights revenge novel to end all novels, as well as a new audio CD from Noam Chomsky.

However, not only are we financially constrained as to what (and how much) we can publish, we already have a huge backlog of excellent material we would like to publish sooner, rather than later. If we had the money, we could publish sixty titles in the coming twelve months.

Projects currently being worked on include: **Morris Beckman's** short history of British Fascism; previously unpublished early anarchist writings by **Victor Serge**; **Raoul Vaneigem's** *A Cavalier History of Surrealism*; two volumes of the collected writings of **Guy Aldred**; first-hand accounts from Kronstadt survivors; an English translation of **Alexandre Skirda's** classic work on anarchist history and organization, and his acclaimed biography of Makhno, *The Black Cossack*; *History's Lost Orgasms*, a history of insurrection from antiquity to the present day; the autobiography of perennial revolutionaries, the Thaelmans; new collage work from Freddie Baer; the first translation in English (running to eight volumes) of the complete works of **Bakunin**; a new edition of the Ex's glorious Spanish Revolution book/CD package; a collection of prison stories from ex-Angry Brigader **John Barker**; new editions of 'outsider' classics *You Can't Win* by **Jack Black** and **Ben Reitman's** *Boxcar Bertha*; a comprehensive look at the armed struggle groups of the 1960s and 1970s, both in Europe and North America; and much, much more. We are working to set up a new pamphlet series, both to reprint long neglected classics and to present new material in an affordable, accessible format.

The Friends of AK Press is a way in which you can directly help us to realize many more such projects, much faster. Friends pay a minimum monthly amount, into our AK Press account. There are also yearly and life-time memberships available. Moneys received go directly into our publishing.

In return, Friends receive (for the duration of their membership), automatically, as and when they appear, one FREE copy of **every** new AK Press title. Secondly, they are also entitled to a 10 percent discount on **everything** featured in the AK Press Distribution catalog, on **any** and **every** order.

To receive a catalog and find out more about Friends of AK Press please write to:

AK Press
PO Box 40682
San Francisco, CA
94140-0682

AK Press
P.O. Box 12766
Edinburgh, Scotland
EH8 9YE